MW01170406

Revolutions in Learning and Education from India

This book offers an important critique of the ways in which mainstream education contributes to perpetuating an inherently unjust and exploitative Development model. Instead, the book proposes a new anarchistic, postdevelopmental framework that goes beyond Development and schooling to ask what really makes a meaningful life.

Challenging the notion of Development as a win-win relationship between civil society, the state and the private sector, the book argues that Development perpetuates a hierarchical world order and that the education system serves to reinforce and re-legitimise this unequal order. Drawing on real-life examples of 'unschooling' and 'self-designed learning' in India, the book demonstrates that more autonomous approaches such as these can help to fundamentally challenge dominant ideas of education, equality, development and what it means to lead meaningful lives.

The interdisciplinary approach pursued in this book makes it perfect for anyone with interests across the areas of education, development studies, radical political theory and philosophy.

Christoph Neusiedl has extensive experience across the field of alternative education, working with 'unschooling' organisations such as Project DEFY, Bangalore, India. He also worked as Development consultant in Bangladesh. His PhD thesis in Asian and International Studies at the City University of Hong Kong was awarded the City University Outstanding Research Thesis Award 2019.

Routledge Critical Development Studies
Series Editors

Henry Veltmeyer is co-chair of the Critical Development Studies (CDS) network, Research Professor at Universidad Autónoma de Zacatecas, Mexico, and Professor Emeritus at Saint Mary's University, Canada.
Paul Bowles is Professor of Economics and International Studies at UNBC, Canada.
Elisa van Wayenberge is Lecturer in Economics at SOAS University of London, UK.

The global crisis, coming at the end of three decades of uneven capitalist development and neoliberal globalisation that have devastated the economies and societies of people across the world, especially in the developing societies of the Global South, cries out for a more critical, proactive approach to the study of international development. The challenge of creating and disseminating such an approach, to provide the study of international development with a critical edge, is the project of a global network of activist development scholars concerned and engaged in using their research and writings to help effect transformative social change that might lead to a better world.

This series will provide a forum and outlet for the publication of books in the broad interdisciplinary field of critical development studies – to generate new knowledge that can be used to promote transformative change and alternative development.

The editors of the series welcome the submission of original manuscripts that focus on issues of concern to the growing worldwide community of activist scholars in this field.

To submit proposals, please contact the Development Studies Editor, Helena Hurd (Helena.Hurd@tandf.co.uk).

1. Postdevelopment in Practice
Alternatives, Economies, Ontologies
Edited by Elise Klein & Carlos Eduardo Morreo

2. Buen Vivir and the Challenges to Capitalism Latin America
Edited by Henry Veltmeyer and Edgar Zayago Lau

3. Deconstructing Human Development
From the Washington Consensus to the 2030 Agenda
Juan Telleria

4. Revolutions in Learning and Education from India
Pathways towards the Pluriverse
Christoph Neusiedl

https://www.routledge.com/Routledge-Critical-Development-Studies/book-series/RCDS

Revolutions in Learning and Education from India

Pathways towards the Pluriverse

Christoph Neusiedl

Routledge
Taylor & Francis Group

LONDON AND NEW YORK

First published 2021
by Routledge
2 Park Square, Milton Park, Abingdon, Oxon OX14 4RN

and by Routledge
52 Vanderbilt Avenue, New York, NY 10017

Routledge is an imprint of the Taylor & Francis Group, an informa business

British Library Cataloguing-in-Publication Data
A catalogue record for this book is available from the British Library

Library of Congress Cataloging-in-Publication Data
Names: Neusiedl, Christoph, author.
Title: Revolutions in learning and education from India: pathways towards
the pluriverse / Christoph Neusiedl.
Description: Abingdon, Oxon; New York, NY: Routledge, 2021. |
Series: Routledge critical development studies | Includes bibliographical
references and index. |
Identifiers: LCCN 2020040499 (print) | LCCN 2020040500 (ebook) |
ISBN 9780367648770 (hardback) | ISBN 9781003126744 (ebook)
Subjects: LCSH: Education–Aims and objectives–India. |
Educational equalization–India. | Self-managed learning–India. |
Education and state–India.
Classification: LCC LA1151 .N393 2021 (print) | LCC LA1151 (ebook) |
DDC 370.954–dc23
LC record available at https://lccn.loc.gov/2020040499
LC ebook record available at https://lccn.loc.gov/2020040500

ISBN: 978-0-367-64877-0 (hbk)
ISBN: 978-1-003-12674-4 (ebk)

Typeset in Times New Roman
by Deanta Global Publishing Services, Chennai, India

Contents

Foreword by Ashish Kothari   viii
Acknowledgements   xii
Abbreviations   xiv

Introduction: Moving beyond development and modern education   1

1   Between neoliberalism and Hindutva: Deconstructing India's
    development paradigm   17

2   Anarchistic postdevelopment and the ontological politics of
    equality   43

3   From OWW Development to OWW Education   68

4   The axiom of (in-)equality: Towards an anarchistic
    postdevelopmental education (ANPED)   99

5   ANPED in practice: Radical unschooling among families   127

6   ANPED in practice: Unschooling in marginalised communities   156

7   ANPED in practice: The Swaraj (Un-)University model   177

Conclusion: Crafting new pathways towards the pluriverse   203

Index   207

Foreword

Ashish Kothari

Radical transformation needs radical learning

Writing in the midst of an interregnum the likes of which humanity has never faced before, I am acutely aware that the pathways out of the COVID-19 pandemic could be broadly along two violently clashing paradigms. One, already seen in the response of many states and corporations, an attempt to return to 'normal' with even more authoritarianism, profit-making and ignoring planetary ecological limits. The other, seen more in the responses of people's movements, indigenous peoples and civil society, are actions and advocacy based on fundamental shifts towards solidarity, justice, equity and sustainability. We will likely see both clashing for quite some time to come, and which one eventually prevails depends a lot on what today's youth and the generations to come make of humanity's place on earth.

This is where *learning*, in all its forms, becomes so pivotal. What we are all learning (or not) from the current crises, what lessons are conveyed to today's youth, what gets written in history books (or more likely, embedded in video clips and memes and all the other new communication forms in use today), will provide a foundation for what pathways people will adopt. It is in this context that Christoph's book provides valuable insights for what we must change in education and learning, if we are to have a fighting chance of moving to a just, sustainable world.

Christoph paints a stark contrast between what he calls the One-World world (OWW) and the Anarchistic Postdevelopmental Education (ANPED) approaches. Just like developmental discourses of 'sustainability' and 'inclusiveness' are seductive distractions at best and dangerous diversions at worst, leading us away from the essential task of changing the economic, political and cultural foundations of today's crises, similarly much of the talk of 'reforms' in education does not enable us to challenge its fundamentally alienating character. The cleverest of rulers are those who can seduce and subjugate the minds of their subjects, rather than having to use physical force. This was Thomas Macaulay's clever insight that prompted the British colonial powers to introduce the western system of schooling in India (a curious if rare omission of significance in this book). Despite trenchant critiques of such a system by Gandhi, Tagore and others, it was retained in its core essentials after independence, and still prevails.

As Christoph lucidly shows, this OWW Education is one of the main reasons for the often unquestioning attitude of a large section of India's population, even when the country's rulers take some blatantly regressive decisions. When it is drilled into one's head from childhood, that one has to listen to figures of authority, one tends to grow up following this for life. As bad, such education has also been the primary weapon in the transformation of an incredibly diverse cultural population into a more homogenous way of thinking and aspiring. And now, increasingly, it has become fertile ground for seeding regressive stereotypes about religious, ethnic, and gender/sexuality minorities, such that an entire generation is growing up demonising 'the other'. All of this is well suited to the continued concentrations of power in the hands of the political, gender, economic and caste elites.

In contrast, ANPED challenges the structures and relations of hierarchy and homogenization. Christoph's detailed empirical and analytical treatment of various initiatives of 'radical unschooling' shows that they not only challenge, reject and resist domination, but at the same time demonstrate the viability of alternative pathways. The examples in India that he describes are clearly working, not only in enabling children and youth to learn, but to learn in ways that enable them to contribute meaningfully to a better world, all the while enjoying themselves and expressing their innate creativity. This reminds me of the shock I got when I first learnt that the Greek root of the word 'school', *skhole*, meant both a leisure and a lecture place!

ANPED forms of learning, then, provide a solid foundation for ways of knowing, doing, being – and I dare say, dreaming and imagining[1] – that are crucial for what the author calls an "ontological politics of equality". They are indeed essential for processes that help in transforming society towards radical equality, as envisioned in anarchist political thought. The best traditions of anarchist, Marxist and Gandhian philosophy, as well as indigenous movements for autonomy rooted in their own worldviews – are not about chaos and mayhem (the popular distortion of the term 'anarchy'), but about each of us claiming the power of decision-making that is inherent in us, but while doing so, also being responsible to others. In emphasizing integrated and holistic learning that makes the best use of not only our heads but also our hearts and hands and feet (very much in the spirit of Gandhi's Nai Talim approach), and in creating spaces for collaborative and joyful growing up. ANPED forms of learning help create more complete human beings that will likely put the sacredness of life ahead of selfish pursuits. Crucially, they also enable the agency of the most marginalised, evident in initiatives like the Nook model of learning, eloquently described in Chapter 6 of this book.

Of course, spaces of learning (and doing and being and …) do not only exist in schools and colleges or in the alternative processes of ANPED-like initiatives, but in all aspects of our lives. Transformations towards social justice, sustainability and equality, towards eco-swaraj or Radical Ecological Democracy[2], have to take place across the entire range of political, economic, social and cultural relations and domains we engage in. A young person going through some of the radical unschooling experiences described in this book will encounter many other spaces and moments in her/his life, and if these are violently unjust or exploitative in contrast, it could reverse the learning in the former, or cause massive confusion and uncertainty. It is interesting therefore that Christoph devotes a part of the book to 'radical equality' in general, not only in learning and education.

Across the world, there are thousands of initiatives of both resistance and creation or reconstruction; resistance to the structures of patriarchy and masculinity, capitalism, racism, statism, casteism and anthropocentrism, and revival or co-creation of alternatives for meeting human needs and aspirations without trashing the earth and without creating ever-more shameful inequalities. These alternatives are enormously diverse, as they ought to be if they are to respond to the diversity of cultural, economic and ecological situations people find themselves in. They form a *pluriverse*,[3] and they resist any attempt at imposition of one model, however alternative it may be; no 'mainstreaming' for them!

Practices like agroecology and indigenous agriculture, energy and food sovereignty, community-led conservation and water governance, commoning, open source technologies, transition towns, and many more, complement and are bolstered by worldviews or concepts like swaraj, ubuntu, buen vivir and sumac kawsay, kyosei, sentipensar, ecofeminism, degrowth, and many many others. They range from a tiny individual effort to millions of people in initiatives such as the Kurdish and Zapatista autonomous movements.

This diversity and plurality, however, also mean that individually they may not be able to effectively challenge the macro-structures of inequality and unsustainability. Are there common threads that could enable confluences, collaborations, and collective processes to become a greater critical mass for macro-transformation? Perhaps there are a set of ethics or values at the base of most or all radical alternatives: interconnectedness, holism, equality, respect, dignity, agency, rights and responsibilities, autonomy, sacredness of life, seeing ourselves as part of nature, solidarity, a balance between individual identity and the flourishing of the collective, and so on. A number of processes are underway to provide platforms for global confluences, and it is likely that those respecting the uniqueness of each movement along with common ethical threads, will go further than those that try to impose conventional politburo-like institutional frameworks.

And as Christoph emphasizes, such ethics are also the foundations of ANPED. Radical transformations in various aspects of life are therefore both a context for ANPED, and in turn can be fed by it in a mutually reinforcing manner. The difficulty of course is that the multi-dimensional processes required for holistic transformation are unlikely to all be in place at any given time or place, so the movement towards radical justice and equality is going to be a struggle, a constant searching, continuous innovation and improvisation. This is precisely what ANPED provides a fertile ground for.

India has always been a place of explosive innovation, even as it is also one of depressing inequality, imposition and fatalism. As in many other fields, in education too it demonstrates this stark contrast. But the exciting alternative initiatives in education that are scattered through the country have rarely been understood and revealed in detail, even as platforms like Vikalp Sangam[4] do provide many brief stories and a handful of case studies. In providing a detailed and analytical exposition of some ANPED initiatives, this book does an enormously important service. I hope it is widely read, especially in the musty corridors of educational institutions and government policy-makers; and equally important, converted into many accessible forms for communities and civil society to spur them to try out their own radical experiments.

Ashish Kothari
Kalpavriksh, Vikalp Sangam, and Global Tapestry of Alternatives
October 2020

Notes

1 We need much more of these! For an example of imagining a utopian future in India, and possible pathways to it, on 30 different aspects of social, cultural, economic, ecological, and political life, see Kothari and Joy (2018).
2 See Radical Ecological Democracy (2018); and Kothari (2016).
3 For over 90 examples of such radical alternatives around the world, see Kothari et al. (2019).
4 See www.vikalpsangam.org

References

Kothari, A. (2016). 'Reflections from the South on Degrowth'. https://www.degrowth.info /en/dim/degrowth-in-movements/radical-ecological-democracy/

Kothari, A. and Joy, K.J. (eds). (2018). *Alternative Futures: India Unshackled*. New Delhi: AuthorsUpFront.

Kothari, A., Salleh, A., Escobar, A., Demaria, F., and Acosta, A. (eds). (2019). *Pluriverse: A Post-Development Dictionary*. New Delhi: Tulika Books.

Radical Ecological Democracy. (2018). 'RED Conversations Series – The Emerging Idea of "Radical Well-Being"'. https://www.radicalecologicaldemocracy.org/red-conversa tions-series-the-emerging-idea-of-radical-well-being/

Acknowledgements

This book could not have been written without the openness, support and encouragement of many people. I would like to use this opportunity to express my gratitude and appreciation to some of the people who made this possible and to apologise to the ones who I will inevitably forget to mention.

First, I want to particularly mention Manish and Vidhi Jain of *Shikshantar: The Peoples' Institute for Re-thinking Education and Development*. I still vividly remember the first time I came to Shikshantar in Udaipur. As the schooled researcher I was at the time, I talked to Manish and Vidhi about scheduling interviews and other research activities. The response I got from them was 'we will not do any formal interviews with you or join any formal research activities, but you are welcome to be here, meet people, make friends, and join our activities'.

This has probably been the best 'advice' they could have given me. Instead of seeing my research about Shikshantar and the unschooling movement as 'just another case study' to get done with – as I initially did – I actually started to deeply engage with the people that are part of this movement, to learn from and with them and see them as equals, rather than as 'research subjects' (or all too often rather 'research objects' on which pre-given theories and assumptions are imposed). More than that, I was able to develop true and long-lasting, continuing friendships with many people I met through the vast Shikshantar network.

The Creativity Adda in Delhi has become another place close to my heart. Thank you to Ashish Tiwari, Prakash, Saadat, Priyank, Bhim, Shashank, Ankit, Vijaya Aunty and Kamran for allowing me to be part of the Adda and learning from and with you. I also fondly remember all the learners of Creativity Adda with whom I shared so many fun times, and from whom I likewise learned a lot: Faiz, Sakib, Chirag, Salman, Sajid, Sachin, Akash, Chintu, Manish, Rahul, Avdesh, Manoj, Nitesh, Bobby, Abhishek, Piyush, Aryan, Aman, Nikhil, Chaman, Vipul, Himanshu, Faizaan, Rahul, Ishant, Ayaan, Labhansh, Vineet, Ishan, Anuj, Sumit, Rahmat, Raj, Deepak, Satyam, Vipin and many more who make Creativity Adda into the beautiful, unique space it is.

Likewise, I was able to get much inspiration and learned a lot from everyone at Swaraj University. My gratitude goes to many people there – to Chetan Kanoongo for his friendship and support and for giving me a home in Delhi and later welcoming me to Swaraj; to Sonika, Rahul H., Mohit, Bhawna, Rahul K., Ankit, Muthok, Aakarsh, Yash, Arti, Aditi, Ruchita, Sumit, Ravi, Nidhi, Shraddha,

Basant, Rajat, Aum, Nikshit, Madhur, Stanzin, Arjun, Anuj, Harsh, Ritesh, Nikhil, Niom, Samyuktha, Snehal, Pratik, Bhupender, Satyam, Devika and many more khojis and friends.

The five-day-long 'Reimagining Education' retreat and workshop at Swaraj University in May 2018 was another important platform to meet many practicing unschoolers from across India. I want to especially thank Sharmila Govande who not only patiently endured and answered all my endless questions about unschooling both in person as well as through email and Facebook, but who also showed me enormous trust in sharing her thoughts with me. I am also grateful to have met Bayo and EJ Akomolafe, who gave me tremendous encouragement to follow through with my project. Special thanks also to Munish for his encouragement and energy.

Another important station in my research and indeed life journey was Project DEFY in Bangalore. Thank you to Abhijit Sinha, Answer Nzuma, Megha Bhagat and the entire team for inviting me with open arms and trusting in me.

I spent some time at the beginning of my research in India at Kalpavriksh in Pune which gave me an important and valuable insight into the many emerging alternatives to Development in India. Thank you to Ashish Kothari, Shruti, Meenal, Shrishtee, Eleonora, Sneha, Milind, Sujatha, Govind, Neema, Prajakta, Pradeep, Radhika, Sharnamma, Mithila and the entire team.

There is a number of other friends and companions whom I would like to mention: Qudrat Sumichandresh and Avinash Almeida who answered all my unschooling-related questions and (despite this) became good friends; Nivedita, Arun, Abhimanyu, Aastha Pragati, Prayanshu, Atreyee, Rayn, Dharmik, Vibhuti, Deepankar, Aaditya, Deepa, Ikieu, Joe, Shoba, Ajay, Darpan, Akshat, Ajanmya, Ratheesh, Harshit, Chaitanya, Ankit, Arnaz, Pavan, Prabhakant, Pia, Chiara, Meghna, Pankaj, Urmila, Sandhya, Tarun, Rajni, Adil, Farah, Rishin, Nikita and so many others who are in one way or the other part of my own unlearning journey.

I also want to appreciate some good friends who accompanied and encouraged me throughout this journey: Ehsan Kabir, Rashidul Karim, Boicha Huidrom, Harsh Wardhan and Jerome Geyer-Klingeberg. My family, and especially my parents, sister and grandmother also helped me in their own, very important ways, to write this book.

Most of the field research I draw on in this book has been part of my PhD project at the Department of Asian and International Studies, City University of Hong Kong. Thank you to the many people in the department with whom I discussed my work and who helped and encouraged me in one way or the other during my journey: Federico Ferrara, Bradley Williams, Ruben Gonzalez Vicente, Thomas Patton, Jun Zhang, Sean Starrs and Linda Tjia.

Most of all, I would like to express my gratitude to my PhD supervisor Toby Carroll who provided important feedback and suggestions for this book. In him I have found not only an academic supervisor and wonderful 'ignorant schoolmaster', but a good friend who supported me all the way in my PhD journey as well as beyond.

Last but not least, I would like to particularly thank Saul Newman, David Brenner, Bruno Dorin, Jörg Nowak and Judith Suissa for their helpful feedback, encouragement and support of this book project.

Abbreviations

ANPED	Anarchistic postdevelopmental education
Ark	Absolute Return for Kids
CA	Creativity Adda
ePPP	Public-private partnership in education
NGO	Non-governmental organisation
OWW	One-World world
PPP	Public-private partnership
SDGs	Sustainable Development Goals
SDL	Self-designed learning/self-directed learning
SU	Swaraj University
TINA	'There is no alternative'

Introduction

Moving beyond development and modern education

This book emerged out of one simple – or rather not so simple – question: why is it, as Fredric Jameson so eloquently put it, *easier to imagine the end of the world than the end of capitalism?*

As we all can increasingly hear, see, feel and experience ourselves, we are living in a world of manifold and multiple crises – be they political, social, cultural, economic, spiritual or ecological. Across the globe, we can observe – to name just a few examples – an increase in right-wing populism and xenophobia;[1] ever-escalating social and economic inequalities within and between countries;[2] more and more people living in poverty and poverty-like conditions;[3] a drastic increase in mental health-related issues;[4] an intensifying loss of cultural[5] as well as biodiversity;[6] the continuously growing effects and dire consequences of climate change and environmental degradation;[7] and, often, a certain apathy of and disillusion with (modern) life in general.

The coronavirus pandemic which started to afflict the world in early 2020 is but another symptom of these interconnected crises. They are rooted in the way our imagination has been captured and co-opted by a subjective and narrow worldview which – as this book will show – creates artificial hierarchies between humans and nature as well as among human beings.

The relentless conversion of natural habitats into anthropogenic land as well as the uncontrolled wildlife trade – which both exemplify how nature has been made into something to be conquered and ruled over in the name of 'Development' and 'Progress' – enabled the spread of the coronavirus from animals to humans in the first place. The ever-increasing inequalities among human beings, then, predetermined who would be mostly affected by it.

Coalitions of governments, large corporations, mainstream media and 'experts' of all sorts – all the ones who have a stake in preserving the pre-coronavirus status quo – reacted as we would expect them to do. Governments such as in India, fearing the collapse of the country's grossly inadequate, decades-long defunded healthcare system, initially imposed a strict lockdown for months that sheltered the ones who have adequate, comfortable shelter, while a majority of the population was and is left to fend for themselves. Soon after, the new global maxim endorsed by the above coalitions was about 'going back to normal' as fast as possible to 'save the economy' – in other words, save corporate profits and ensure a return to economic growth.[8] Nowhere in these circles, of course, did there emerge a doubt that this 'normal' – with all its absurdities and perversities which wreaked havoc across the world long time before the virus – was something not desirable.

The COVID-19 crisis, indeed, seems to have become another textbook example of what Naomi Klein has termed *disaster capitalism*.[9] In India and elsewhere, labour laws and protections are already being diluted, what is left of environmental protection is further cannibalised and corporate bailouts and additional regulatory rollbacks are pushed through without much questioning and opposition. At the same time, what we can see in India is not only an increase in disaster capitalism but what Jayati Ghosh calls disaster authoritarianism, bolstering the government's nationalist, strong-state agenda.[10] This shows how neoliberal and nationalist agendas indeed nurture and reinforce each other, in times of disaster and also during the 'normal' times to which the elites want to go back.

At the same time, the way in which state and corporate elites have responded to the COVID-19 pandemic is only one – although the dominant – way of how this global crisis is being addressed. As we can always see when disasters of any kind strike, people come together and help each other in manifold ways. This is what anarchists refer to as mutual aid:

> mutual aid – solidarity, free cooperation – is a core concept of anarchist thought. It is the principle around which just social organization must be built. To embrace mutual aid as the sole legitimate organizing principle of society is to reject the institutionalization of any means of coercion, or of violence and the threat of violence. It is to embrace the idea that we can cooperatively reason with one another, and thereby instantiate our common inclination to build a society that benefits all without instituting any sort of hierarchy that functions to enforce such arrangements.
>
> (Jun and Lance 2020)

The coronavirus pandemic is another example in which we can see mutual aid in action, even if the very nature of a pandemic makes it more difficult for people to come together.[11] The mutual aid activities we could observe include everything from grocery shopping and offering rides for at-risk neighbours to fabricating medical equipment such as masks, distributing food to the poor, engaging in online and offline skill-sharing sessions, providing emotional support to people in distress during the lockdown, taking care of the elderly, cooking and sharing food with others and much more.[12]

In India, we could also see how countless individuals came together and solidarity groups were formed to support migrants stranded in the cities, as well as those going on their long, perilous journeys home. Migrants were supported in many ways from distributing food to supplying sanitary kits or raising money for lost wages. As Debarati Roy observes, while

> India grapples with containing the coronavirus pandemic, stories of hope and solidarity are emerging from the country. The situation has underlined a

crucial element – the power of solidarity, hope and humanity. What is particularly remarkable in this moment is how people from all sections of society have come together and organized mutual aid projects across the country.

(Roy 2020)

The question then becomes how we can nurture aspects of mutual aid, of direct action and – ultimately – of more solidary, cooperative ways of life beyond the times when disasters strike. How can we co-create, nurture and build alternatives to a further looming neoliberalisation, often coupled with the rise of right-wing nationalism? And how can we build these alongside with the many, yet often marginalised cases of local communities and social movements which already practise these aspects in the here and now against the onslaught of 'Development'?

As this book suggests, an important part of the answer to these questions can be found by looking more closely at how we educate ourselves and our children. It is no coincidence that governments around the world had as one of their highest priorities during the COVID-19 pandemic to re-open schools as soon as possible. This is both because – as became obvious during the pandemic – schools serve as spaces where parents can park their children to pursue 'productive work', as well as because schools play a pivotal role in socialising young people into the given, hierarchical order so they accept their – usually subordinate – roles within it and contribute to its permanent re-creation.

'Education', in other words, has become an extremely subjective and narrow, top-down approach towards learning which is rooted in a particular worldview that puts the capitalist social and economic order and the status quo above all. Mark Fisher describes this worldview as *capitalist realism*, 'the widespread sense that not only is capitalism the only viable political and economic system, but also that it is now impossible even to *imagine* a coherent alternative to it' (Fisher 2009: 2; emphasis original). In order to break out of capitalist realism and open up new imaginations of what makes meaningful lives beyond late capitalism, we therefore need to change the way we think about as well as practise education and learning.

Drawing on the anarchistic perspective on education, Judith Suissa suggests that

> before we even engage in the enterprise of philosophy of education, we must question the very political framework within which we are operating, ask ourselves what kind of society would embody, for us, the optimal vision of 'the good life', and then ask ourselves what kind (if any) of education system would exist in this society.
>
> (Suissa 2010: 4)

The book sets out to do exactly this. Before beginning to imagine what kind of society we would want, we will first analyse what kind of society we currently have and how it comes into being by deconstructing the prevailing neoliberal Development paradigm which reigns in India and elsewhere. This will be followed by mapping out how postdevelopmental visions of meaningful lives beyond Development alongside anarchist ideas and practices of non-hierarchical community-building can provide us with a flexible framework to imagine what kind of society we want. This, however, will not take the form of yet another blueprint of the 'ideal society', but consist of a broad model – or what postdevelopment scholars and activists call '*the pluriverse*' – which allows the flourishing of manifold ways of life based on minimising hierarchies among human beings as well as between humans and nature.

Next, it is important to understand the historical and contemporary role of mainstream education in preserving and indeed permanently re-creating the status quo of the (liberal and neoliberal) society we currently have and aim to transcend. After this, we will explore what an education in and for the pluriverse can look like in theory. Finally – by analysing real-life case studies of various alternative education and learning initiatives in India – we will experience which forms such an education can take in practice and examine how the educational activities identified in the various examples serve as *pathways towards the pluriverse*.

As such, this book does not aim to devise yet another theory which will tell the ones considered 'not (yet) developed' what to do, or what kind of education they should follow, or criticise their models and approaches towards education, finding something that the 'enlightened scholar' can dismantle and change.

Instead, this book is written out of the motivation that 'we' – the people living in what I will call below *the One-World world*, i.e. those who have a stake in the current system and stand to benefit from it, which certainly includes myself as a white, German, European, former PhD researcher and former Development practitioner, as well as many of my readers in the Global North and South who are able to access and afford this book – can be inspired and learn from the examples and case studies featured in the book to build our own paths towards the pluriverse and support others who already do so.[13]

With this in mind, I aim to follow and apply David Graeber's understanding how

> one obvious role for a radical intellectual is to do precisely that: to look at those who are creating viable alternatives, to try to figure out what might be the larger implications of what they are (already) doing, and then offer those ideas back, not as prescriptions, but as contributions, possibilities – as gifts.
>
> (Graeber 2004: 12)

Book structure

The first two chapters centre around the philosophy of Development. They serve to both question the dominant, political framework within which Development operates as well as to offer a new, alternative and emancipatory framework to replace it.

The postdevelopment school of thought provides the point of departure for this venture. Postdevelopment writers argue that the narrow conceptualisation of

Development as economic growth and progress – embedded within a modernist, today most often capitalist-neoliberal framework – constitutes an apolitical, Western-centric and elitist concept which is being imposed onto 'developing countries' and their populations. It takes away from them any agency to determine their own fate and prevents them from an independent choice of living what they consider as meaningful lives.[14]

Adding to postdevelopment's body of work, the first chapter will harness the political philosophy of Jacques Rancière and Todd May to demonstrate how we can further make sense of Development as a politics based on '*the presupposition of inequality*'. This presupposition masquerades as equality by conceptualising the latter as a good that is to be distributed from an authority (i.e. the modern nation-state) to its citizens. Such an understanding posits that some people – the ones with political, economic and juridical clout – are already more equal than others. Therefore, they can 'award' equality to the vast majority of people who in the process become mere spectators and supplicants of equality.

This 'hidden inequality' is an inherent characteristic of liberal philosophy and liberal democracy and – as we will see – all too willingly lends itself to be incorporated into the current Indian government's right-wing, nationalist agenda. Ultimately, it is used as a key strategy in order to reinforce and perpetuate the hierarchical, inherently unjust and exploitative status quo that mostly serves a small elite by promising to everyone else an equality never-to-come.

By implication, the assumption that equality is a right that needs to be awarded from an authority above – and not something that everyone always and inherently possesses – entails the powerful myth and self-fulfilling prophecy that ordinary people are not able to create their own meaningful lives. Instead, they are assumed to be in need of authoritarian institutions and their experts to do so. As we will see, this idea – which has become ingrained as natural and common-sense across large parts of society and therefore serves to perpetuate the world of capitalist realism – ultimately constitutes Development's very *raison d'être by normalising, legitimising and justifying its expert-led interventions in peoples' lives*.

These interventions then always follow the same pattern, rooted in the idea that everyone should become 'equally developed', which today means that everyone becomes an equal 'good consumer-citizen' in and of the marketplace. I will further demonstrate how this particular approach to equality is embedded in what we will call 'the ontological politics of inequality' as a world-making practice. The result of this politics can be described as what John Law calls the One-World world (OWW).[15]

The OWW is deeply rooted in a dualist ontology or worldview based on the artificial establishment of various strict hierarchies between human beings as well as between humans and nature. These hierarchies, in turn, structure our everyday fields of experience, or what Jacques Rancière calls the partitioning of the sensible as 'our perception of things that reinforces social hierarchies' (May 2010: 9).

In other words, the various partitions of the sensible are the everyday visible expressions, actions and other concrete, graspable manifestations – such as

'Development' – of the dualist and hierarchical OWW. The latter then constitutes not a natural existing phenomenon but a specific and selective worldview reflected and re-created by various world-making practices such as Development and modern education. The OWW ontology, moreover and as we will see, is quite compatible with the 'Hindutva', Hindu-nationalist 'way of life' promoted by the current Indian government.

Based on this, I draw on the research areas of political ontology, pluriversal studies and eco-feminist philosophy to unwind the notion of Development as 'natural order' by showing how we can understand it indeed as *OWW Development* grounded in the ontological politics of inequality which aims to re-create, reinforce and perpetuate the OWW. OWW Development's ontological politics then aims to negate, co-opt, transform, marginalise and destroy any other ways of life that exceed the OWW's ontological limits while aiming to fit anyone and everyone into pre-given roles and identities based on an inherently hierarchical, exploitative order.

This, I contend, lies at the roots of why we cannot reimagine Development and think beyond capitalism – to say it in the (alleged) words of Einstein, 'we cannot solve our problems with the very same thinking that created them'. As such, we need to understand how the ontological politics of inequality manifests itself as a deeply rooted belief system and ideology that structures both the lives of many people in the so-called Global North as well as in the so-called Global South.[16]

Whereas the former is pervaded by the ingrained presupposition of inequality that structures the 'modern' way of life and legitimises its expansion to the South, the latter – while suffering from OWW Development's creation of poverty, inequality and 'underdevelopment' – still is full of pockets of resistance which refuse to accept the hierarchical OWW order, weaken its impact and therefore also provide important examples of 'living otherwise'.[17]

The second chapter then takes up the challenge to outline an emancipatory politics that counters OWW Development's ontological politics of inequality. It does so by developing a theoretical framework grounded in postdevelopment thought and anarchist philosophy. As I will demonstrate, this *anarchistic postdevelopment* is operated and acted out through Jacques Rancière's principle of the 'presupposition of equality'.

It posits that everyone and anyone is equally capable of creating meaningful lives alongside others. Once people act out of this presupposition, they rearrange one or more given partition(s) of the sensible within the OWW's dualist ontology. As such, movements, groups and communities that act out of their own equality 'rearrange what and how we perceive, make us see something new or different, reconfigure the field of our experience' (May 2010: 40).

This, in turn, directly challenges the OWW and its hierarchical order. Therefore, I conceptualise anarchistic postdevelopment under the presupposition of equality further as *the ontological politics of equality* which ultimately serves to (re-)create and nurture more egalitarian ways of life outside the OWW. This concept can be applied both theoretically as a way to analyse already existing struggles against and alternatives to OWW Development, as well as harnessed as a practical framework particularly for people within the OWW in order to leave the ingrained presupposition of inequality behind them and start creating their own meaningful lives.

One essential question that remains open after having established this framework of emancipatory politics is how the OWW has achieved such widespread hegemony in the first place and, accordingly, how this hegemony can be undermined and broken in the long term. In other words, how can what I term anarchistic postdevelopment take place not only on the margins of OWW Development, but how can it, alongside other 'alternatives to Development', replace the former in order to bring about substantial and impactful change to a larger part of society across the Global North and South?

Here, I will suggest that we need to examine the often-overlooked role of *education* and its contribution to either reinforcing or overthrowing the status quo. Both these aspects will be addressed and analysed in the second part of the book, which brings together the 'philosophy of Development' with the 'philosophy of education'.

As Derek Jensen points out,

> more is at stake in the process of schooling than mere booklearning or even the development of character. The process of schooling gives children the tools they can – and often must – use to survive after graduating into 'the real world', and teaches them what it is to be a member of our culture.
>
> (Jensen 2004: 3)

In a globally hegemonic mono-culture that is so pervaded by the OWW ontology that it cannot imagine any alternatives to it, education thus becomes a tool to merely reproduce the status quo.

Following Gert Biesta, we can therefore characterise modern education as 'evidence-based practice'.

> It assumes that the ends of professional action are given, and that the only relevant (professional and research) questions to be asked are about the most effective and efficient ways of achieving those ends. In this respect, evidence-based practice entails a *technological model of professional action*. (Biesta 2016: 34; emphasis original)

In other words, whilst there are continuously discussions and debates, initiatives and interventions around 'how to provide increased or universal access to education', 'how to make education more effective' or 'how to achieve and safeguard global education standards' and so on, what is almost never being questioned and analysed is the *kind of education* that is being imparted and distributed. This is no wonder given the hegemony of OWW Development where education can have only but one objective, which is – today – to prepare children for their future role in the global economy – i.e. to make (productive, subservient) workers.

According to Underhill (2016: 158), both the Millennium Development Goals (MDGs) and the Sustainable Development Goals (SDGs) for education illustrate how dominant discourses of Development utilise formal education as a tool that connects the delivery of schooling to processes of capitalist-neoliberal economic Development. As Manish Jain, co-founder of unschooling organisation *Shikshantar: The Peoples' Institute for Re-thinking Development and Education*, puts it more bluntly for the case of the modern education system in India,

> it sees people as part of this larger model of economic growth. It comes basically from three ways. From stupid consumers, from people who have no regard for their ecological systems and want to mine the hell out of them, and from people who can only find happiness through addiction. That's a growth economy in India basically, and that's what education prepares [for].
>
> (quoted in Hopkins 2018)

This means that the expansion of modern education across the globe is at the same time one of the key factors for what Arturo Escobar calls the 'mono-ontological occupation of the OWW'.

Instead of serving as a tool and platform to question, challenge and overcome dominant hierarchies and injustices, education has become an instrument of the elites to justify, preserve and perpetuate the status quo: 'the rhetoric of education and development claims to improve and transform people's lives, but the reality is often the opposite; education's latent function is to reinforce people's subordination and oppression' (Roig and Crowther 2016: 77).

Therefore, the goal in the second part of the book will be both to analyse and deconstruct the key role of education for OWW Development as well as to draft and apply a framework for an anarchistic postdevelopmental education (ANPED) that can anchor, support and strengthen the ontological politics of equality which lets us build new pathways towards the pluriverse.

In Chapter 3, we will explore how the modern education system has become a central tool of OWW Development actors to reinforce the key principles on which the current Development paradigm rests and to impose the related idea that there is only one way – the OWW way – to lead a meaningful and worthwhile life.[18] I will provide an example of the current form this takes in India through a mini case study of 'Absolute Return for Kids' (Ark) India, a philanthrocapitalist organisation operating three schools in Delhi under the public-private partnership (PPP) model.

The chapter will show how the ostensibly objective, positive and benign instrument of modern education – in parallel to the ostensibly neutral and positive tool of Development we will have deconstructed in the first part of the book – needs to be understood as *OWW Education* which lays the foundation for OWW Development to come into being, expand and thrive. Ultimately,

> by 'education', what is actually meant is the introduction of Western-style schooling around the world. It is a building block of 'development' or

'aid', which in turn is linked to corporate-led globalisation (Edelman and Haugerud, 2005). The erosion of traditional skills is an inevitable consequence of a global economic system which concentrates capital, energy and job opportunities in ever-larger urban centres. This form of education represents a systematic transition away from a deep knowledge of how to survive using local, natural resources towards a dependence on fossil fuels and large anonymous businesses and government bureaucracies. In order to sustain life on this planet, we need to become aware of these connections.

(Norberg-Hodge 2016: 50)

While today's dominant form of OWW Education takes the shape of preparing children for their role within a global, neoliberal economy, I further contend that one of the main goals of OWW Education in all its forms was, is and always will be to 'produce' docile, subservient-authoritarian subjects that would not threaten the status quo, be it the hegemonic order of the nation-state or the dominant order of the global economy (which today go hand in hand together).

Drawing again on the philosophy of Jacques Rancière, the fourth chapter further substantiates this point by analysing the structural role of 'explanation' in perpetuating inequality and creating what Rancière calls 'the pedagogicisation of society' or the belief that we are in need of institutions and their experts to tell us and *explain* to us what to do. This ingrained idea takes shape in our schools and classrooms and from there spreads to all areas of life – it thus forms the basis for the ingrained presupposition of inequality.

The central roles of explanation and the hierarchical model of teacher–student relations can be found in every and all cases, forms and shapes of OWW Education rather than being an exclusive feature of contemporary neoliberal education models. Therefore, after making the case that OWW Education in all its forms and guises is based on the presupposition of inequality, the question naturally becomes what an *anarchistic postdevelopmental education* (ANPED) can look like.

The remainder of Chapter 4 lays this out in both theory and practice. After establishing the theoretical framework of ANPED, I will introduce the 'unschooling' mode of learning and education as a practical application of it, drawing on a case study of Delhi-based Creativity Adda, a self-designed learning space for children from marginalised backgrounds.

Following this, the next three chapters will introduce and analyse further examples of 'ANPED in practice' by analysing various forms of and approaches towards unschooling in India.

Across India, there exists an abundance of social and grassroots movements and local and indigenous communities that reject the idea of education as creating good or virtuous consumer-citizens. Instead, they design their own learning models outside of and against mainstream education. These learning approaches are often rooted in and further build on India's long history of education that includes approaches completely at odds with the modern education system, from what can be found in ancient sacred texts to indigenous knowledges and the more contemporary thoughts of Tagore, Gandhi, Krishnamurti, Sri Aurobindo, Bhave and many others. As Manish Jain points out, the concept of unschooling is one contemporary expression of this:

> the idea of unschooling, or self-designed learning, is at least 4000 years old. It's not a new idea that we're coming up with. If you go back and look at Upanishads, Mahabharata and the Bhaghavad Gita and other sacred texts, you'll find tons and tons of stories of self-designed learners in that, and even radical critiques of the formalised education system even of that time … Then we have other people, I'm sure you've heard of Kabir. He's a 15th century Sufi weaver. He never went to any school. He's a self-designed learner. There are lots and lots of examples historically of people like that, even then going into the works of Gandhi and Tagore, and other inspiring leaders. Most of them are advocating this much more radical approach to learning.
>
> (quoted in Hopkins 2018)

Contemporary unschooling, in all of its forms, is connected to an explicit critique of the OWW Development model and the simultaneous co-construction of ways of life outside the OWW. As Manish Jain further states,

> unschooling is one mode which means that we consciously choose not only not to send our children to school, but also to look at the impacts – how school plays out in not only the school setting, but also how it's infiltrated into many aspects of our lives and our mind sets – what I call the culture of schooling … We are actually trusting the children and co-creating learning programmes with each other based on their personal needs, and also based on how we try to rebuild a larger connection with community, culture and ecology … In India we've really been trying to link it to larger questions of sustainable life-style, reimagining economy, love, re-looking at reconnecting to a different sense of what is spiritual and sacred. So many other questions as well. Once you take your child out of school, what's your alternative? The alternative is Life. We started this journey wanting to live our lives differently.
>
> (ibid.)

Chapter 5 will provide an introduction and detailed analysis of the concept and practice of *radical unschooling among families*, in which parents and their children consciously and together decide to seek an education outside the schooling system based on the principles of children-led, self-designed learning (SDL).

While Chapter 5 thus looks at a largely individual, unstructured form that unschooling takes when practised among (middle-class) families whose children never or only for some very limited time attended mainstream schooling, Chapter 6 looks at the 'Nook' model of unschooling in the form of self-designed learning spaces catering to marginalised communities. As I will show, the philosophy of this model comes probably closest to the 'ideal' of ANPED by very consciously aiming to avoid the creation of hierarchies and of any sort of 'mould-ing of learners' at all costs.

The final chapter will introduce an unschooling model for higher education through a case study of Swaraj University, a semi-structured unschooling space for urban, middle-class young people who most often went through the OWW Education system. Swaraj University helps its learners, referred to as *khojis* ('seekers') to escape from the deeply ingrained presupposition of inequality with its pre-assigned roles and identities in order to discover their own ways of creating meaningful lives, what Swaraj University refers to as 'Alivelihoods'.

As such, the khojis' individual stories

> introduce turbulence to the linearity and one-dimensionality imposed by glo-balizing narratives about life-trajectories. They are not the kinds of decisions one would expect young persons to make in a cultural milieu increasingly defined by rapid urbanization, internet-mediated social networks, mushroom-ing shopping malls, and budding incentives to escape the boredom of village life.
>
> (Jain and Akomolafe 2015)

Ultimately, unschooling makes visible that 'education', 'knowledge' and 'learn-ing sources' are much more abundant than we are taught through the OWW Education model. This realisation can positively affect and impact both the ones who have a part in the OWW – in whatsoever subservient role – as well as the ones more intensely marginalised by OWW Development.

> We're told there's a shortage of teachers everywhere in India and every other country. But if you go on the streets, there's so many people who know how to do things. Who are brilliant, amazing, doing beautiful things. Our spiritual gurus, awesome mechanics, who know how to fix everything you bring them, who are fantastic artisans, farmers. But none of these people are regarded as teachers by the existing system. We find that once we step out of the bounda-ries of school, we're no longer poor, backward, underdeveloped people. We actually have very brilliant, abundant resources of learning all around us. For us at least it's very important to step out and see that we have so much poten-tial. In India, the apprenticeship learning system is humungous … But none of our educationists, nobody can see that this is an entire system that's work-ing in parallel in this country to support young people's learning. So we have a lot of other resources. Part of our work is an imagination census to remind ourselves that we have much more to work with than just working within this monoculture system.
>
> (Manish Jain, quoted in Hopkins 2018)

As a result, once we can shed our preconceived notions of what is actually worth-while and meaningful to learn, we also start to look at what is worthwhile and meaningful to do in and with life from a different perspective. Once we look at and thus drastically broaden our understanding of what is meaningful in life, we are able to create our own meaningful lives alongside others rather than competing against others to get a share in what others tell us is a meaningful life. In this spirit, this book aims to contribute its part to shed our preconceived notions of 'development', 'education' and what makes a meaningful life and to make visible, in turn, what seemed indeed impossible – to imagine the end of capitalism rather than the end of the world.

Notes

1 As Saul Newman puts it, 'the impotence of our lives also seems to encourage not the rejection of the current order, which renders us as such, but rather a seething resentment against certain marginalized groups – the poor, immigrants – which comes out in increasingly xenophobic and racist, even fascistic forms of politics' (Newman 2016: 28).

2 See Goldberg and Pavcnik (2007); Hickel (2019a); Oxfam (2019).

3 Measured from a more realistic, still moderate poverty line of USD 7.40 per day, 'we see that the number of people living under this line has increased dramatically since measurements began in 1981, reaching some 4.2 billion people today' (Hickel 2019b).

4 See Fisher (2009); Monbiot (2016); Bailes (2017); Cain (2018).

5 As Mohanty (2002: 34) contends, 'the world has gone from a patchwork of cultures to almost a monolith. Today the situation is such that there is (almost) one right way of growth, one right way of governance, one right way to acquire and use knowledge, one right way to learn, one right belief, one right way to build relationships, one right way to live'. Santoshi Markam provides one of many contemporary examples for this, looking at how many Adivasis – the indigenous people of India – are 're-educated' in ways similar to the crimes committed against Australia's and Canada's indigenous populations: 'by the time they graduate from school, there is very little "tribal" left in them. Their ways change so much that they begin to detest their native villages. Indigenous food habits seem strange or unknown to them. They develop a disdain towards their own culture. They do not find any aspect of their identity – language, customs, dress or food habits – worthy of pride. This is a direct result of the twelve years of brainwashing they are put through. This was my personal experience too. While studying, when I visited my home during holidays, the traditions looked "bad". However, as I grew up and became politically aware of my identity, I was able to analyse what "education" had transformed me into' (Markam 2020). A prominent example for this re-education taking place in contemporary India is the Kalinga Institute of Social Sciences (KISS) located in Bhubhaneshwar, 'a factory of a school for indigenous students' (ibid.).

6 See Sánchez-Bayo and Wyckhuys (2019).

7 See IPCC (2018).

8 As Spash (2020) argues, 'even as the general inadequacy of initial government policy led to global lockdown the primary aim was already to reassure stock markets, get "the economy" back to normal and re-establish "growth". Supposedly non-interventionist, "free-market", pro-corporate, anti-government business executives, billionaires and politicians united in supporting public policy packages offering trillions to save "the economy"'.

9 Another example for this is the further rise of India's e-commerce sector, catering to the middle and upper classes, which has received special protection from the government. As Gurumurthy and Chami (2020) observe, 'during the COVID-19 crisis, disaster capitalism is evident in the zeal that e-commerce platforms in India have displayed. For these companies, the lockdown is the moment to consolidate their dominance in

the market. The pot at the end of the rainbow must be claimed now, and the traditional retail sector – grocers, pushcart vendors, neighborhood traders who have actually been catering to the public in these trying times – rendered irrelevant'.

10 See Sampath (2020).

11 This is not to claim that mutual aid is practised as a conscious pursuit of anarchist politics during the pandemic, but most often simply out of solidarity for and with others.

12 For some concrete examples from around the globe, see Desta (2020); Sitrin and Colectiva Sembrar (2020); Solnit (2020); Jun and Lance (2020); Rickett (2020).

13 As such, it is important to recognise that even as most of us are part of the OWW and 'have a stake', we are so in a subservient role and we are so as often unwilling supporters of a seemingly natural system that damages our own lives (again, we just need to look at the rise in mental health issues, depression, increasing levels of frustration and anger and the feeling of meaninglessness that many of us as part of the OWW encounter in one way or the other).

14 See Escobar (1995, 2008 and 2018); Sachs (1992); Latouche (1993); Ferguson (1994); Rahnema and Bawtree (1997); Esteva and Prakash (1998); Rist (2006); Li (2007); Ziai (2007 and 2016); Esteva, Babones, and Babcicky (2013); Kothari et al. (2019).

15 See Law (2015).

16 As is important to note, 'there exists a significant North within the Global South, and a significant South within the Global North. That is, within the Global South, there exists a group of people who live in material and social conditions that are quantitatively and qualitatively more characteristic of the Global North … Likewise, within the Global North, there exists communities who live in material and social conditions which are quantitatively and qualitatively more characteristic of the Global South' (Aubrey 2002: 196–197).

17 As Ashish Kothari and Aseem Shrivastava note, 'India and the rest of the so-called developing world are strangely better off in one sense, compared to the West. The latter is deeply vested in the unsustainable modern industrial system, whereas countries of the global South are less entrenched … India … is among the few places in the world … where indigenous peoples and other traditional or small-scale communities have survived the onslaught of industrial modernity to this day' (Shrivastava and Kothari 2012: 316).

18 I focus my critique against the modern education system mostly but not exclusively on the idea and practice of compulsory schooling.

References

Aubrey, L. (2002). 'Moving beyond collective learning from the global north and bringing humanity back to itself: Pan Africanism, women, and co-development'. In Jain, M., and Jain, S. (eds.), *Unfolding Learning Societies: Experiencing the Possibilities*. Udaipur: Shikshantar, pp 194–209.

Bailes, J. (2017). 'Mental health and neoliberalism: An interview with William Davies'. https://www.counterpunch.org/2017/10/18/mental-health-and-neoliberalism-an-interview-with-william-davies/.

Biesta, G. (2016). *Good Education in an Age of Measurement: Ethics, Politics, Democracy*. London: Routledge.

Cain, R. (2018). 'How Neoliberalism is Damaging Your Mental Health'. https://theconversation.com/how-neoliberalism-is-damaging-your-mental-health-90565.

Desta, J. (2020). 'Is another world possible? Pandemic communalism as a cure to corona capitalism'. https://anarchiststudies.org/is-another-world-possible-pandemic-communalism-as-a-cure-to-corona-capitalism/.

Edelman, M., and Haugerud, A. (eds) (2005). *The Anthropology of Development and Globalisation: From Classical Political Economy to Contemporary Neoliberalism.* Oxford: Blackwell.

Escobar, A. (1995). *Encountering Development: The Making and Unmaking of the Third World.* Princeton, NJ: Princeton University Press.

Escobar, A. (2008). *Territories of Difference: Place, Movements, Life, Redes.* Durham: Duke University Press.

Escobar, A. (2018). *Designs for the Pluriverse: Radical Interdependence, Autonomy, and the Making of Worlds.* Durham: Duke University Press.

Esteva, G., and Prakash, M.S. (1998). *Grassroots Post-Modernism: Remaking the Soil of Cultures.* London: Zed Books.

Esteva, G., Babones, S., and P. Babcicky. (2013). *The Future of Development. A Radical Manifesto.* Bristol: Policy Press.

Ferguson, J. (1994). *The Anti-Politics Machine: "Development," Depoliticization, and Bureaucratic Power in Lesotho.* Minneapolis: University of Minnesota Press.

Fisher, M. (2009). *Capitalist Realism: Is There No Alternative?* Winchester: 0 Books.

Goldberg, P.K., and Pavcnik, N. (2007). 'Distributional effects of globalization in developing Countries'. *Journal of Economic Literature*, XLV, pp. 39–82.

Graeber, D. (2004). *Fragments of an Anarchist Anthropology.* Chicago: Prickly Paradigm Press.

Gurumurthy, A., and Chami, N. (2020). 'Profiteering from the Pandemic: How India's lockdown paved the way for big e-commerce disaster capitalism'. https://us.boell.org/en/2020/06/19/profiteering-pandemic-how-indias-lockdown-paved-way-big-e-commerce-disaster-capitalism.

Hickel, J. (2019a). 'Bill Gates says poverty is decreasing. He couldn't be more wrong'. https://www.theguardian.com/commentisfree/2019/jan/29/bill-gates-davos-global-poverty-infographic-neoliberal.

Hickel, J. (2019b). 'Global inequality: Do we really live in a one hump world'? https://www.jasonhickel.org/blog/2019/3/17/two-hump-world.

Hopkins, R. (2018). 'Manish Jain: "Our work is to recover wisdom and imagination"'. https://www.robhopkins.net/2018/01/31/manish-jain-our-work-is-to-recover-wisdom-and-imagination/.

Intergovernmental Panel on Climate Change. (2018). *Global Warming of 1.5°C. An IPCC Special Report on the Impacts of Global Warming of 1.5°C above Pre-industrial Levels and Related Global Greenhouse Gas Emission Pathways, in the Context of Strengthening the Global Response to the Threat of Climate Change, Sustainable Development, and Efforts to Eradicate Poverty.* Geneva: Intergovernmental Panel on Climate Change.

Jain, M., and Akomolafe, B. (2015). 'This revolution will not be schooled: How we are collectively improvising a "new story" about learning'. http://bayoakomolafe.net/project/this-revolution-will-not-be-schooled-how-we-are-collectively-improvising-a-new-story-about-learning/.

Jensen, D. (2004). *Walking on Water: Reading, Writing, and Revolution.* White River Junction, Vermont: Chelsea Green Publishing Company.

Jun, N., and Lance, M. (2020). 'Anarchist responses to a pandemic: The COVID-19 crisis as a case study in mutual aid'. https://kiej.georgetown.edu/anarchist-responses-covid-19-special-issue/.

Kothari, A., Salleh, A., Escobar, A., Demaria, F., and A. Acosta. (eds.) (2019). *Pluriverse: A Post-Development Dictionary.* New Delhi: Tulika Books.

Latouche, S. (1993). *In the Wake of the Affluent Society: An Exploration of Post-Development*. London: Zed Books.

Law, J. (2015). 'What's wrong with a one-world world'? *Distinktion: Journal of Social Theory*, 16 (1), pp. 126–139.

Li, T.M. (2007). *The Will to Improve: Governmentality, Development, and the Practice of Politics*. Durham: Duke University Press.

Markam, S. (2020). 'The alienation of adivasis from our identity, or how I unlearned my Hinduisation'. https://thewire.in/culture/alienation-adivasis-identity-culture-hinduisation-education.

May, T. (2010). *Contemporary Political Movements and the Thought of Jacques Rancière: Equality in Action*. Edinburgh: Edinburgh University Press.

Mohanty, S. (2002). 'The altars of constructs'. In Jain, M., and Jain, S. (eds.), *Unfolding Learning Societies: Experiencing the Possibilities*. Udaipur: Shikshantar, pp. 26–39.

Monbiot, G. (2016). 'Neoliberalism is creating loneliness. That's what's wrenching society apart'. https://www.theguardian.com/commentisfree/2016/oct/12/neoliberalism-creating-loneliness-wrenching-society-apart.

Newman, S. (2016). *Postanarchism*. Cambridge: Polity Press.

Norberg-Hodge, H. (2016). 'Practitioner perspective: Learning for life'. In Skinner, A., Smith, M.B., Brown, E., and T. Troll (eds.), *Education, Learning and the Transformation of Development*. New York: Routledge, pp. 50–57.

Oxfam. (2019). *Public Good or Private Wealth?* Cowley, Oxford: Oxfam GB.

Rahnema, M., and Bawtree, V. (eds.) (1997). *The Post-Development Reader*. London: Zed Books.

Rickett, O. (2020). 'These local heroes are protecting people because the government won't'. https://www.vice.com/en_uk/article/4agjwq/mutual-aid-groups-coronavirus-uk.

Rist, G. (2006). *The History of Development: From Western Origins to Global Faith*. 2nd ed. London: Zed Books.

Roig, S., and Crowther, J. (2016). 'Can dreams come true? Exploring transformative education and development through the experiences of La Verneda-Sant Martí, Catalunya, Spain'. In Skinner, A., Smith, M.B., Brown, E., and T. Troll (eds.), *Education, Learning and the Transformation of Development*. New York: Routledge, pp. 77–92.

Roy, D. (2020). 'Rethinking minority and mainstream in India'. In Sitrin, M., and Colectiva Sembrar (eds.), *Pandemic Solidarity: Mutual Aid during the Covid-19 Crisis*. Kindle ed. London: Pluto Press.

Sachs, W. (1992). *The Development Dictionary: A Guide to Knowledge as Power*. London: Zed Books.

Sampath, G. (2020). 'Comment: The "shock doctrine" in India's response to COVID-19'. https://www.thehindu.com/podcast/comment-the-shock-doctrine-in-indias-response-to-covid-19/article31831402.ece.

Sánchez-Bayo, F., and Wyckhuys, Kris A.G. (2019). 'Worldwide decline of the entomofauna: A review of its drivers'. *Biological Conservation*, 232, pp. 8–27.

Shrivastava, A., and Kothari, A. (2012). *Churning the Earth: The Making of Global India*. New Delhi: Penguin.

Solnit, R. (2020). 'The way we get through this is together': The rise of mutual aid under coronavirus'. https://www.theguardian.com/world/2020/may/14/mutual-aid-coronavirus-pandemic-rebecca-solnit.

Spash, C.L. (2020). '"The economy" as if people mattered: Revisiting critiques of economic growth in a time of crisis'. *Globalizations*, DOI: 10.1080/14747731.2020.1761612.

Suissa, J. (2010). *Anarchism and Education: A Philosophical Perspective*. 2nd ed. Oakland, CA: PM Press.

Underhill, H. (2016). Learning in the praxis of diaspora politics: Understanding development as social justice. In Skinner, A., Smith, M.B., Brown, E., and T. Troll (eds.), *Education, Learning and the Transformation of Development*. New York: Routledge, pp. 158–171.

Ziai, A. (2007). *Exploring Post-development: Theory and Practice, Problems and Perspectives*. New York: Routledge.

Ziai, A. (2016). *Development Discourse and Global History: From colonialism to the Sustainable Development Goals*. New York: Routledge.

1 Between neoliberalism and Hindutva

Deconstructing India's development paradigm[1]

This chapter aims to provide a refined understanding of both the current Development paradigm as applied across the world, and its specific application and ramifications in the contemporary Indian context. Building on a mix of post-development theory, the political philosophy of Jacques Rancière and Todd May, as well as on political ontology, I conceptualise Development as *ontological politics of inequality,* a 'world-making practice' that reinforces a subjective and hierarchical worldview and thereby takes away people's capacity to co-create their own meaningful lives outside the developmental purview explored below.

To begin with this endeavour, I draw on the postdevelopment school of thought in order to deconstruct the hegemonic conceptualisation of Development as purportedly neutral, objective and overall 'benign' discourse and practice, a win-win situation that benefits everyone involved, from civil society and the state to the private sector. At the same time, I will draw attention to how the mainstream education system, seen as the silver bullet of Development by both private and state actors, is inherently tied to the at the time prevailing Development model and serves as a powerful tool that both reflects and, even more importantly, recreates and extends it across society.

After this, we will look at the current, specific forms that the Development model takes in India. With the rise to power of the nationalistic Bharatiya Janata Party (BJP) and its Hindutva ideology – as with the rise of nationalist governments elsewhere – there is much speculation about the potential end of neoliberal Development, seeing right-wing populism and nationalist capitalism oftentimes as a counter-reaction to the adverse impacts of neoliberalism on large parts of the population. However, as I will suggest, instead of a departure from neoliberal Development policy, what we can observe is an intensification of the latter fused with a cultural accoutrement in the form of a Hindu-nationalist framework aimed to create 'virtuous market citizens'.

At the same time, I demonstrate how all forms of Development – liberal, neoliberal or virtuous neoliberal – follow a specific liberal notion of 'equality'. This indeed represents a very narrow and subjective interpretation of its potential meaning, 'put to cynical use … in order to justify … the virtues of the capitalist market' (May 2010: 152).

Ultimately, I propose to make sense of Development as a specific social practice or ontological politics which both reflects as well as reinforces and expands a certain worldview or ontology rooted in Western modernity, showing how this specific worldview is very much compatible with and often even conducive to the Hindutva 'way of life'. This understanding sets out the scene for the next chapters to both further deconstruct how mainstream education is closely intertwined with Development, as well as to envision a postdevelopmental politics and a related mode of education that can counter the hegemonic Development–education nexus and let us build meaningful lives beyond Development.

Postdevelopment and the deconstruction of global Development

The origins of postdevelopment theory can be found in Wolfgang Sachs' now infamous obituary of the post-World-War-II (PWWII) Development project:

> the last 40 years can be called the age of development. This epoch is coming to an end ... The idea of development stands like a ruin in the intellectual landscape. Delusion and disappointment, failures and crimes have been the steady companions of development and they tell a common story: it did not work.
>
> (Sachs 1992: 1)

This verdict is based on a mix of both socio-economic analyses of the impact of Development on local communities and discursive analyses of the very concept and structure of Development. Regarding the former, postdevelopment writers draw attention to the many negative socio-economic effects of Development. As Berger and Weber, for example, argue, the many promises that Development has made for almost eight decades now are still not fulfilled.

> Even if we take the orthodox measurement of development, and even if we do it in cases where economic growth rates have increased, this does not necessarily translate into improvements in the day-to-day lived experiences of very large numbers of people across the planet ... On the contrary, inequalities have increased, in some cases dramatically, and new challenges (for instance in health, nutrition and environmental safety) have arisen.
>
> (Berger and Weber 2014: 14)

Focussing on India, Shrivastava and Kothari (2012: 116–117) contend that

> given the sheer number of people who have been paralysed by debt, dispossessed, displaced or otherwise impoverished, it would scarcely be an overstatement to say that development, far from reducing poverty, has actually been creating new, modern forms of it.

Coming to a similar conclusion, Padel and Das (2010: xviii) state that the reality of Development in India 'spells communities torn apart, families thrown into squalor, grinding menial jobs and chronic food shortage'. Finally, current research provides compelling evidence that in India, 'neoliberal capitalism, far from ena-bling the benefits of its growth rates to trickle down to all groups, has further entrenched inequalities based on pre-existing unequal social divisions' (Shah and Lerche 2018: 1).

Connecting the socio-economic analysis with a poststructural critique against Development, postdevelopment shows how, instead of enhancing people's lives in meaningful ways, the practice of Development works in the same way as Foucault argues the practice of rehabilitation works for the prisoner, or the practice of 'schooling' works for the student: it is 'molding people's behaviour and conception of themselves along narrow predefined pathways ... It constrains people to act in accordance with the needs of an industrialised capitalist society' (May 2016: 154).

Building on this line of inquiry, postdevelopment scholars equally empha-sise the indirect, psychological/cultural-turned-material impact on 'Third World Populations', resulting in a 'dispossession of meaning' (Da Costa 2016: 188), a 'de-ontologising' and 'de-culturing' of non-Western, non-modern ways of life by instilling that ostensibly underdeveloped, inferior people can only 'become developed' by giving up their cultures, life-experiences and place-based exist-ence. When these processes of Development unfold, as they do on a daily basis, 'cultural platforms are deformed or destroyed ... [and] people's lives may cease to exist in ways that benefit them and may only function to advantage those who caused the problems in the first place' (Abdi 2016: 231).

Taken together, this results in the radical critique of postdevelopment against each and every form of Development, including 'participatory', 'community' and other, 'alternative' forms of it. As Aram Ziai argues,

> alternative development merely looks for different roads to arrive at the same goal. However, if this goal is unambiguous and defined by modern, indus-trial capitalist societies, then even alternative development remains firmly grounded in the Western, or more precisely hegemonic, models of politics (nation state and liberal democracy), the economy (neoliberal, globalised capitalism) and knowledge (Western science).
>
> (Ziai 2017: 2552)

Similarly, postdevelopment scholars criticise the latest reincarnation of Development under its 'sustainability' tag for appropriating the originally radical idea of the latter to fit economic imperatives of growth instead of pushing envi-ronmental or social issues on top of the sustainability agenda. This is exemplified in the 2012 final report of the global 2012 Rio+20 sustainability summit:

> the report did not acknowledge that infinite growth is impossible in a finite world. It conceptualised natural capital as a 'critical economic asset', open-ing the doors for commodification (so-called green capitalism), and did not challenge unbridled consumerism. A lot of emphasis was placed on market

mechanisms, technology and better management, undermining the fundamental political, economic and social changes the world needs.

(Kothari et al. 2015)

The SDGs agenda by the United Nations is another case in point. According to
Ziai (2016: 204), it features some central discursive structures which date back
to the origins of development aid in the middle of the 20th century. Thereby, it
emphasises again technical, top-down solutions focused on sustaining economic
growth and the modernist, Western way of life above everything else.

Finally, Marxist and socialist-statist approaches towards Development are
likewise rejected based on their pursuit of modernisation and economic growth,
albeit through other means, and on the top-down nature of the interventions by the
'developmental state'.[2] This is most pronounced in the work of Gustavo Esteva,
denouncing the state as 'a mechanism for control and domination, useless for
emancipation' (Esteva and Escobar 2019: 24).[3]

Consequently, postdevelopment rejects all forms of Development – be it capitalist, Marxist, socialist or alternative – which conceptualise countries, regions
and peoples as underdeveloped and inferior, and in need of more Development to
catch up to some predefined and imposed role model.

> The PWWII development project encompasses them all – the term is meant
> to refer to the various ideas and practices which have been premised upon the
> belief that some areas of the world are 'developed', and others not, and that
> those which are not can and should set about achieving the 'development'
> which has thus far eluded them. This whole body of knowledge (with all its
> various strains) is rejected by post-development theorists, but the idea that it
> is possible for a society to undergo some or other process of transformation,
> which will result in a better life for its inhabitants, is not.
>
> (Matthews 2004: 375)

Based on this, postdevelopment writers argue that the concept of Development
needs to be completely abandoned as it is so deeply rooted in a Eurocentric,
depoliticising and authoritarian ideology or worldview that it cannot be 'rescued'
anymore.[4]

The Development–education nexus

India's modern 'Development history' almost reads like a 'history of Development'
itself. During the colonial period, Gandhian postdevelopmental positions based
on the ideal of the Indian village featured prominently in public discourse. After
independence, however, Gandhi's village model – pursuing ideas of self-governance, autonomy, decentralisation and economic self-sufficiency – was soon
discarded by the Nehruvian developmental state.

Fully embracing a Westernised, modernist vision of Development, the latter
can be considered as a mixed-economy model, grounded in a strong belief in

technological progress, rationality, modern science and the miracles of industrialisation, and measured against the ups and downs of the gross domestic product. The seamless combination of capitalist and socialist ensembles in Nehru's Development model, in fact, reveals their similarity in Development-thinking, justifying once more the postdevelopmental rejection of both.

Turning more and more into a fully capitalist Development model in the 1970s and 1980s, the last three decades then marked the neoliberal turn in and of Development, beginning in July 1991 with the World Bank-imposed structural adjustment programme (SAP) to address India's external debt and foreign exchange crisis. As we will see below, the most recent turn towards right-wing populism and nationalist capitalism does not mark the end of the neoliberal mantra of free markets, privatisation and private sector-led growth, but rather its intensification and modification along Hindu-nationalist lines.

But before turning to a more in-depth analysis of India's most recent, current history of Development, it is instructive to briefly look at the closely intertwined relationship between Development and education in India over the last decades. As such, we can see how education both reflected and reinforced and recreated the then-prevailing Development paradigm.

Gandhi's *nai talim* – which can be freely translated as 'new decolonised system of learning'[5] – therefore was envisioned to lay the foundations for the 'village republic' to function and flourish. Geared primarily towards the needs and interests of the rural population – and not the colonial powers or urban elites – *nai talim* focused on the acquisition of practical, relevant skills to achieve self-sufficiency on the village level. Beyond this, however, it served as a holistic philosophy of localised learning and living that was intended to combine 'head, heart, hands and home'.[6]

As Gandhiji put it,

> when our villages are fully developed there will be no dearth in them of men with a high degree of skill and artistic talent. There will be village poets, village artists, village architects, linguists and research workers. In short, there will be nothing in life worth having which will not be had in the villages. Today the villages are dung heaps. Tomorrow they will be like tiny gardens of Eden where dwells the highly intelligent folk, whom no one can deceive or exploit. The reconstruction of the villages along these lines should begin right now. That might necessitate some modification of the scheme. The reconstruction of the villages should not be organized on a temporary but permanent basis. *Craft, art, health and education should all be integrated into one scheme. Nai Talim is a beautiful blend of all the four and covers the whole education of the individual from the time of conception to the moment of death.* Therefore, I would not divide village uplift work into water-tight compartments from the very beginning but undertake an activity which will combine all four. *Instead of regarding craft and industry as different from education, I will regard the former as the medium for the latter.*
>
> (Gandhi [1946] 2009: 97–98; emphasis added)

As Gandhi lost much of his influence in the nationalist movement over the final years of the independence struggle and his model of (post-)Development was relegated to the sidelines, so too has the idea of *nai talim* been marginalised and largely ignored by the Indian state after independence.

Under Jawaharlal Nehru's vision of progress and modernisation, school-based learning and the setup of higher education institutions became the means to catch up to the 'developed countries', and classrooms soon became some of the 'new temples of modern India'. Accordingly, in Nehru's developmental state,

> the post-Independence educational agenda was a nationalist project having broadly two components: (a) it attached 'great importance to modernity', trying to put forth the image of an industrially advanced modern state having a scientific and rational paradigm of development; and (b) it was deeply concerned with the issue of national integration, which meant 'overcoming all local identities and regional differences; realising our shared Indianness and strengthening the centrality of the new nation-state' (Pathak 2002: 95).
>
> (Kumar 2006: 20)

With the arrival of neoliberalisation and the implementation of the draconian SAPs in the 1990s, the agenda of and in education shifted likewise. A massive defunding and destabilisation campaign against the public school system – actively pursued by the Indian state in coordination with key Development actors such as the World Bank – saw the rise of private players and public-private partnerships in education (ePPPs). Alongside this came a shift of education's main role from creating 'good citizens' of the developmental state towards creating 'good market citizens' through incorporating the neoliberal mantras of 'competition', 'choice' and business-like logic and language in the curriculum (see Chapter 3).

While the latter still constitutes the main thrust of India's contemporary education landscape, we can see how an increasingly assertive Indian state not only aims to create more 'enabling environments' for private education actors, but additionally intervenes to tame and control 'free-thinking' institutions, especially universities and colleges. Moreover, the government has set out to actively change parts of the school curriculum to promote a Hindutva-influenced understanding of history.

As I will show in the next section, these changes reflect the newest reincarnation of the Indian Development paradigm under what we can call, following Priya Chacko, *virtuous neoliberalism*. However, rather than merely reflecting these changes, I contend that modern education, especially in its form of obligatory schooling, indeed reinforces and attempts to *socialise* its subjects into the given, hierarchical order of Development, thereby indeed co-creating and co-constituting it at the same time.

As Derek Jensen so vividly asks us, imagine 'to make a nation of slaves' using direct force, dispossession or other less subtle means –

> the primary drawback of each of these approaches is that the slaves still know they're enslaved, and the last thing you want is to have to put down a

rebellion. Far better for them to believe they're free, because then if they're unhappy the fault lies not with you but with themselves. It all starts with the children. If you don't start young enough, you'll never be able to acculturate them sufficiently so that they disbelieve in alternatives. And if they honestly believe in alternatives – those not delineated by you – they may attempt to actualize them. And then where would you be?

(Jensen 2004: 9)

This means that in order to nurture, advance and bring about the alternatives to Development that postdevelopment envisions, education becomes an immensely important site of struggle. It is therefore essential to understand both the current Development model which education both recreates and reflects, as well as to co-create, make visible and promote new models of education and learning that are, in turn, reflecting, reinforcing and actively building postdevelopmental visions of what makes meaningful lives. This book sets out to do both.

Virtuous-neoliberal Development and the presupposition of inequality

Despite the numerous postdevelopmental obituaries of Development, the latter – especially in its current neoliberal form – seems to be alive and kicking.[7] In India, this becomes evident through what Ranabir Samaddar terms 'the governmentalisation of party politics', referring to a consensus on the neoliberal Development model across the entire political spectrum, from Hindu nationalists to centrists and Communists.[8] This consensus finds its expression in an explosion of social policies by various government coalitions, targeted 'to prepare everyone (ideally equally) for the market-driven order' (Samaddar 2016: 158).

The neoliberal consensus also continues under the current BJP-led National Democratic Alliance's reign in India. While there has been much debate about the question of whether the contemporary rise of right-wing populism alongside nationalist capitalism in India and elsewhere signals a shift away from neoliberalism, what we can see in today's India under Prime Minister Narendra Modi and Home Minister Amit Shah is an intensification of the neoliberal agenda paired with Hindutva ideology.[9] As such, neoliberalism – not to be confused with a more internationalist liberalism – and right-wing populism are often two mutually reinforcing philosophies.[10]

Harmes (2012: 63), on the one hand, shows how nationalist policies are often compatible with and even conducive for neoliberalism understood as a normative concept of 'individual freedom and, in particular, freedom from "progressive" forms of government intervention designed to redistribute wealth and correct market failures'. On the other hand, the case of India demonstrates how neoliberal policies actively help to further the BJP's communal agenda. This becomes particularly visible in the abolition of the Planning Commission[11] and the roll-back of many of the former Indian National Congress-led, United Progressive Alliance government's social policy schemes that aimed to abate some of the most egregious effects of its otherwise neoliberal agenda.

Instead, many of these basic social welfare schemes are replaced by neoliberal, 'community-based empowerment programmes' aiming for the hierarchical inclusion of the so-called 'neo-middle classes', consisting mainly of what is referred to as the 'Other Backward Classes', and the targeted exclusion of others, especially non-Hindu minorities and the ultra-poor. This leaves existing hierarchies firmly in place and often even reinforces them.[12] In sum,

> the BJP-led government seeks to insulate neo-liberal policies and practices from dissent while also building consent for neoliberalisation and authoritarian statist practices through a populist discourse that pits a 'people', encompassing the poor, the newly urbanised 'neo-middle classes' and middle-class Hindus. These groups are cast as entrepreneurs and consumers, against a secular, 'anti-national' liberal 'elite' who are seen as corrupt because they monopolise power, resources and prevent 'development' while pandering to non-Hindu minority groups.
>
> (Chacko 2018b: 543)

What becomes evident is that this model of Development is still clearly based on the neoliberal paradigm, with some modifications and additions. This neoliberal Development model, as I lay out next, has its roots in liberal philosophy that promises to deliver Development-as-equality, i.e. 'making everyone equally developed'.

Contrary to what it promises, however, Development does not deliver 'equality', but takes away people's freedom to pursue their own ways of leading meaningful lives by *forcing* them to become equals in a predefined and predetermined project. As such, the one and only equality that Development today offers to its objects is equality before the market, i.e. having equal access to markets, finance, products and opportunities that the market offers.

As Jacques Rancière and Todd May, who builds on the thoughts of the former, argue, the contemporary, liberal and common-sense understanding of equality implies a technical, manageable, top-down, elitist approach (note the similarity to postdevelopment's critique of Development):[13] 'there is general agreement that equality is, first and foremost, a matter of what people deserve. Otherwise put, it is a matter of what they should receive' (May 2010: 4).

Equality thus becomes a distributive good, a right that can be awarded by someone to someone else. This implies both the need of a duty-bearer or distributor (often, but in the age of late capitalism equally often challenged, the state, replaced or complemented more and more by the private sector or civil society), and the need of a (passive) receiving end that awaits to obtain the distributable goods. This receiving end is the vast majority of the world's population, in the process becoming a mere object that is expected to receive equality from an authority above, rather than 'possessing' or 'seizing' equality on their own. The consequence of this is a hierarchical society in which 'there are those who distribute equality, and those who receive it. Once you start with that assumption, the hierarchy is already in place' (May 2010: 5).

Such a passive, hierarchical conceptualisation of equality is an inherent part of liberal philosophy which legitimises and normalises the modern nation-state by taking its role in guaranteeing and even *awarding equality* to its citizens as granted, as the point of departure for all political action. Similarly, for libertarian philosophers, the role of awarding equality to others is being granted to the markets (through the state that transfers this role to markets as, for libertarians, they are seen as more efficient in distributing equality).

What all of these liberal and libertarian notions of equality, from John Rawls to Amartya Sen and Robert Nozick, then have in common is that they take the institutions of the state and the market respectively as a pre-given, pre-existing entity whose role is never questioned as such and who then are legitimised to distribute a pre-given form of equality to others. In all these conceptualisations, be it as 'equal liberty, opportunity and access' (Rawls), 'equal liberty' (Nozick), or 'equal capabilities' (Sen),

> equality is a debt owed to individuals by the governing institutions of a society or a community … Equality, in these views, lies in what is given to people, what they are entitled to receive from others … While they are not concerned with how much happiness or how many goods people wind up with, they are still concerned with what institutions owe to individuals. If goods or happiness do not lie at the end of the process, people still do.
>
> (May 2009b: 109–110)

Equality, in other words, transforms into *the presupposition of inequality* (of people). As Todd May further points out,

> the people living in a particular society do not, unless they form part of the distributing class, have anything to do with equality other than to be the object of it. We can readily see the politics of traditional liberalism at work in these implications. Taken together, they help sustain a hierarchical view of society in which the members of that society are conceived as individuals pursuing disparate and unrelated ends that the state helps them more or less to achieve.
>
> (May 2009a: 5)

In conceptualising equality as a distributive good or debt, it is not 'ordinary people' themselves who decide about what it is they are owed. Instead, equality is predefined by the very (few) people who distribute it from above. Therefore, while the ends that people may pursue are disparate, they are all firmly rooted within the limits of what we can call for now *liberal modernity* – i.e. market-based, capitalist economies, liberal democracies, the supremacy of private property, sanctity of contracts, rationality, modernity, Western science, linear progress, etc. This is what Arturo Escobar refers to as

> the individual~real~science~economy (market) ensemble [which] constitutes the default setting of much of socio-natural life in late modernity;

they are historical constructs, to be sure, but also beliefs to which we are deeply attached in our every day existence because of the pervasive social processes and practices which hold them in place, and without which we cannot function.

(Escobar 2012: 22)

The various pre-given sets and bundles of equality on offer by those who distribute it, however different they are from each other, are all similarly geared towards realising ends that fall within the parameters of this ensemble. In its neoliberal variant, this means that equality and autonomy are 'defined much more narrowly in terms of economic responsibility … The individual is thrown back upon himself and his own resources and is forced to reduce his entire existence to a marketable and commodifiable set of behaviours and performances' (Newman 2016: 121).

Although the discourse of the Modi/Shah government seems to challenge or even shift some of the above parameters (e.g. challenging the primacy of Western science and modernity in favour of restoring 'India's civilisational identity and past glory'), to date, this often takes more of a symbolic character and serves to appeal to the core base of BJP voters.

After all, Narendra Modi came to power in 2014 through a campaign that highlighted the promise to successfully replicate his 'Gujarat Model for Development' (as then Prime Minister of the state) across the nation:

in the BJP's campaign, the Gujarat-Modi model promised private sector driven growth, high economic growth rates, business-friendly policies, foreign investment, urbanisation and industrial development. It was also linked to a discourse on 'development', which was, in part, conceptualised as market-based, entrepreneurial self-improvement.

(Chacko 2018b: 554)

However, we can increasingly observe the attempt to embed the above market-based ensemble within a cultural framework of Hindu nationalism among the neo-middle classes. This challenges the Western idea(l) of the rational, autonomous individual and shifts it towards what Priya Chacko calls the '*virtuous* market citizen' who relies 'on the market, the private sector and individual self-improvement for well-being … The regime of virtuous market citizenship valorises an entrepreneurial individualised subject whose behaviour is regulated by a Hindu nationalist social framework' (Chacko 2019: 49).

This becomes evident in many of the government's Development projects such as the heavily promoted '*Swachh Bharat Abhiyan*' ('Clean India Mission'). The programme shifts the responsibility for a clean environment, public health and hygiene squarely onto the individual household. Thereby, it promotes 'individual and community responsibility for the provision of public goods and treats cleanliness as a nationalist virtue with Gandhi upheld as a role model … He is appropriated as a Hindu nationalist market citizen' (Chacko 2019: 51).[14]

Another example is the government's '*Pandit Deendayal Upadhyay Shramev Jayate Karyakram*' scheme which aims to enable a 'more friendly' business environment by diluting labour regulations, in turn providing workers with access to training and insurance. It 'was described by Modi as a compassionate approach' that 'would result in the "Shram Yogi" (labourer) becoming a "Rashtra Yogi" [nation labourer] and hence, a "Rashtra Nirmaata" (nation-builder)' (Chacko 2018a: 402).

This is part of a whole range of 'empowerment' programmes recently set up by the BJP-led government. All of these are 'essentially neoliberal programmes, presented as social programmes, with a focus on market-driven supply-side incentives to encourage risk taking while at the same time securitizing risk' (Gudavarthy and Vijay 2020: 474).

As such, the virtuous market citizen is a role model of self-discipline and sacrifice for the greater good. Left mostly to their own devices, without the state's support in terms of traditional welfare programmes, public services delivery, etc., the virtuous market citizen heroically sees it as their own task, as a duty to the greater Hindu nation, to manage their own risks and join the 'empowerment' interventions of the government in order to advance on the path of Development. Advancing on the path of (neoliberal) Development, indeed, becomes synonymous with advancing the project of a Hindu nation.[15]

Be it a liberal, neoliberal or virtuous-neoliberal idea of Development-as-equality, all of them have in common that they fall by and large within the framework of liberal modernity as explored above, with some additions and modifications. In other words, the pre-given, imposed forms of equality are intended to help those who are thought less than equal to become equals only within this very narrow framework, the tenets of which are already set by the very elites that distribute equality from above.

Microloan schemes such as the Indian government's '*Pradhan Mantri MUDRA Yojana*' programme, inaugurated in 2015, are another textbook example of the neoliberal presupposition of inequality disguised as empowerment. Targeted often particularly at women, the microcredit model

> rests on the idea of the individual entrepreneur who, with the help of micro-credit, becomes self-employed, owns private property (the assets she builds with the loans), and sells her labor on the market. The out-of-the-home entrepreneur links seamlessly with the ideology of neoliberalism. She is an owner of petty capital. This production of the ownership ethic is against wage labor, overtime pay, retirement benefits and worker's compensation, i.e. against the very foundations of a welfare state. Failure to succeed now rests solely with the individual and not with the corporation/NGO/state. In this scenario, the state withdraws from the welfare of its citizens to the welfare of capital.
>
> (Karim 2008: 14)

These and many other contemporary examples show how equality in the (neo-) liberal, developmental sense becomes a productive form of power that takes away from people the very matter it purports to give them and attempts to subjectivise them into conformist, consumerist, passive-productive individuals of the neoliberal order based on 'a neoliberal discourse of self-help and individual responsibility' (ibid.). Thus, this is another example where 'there is a hierarchical order in which those who are the object of equality are not its subject. And, of course, if there is such a hierarchical order then there isn't really equality' (May 2010: 4).

Seen in a broader perspective, the various predefined and pre-packaged concepts of equality distributed by the ones more equal than others hence demonstrate another essential aspect: the idea that people are not able to create meaningful lives on their own, but that they need an 'enlightened elite' to help them make sense of the world and lead them towards the proper ends. As such,

> roles are distributed on the presupposition that certain people are just not as intelligent as others. Think, for instance, of the history of gender or racial relations. Think of the assumptions made by managers about the inherent limits of worker ability. The divisions between intellectual and manual labor, between the private and the public sphere, between the government and the governed, are guided by a hierarchy founded in the presupposition of inequality. One of the reasons we find it so difficult to imagine another social order is that these hierarchies present themselves as natural or inescapable, because the presupposition of *in*equality has become ingrained in us.
>
> (May 2010: 8–9; emphasis original)

Other current examples for this presupposition of inequality can be found in how plans for vocational training and skill development programmes by the Indian government, presented under the idea of community-based empowerment, are targeted towards 'modernising' traditional professions of lower-caste communities and other minorities through access to finance, markets and resources.[16]

Similarly, Dalits[17] are targeted through programmes such as the '*Swachhta Udyami Yojana*' ('Cleanliness Entrepreneurship Scheme') and the 'Sanitary Mart' scheme. All these Development initiatives reinforce hierarchies instead of challenging them:

> while occupation-based caste hierarchies remain undisturbed, there is an effort to overcome the stigma attached by modernizing these professions. It is an attempt to lend a sense of inclusivity without breaking free from the ancient normative frame based on purity–pollution hierarchical distinctions (*varna-ashrama-dharma*).
>
> (Gudavarthy and Vijay 2020: 475)[18]

This shows how the presupposition of inequality is based on the assumption and powerful myth that the vast majority of people are less intelligent than an enlightened few, and therefore incapable of co-creating meaningful lives on their own. Instead, they need to be assigned to their (pre-destined) roles and kept in place by the ones more equal than others. Ultimately, this is the justification for why there is a need for institutions and their elites to provide certain pre-packaged forms of equality.

Therefore, Jacques Rancière argues that formal liberal democracies – whose social orders and political systems operate on the presupposition of inequality – do not constitute a form of *democratic politics*. Instead, they are part of what Rancière (1999: 28) refers to as '*The Police*', a process under the guise of democratic politics which 'is generally seen as the set of procedures whereby the aggregation and consent of collectivities is achieved, the organization of powers, the distribution of places and roles, and the systems for legitimizing this distribution'.[19]

We can easily apply this notion to the Development paradigm as a whole. On a general level, the concept of Development – by necessarily having to draw the distinction between 'developed' (Western, modern) selves and 'underdeveloped' (non-Western, non-modern) others – is deeply rooted in the presupposition of inequality. In this process, it is (pre-)selecting and judging a certain way of life based on pre-given values and principles as 'developed' while it marginalises and discredits any other ways of life as 'underdeveloped'. The people designated as leading 'underdeveloped lives' cannot seize equality on their own but are dependent on the 'developed elites' in order to become 'equally developed'.

More specifically, then, the idea of Development is based on the prerogative of the state and its 'Development experts' to speak on behalf of others, to define and determine what a meaningful life is and what it is not – without this in-built presupposition of inequality, Development cannot even exist.[20] The expert-driven nature of Development is tied to the phenomenon that on the global level[21] as well as across most nation-states, at least those that are not 'failed states', Development is conceptualised as a right rather than as freedom. As a subset of the liberal notion of equality, Development thus becomes a good distributed from above.

As such, 'the freedom to pursue Development' is fundamentally different from 'the right to Development'. Keeping aside for a moment the postdevelopmental concerns that Development cannot be saved from its Western, modernist overtones, the former would be built on the understanding that (a) different people have different ideas of Development and can pursue various forms of Development together with and alongside others; and (b) that not everyone wants to and has to pursue Development.

In contrast, the latter is based on the presupposition of inequality – it assumes that everyone lacks, but ultimately needs and wants 'to be developed' in a specific way and is not capable of doing so on their own. Thus, it is the duty of the modern nation-state to 'deliver' Development. We can indeed argue that Development has become a primary legitimising function for most 'developing countries' and their governments after gaining independence.[22]

This holds true up to today, not the least in the case of India, where Prime Minister Modi as self-styled '*Vikas Purush*' or 'Development Man' has successfully campaigned on the promise of '*achhe din aane wale hai*' ('good days are coming') through the heavily promoted theme of '*Sabka Saath, Sabka Vikas*' ('Taking Everyone Along, Development for All').[23]

In order to be able to deliver Development and be acknowledged by the public as a successful deliverer, the nation-state, therefore, needs to, first and foremost, develop a standardised, homogeneous definition of Development. Consequently, the concept and practice of Development – produced and delivered by the nation-state – needs to be one that, seen from within the state's perspective, is rational, achievable and supports the inherent goals and objectives of the nation-state itself – in the case of contemporary India, this led to the recent formation of virtuous neoliberalism.

This already inherently limits the scope of Development and takes the nation-state for granted as one of its central actors as well as one of its central beneficiaries. In India, this further culminated in the equation of Development with the state and the stigmatising of everyone who speaks out against Development projects and policies of the government as 'anti-nationalist' and members of the '*tukde tukde gang*' who are allegedly out to 'divide the nation'.

Secondly, as Development becomes a carefully defined right, and to ensure that this right is protected and can be delivered in a feasible manner, the decision of what Development means and entails and how it is pursued cannot be left up to the (as seen from the nation-state's elitist perspective) irrational, ever-changing, unreliable, uninformed, contradictory, dangerous, unintelligent and unintelligible will of the people. Development as a concept of the formally rational modern nation-state, therefore, needs to be rationally and objectively approached and legitimised – and who could fulfil this task better than the 'expert class' who marks today's epitome of rationality?[24]

Seen from a democratic perspective, there is, however, one big problem with the class of 'Development experts', selected and legitimised by the state and who in turn legitimise – ex officio, through their very 'expertise' – the concepts and ideas of Development they advance, as well as the means to achieve them: they are even less accountable than so-called democratic governments. Nonetheless, part of the (neo-)liberal logic and therefore legitimation of experts is their independence from ordinary people's will, whims and wishes. Governments, alongside the expert class itself, view their 'insulation from public opinion … as a virtue. It is that very insulation that allows them to determine the rights of others in an objective, professional manner. Experts only have to answer to other experts. They are self-referential authorities' (Babones 2018: 21).

This excludes Development – the legitimising function of formally democratic governments – from any democratic influence and makes it into an authoritarian tool under what Salvatore Babones calls 'liberal authoritarianism' or 'the tyranny of experts':

> liberal democracy thus requires the obedience of the voters (or at least the citizens) to expert authority. The people are the passive recipients of those rights the experts deem them to possess. As the domain of rights expands, experts end up making more and more of the decisions … in an ever-increasing number of the most important aspects of public life: economic policy, criminal justice, what's taught in schools, who's allowed to enter the country,

what diseases will be cured, even (in many cases) who will have the opportunity to run for elective office. In these areas and more, experts arrogate for themselves the authority to adjudicate competing claims for public resources and private benefits. As society evolves, the areas reserved to expert adjudication seem only to expand.

(Babones 2018: 10)

Under this tyranny of experts – which in India has been carried out, for example, through the Planning Commission and after its abolition continues through the NITI Aayog think-tank as its replacement – Development has been squeezed into the straitjacket that we have explored above through the postdevelopment school of thought.

The appointment of Arvind Panagariya as first vice chairman of the NITI Aayog (the chairperson being the Prime Minister), is a case in point: 'Panagariya is an internationally renowned free market economist – a neo-liberal blueblood, as it were – and an enduring supporter of Modi from his earliest days on the campaign trail' (Sengupta 2015: 801). In 2017, he was succeeded by Rajiv Kumar, a long-standing principal economist at the neoliberal Asian Development Bank and Senior Fellow at the Delhi Centre of Policy Research who lauds 'the Prime Minister's impressive and "sharp focus" on economic development' (Dhoot 2017).

As with the Planning Commission at least in its late phase from 1991 onwards, the NITI Aayog, therefore, can be equally if not more expected to be filled with experts close to the government's own, virtuous-neoliberal policy positions and visions.

Therefore, there is little hope that Development can ever be something else than the vicarious agent of the nation-state's current agenda which is itself based on the presupposition of inequality. As Blühdorn (2011) points out,

the rule of experts is, and has always been, the rule of vested interests, and no structural change to the established order ... is ever to be expected from those who confine themselves to stimulating ever new cycles of techno-managerial innovation, economic growth and mass consumption.

In sum, by limiting the idea of equality to nowadays mainly an economic function, we can see how liberal, neoliberal and virtuous-neoliberal notions of equality, which are inherent in the various contemporary strands of Development, are based – contradictorily – on *the presupposition of inequality* which assumes that people are inherently unequal and, in turn, that they need to be told what lives they should live. As British anarchist Colin Ward notes,

ours is a society in which, in every field, one group of people makes decisions, exercises control, limits choices, while the great majority have to accept these decisions, submit to this control and act within the limits of these externally imposed choices.

(Ward 1996: 67)

Development, therefore, is based on the *Myth of Equality* while, paradoxically, acting out of the presupposition of *inequality*. India's current Development model, then, is built around both an external and internal presupposition of inequality masquerading as equality. It first accepts and applies most if not all of the hegemonic notions of (neo-)liberal equality coming from modern Western theory and thought, and then imposes on it a Hindu-national framework of hierarchical inclusion and targeted exclusion to mould the subjects of Development into virtuous market citizens.

The presupposition of inequality, however, did not emerge suddenly out of thin air. Practices such as Development that are built on the powerful idea that people are inherently unequal are part, as I will show next, of a modern ontology. This ontology has sedimented itself over time and established various hierarchies and dualisms that structure most of our everyday, modern life and are expressed and reflected in many social practices and ideas such as Development, as well as modern education.

The presupposition of inequality as ontological politics

All accounts of postdevelopment have in common that they conceptualise Development as a thoroughly apolitical process, epitomised, for example, in Ferguson's (1994) notion of Development as an 'anti-politics machine'. In the same vein, Ziai (2016: 151) refers to Development as 'a technical, apolitical intervention based on expert knowledge', and Escobar (1995: 45) contends that 'the professionalization of development also made it possible to remove all problems from the political and cultural realms and to recast them in terms of the apparently more neutral realm of science'.

Such an apolitical understanding of Development is certainly in accordance with Rancière's concept of the police order, seeing Development as a subset of it. However, while I do agree with the overall assessment by postdevelopment scholars that Development is an apolitical concept in the sense of not providing any real choice to people themselves but being based on expert knowledge and a mix of Western and localised nationalist, elitist imaginations and interests, I argue that Development in another sense is thoroughly political.

By deciding which ideas, practices, knowledges and ways of life fit inside its purview, and which don't (hence denying the equal intelligence of those people who attempt to build meaningful lives outside the developmental purview), Development actively performs what we can term '*ontological politics*'. As such, Development under the presupposition of inequality is – like other practices such as modern education – a 'world-making practice' that brings certain relations of thinking-knowing-feeling-doing-being *into being* in the first place.

The concept of world-making practice, or ontological politics, is based on the notion of 'ontology' as 'the understanding of reality'. In simplified terms, there exist myriads of ontologies, some quite similar to each other, some quite different, such as Western or modern ontologies and non-Western, indigenous ontologies (which again can each be rather similar or quite different from each other, or anything in between). Each of these ontologies consist of various social practices and sub-practices that together then bring a specific world and worldview into being, which in turn reinforce certain practices and lead to the creation of new practices.

Following Johanna Oksala and her interpretation of the political philosophy of Michel Foucault, I contend that all ontology 'is achieved in social practices and networks of power rather than being simply given' (Oksala 2010: 447). This denaturalises the notion of ontology and takes away the ground for any onto-logical foundation, understood as 'real reality', or the one and only, 'ultimate truth', an essence which objectively exists 'out there' and therefore just needs to be matched with the 'right' politics.

Instead, ontology becomes historically, geographically and politically con-tingent. This paves the way to 'treat the alternative and competing ontological frameworks as resulting from historical, linguistic and social practices of power' – in other words: 'reality as we know it is the result of social practices always incorporating power relations, but also of concrete struggles over truth and objec-tivity in social space' (ibid.).

Therefore, we can indeed say that ontology and the social practices it consists of *are* politics. Ontologies do not constitute completely closed, unified systems, but they are 'formed by a web of social practices' (Oksala 2010: 463) that exist beside each other and often compete against each other. As such, different social practices may be inspired by different ontologies and vie for the hegemony of one ontology in particular, or they result in hybrid ontologies informed by social practices reflecting and legitimising different ontologies.

Contemporary India is a case in point, where the ontological politics of Development, which draws on the aspiration towards an ideal of Western mod-ernisation and consumerism, combines with the social practices, rituals and sym-bols of Hindutva. This gave way to the powerful imagination and idea

> of a 'Rising India' that was open for business, heading toward 'Development' for all, reclaiming its place on the world stage as a world leader ('Vishwa Guru'), and reflected an awakened Hindu nation that could export its tradi-tional Hindu values.
>
> (Kaul 2017: 528)

The creation of this hybrid ontology – with all its complementarities as well as contradictions – is indeed what secured the 2014 landslide election victory of Narendra Modi.[25]

Development as a modern, Western concept, therefore, needs to be seen as a social practice and ontological politics that has gained unprecedented hegemony across the globe, drawing on a global network of governments, institutions, think-tanks, development agencies, non-governmental organisations (NGOs) and so on that spread Development and therefore also the ontology it is based on across the world.

This, along with other social practices, provides Development with enor-mous influence and power to reinforce, recreate, stabilise, normalise and expand the specific ontology on which it is based. As such, I suggest understanding Development, operating under the presupposition of inequality, as *ontological politics of inequality* which reflects a certain ontology and ensures both its continuous stabilisation and expansion by competing with and often suppressing other social practices outside the developmental purview that reflect other ontologies and thereby other ways of making sense of reality and – ultimately – other ways of life.

The ontology on which Development and its politics of inequality are based, which it recreates and reflects, is paradoxically itself based on the assumption that it is the only one and indeed constitutes 'real reality' as an objective, measurable and discoverable state. This also means that Development as ontological politics *considers itself the whole* – everything else (i.e. 'alternatives to Development') is ontological excess and therefore almost non-existent.

Following John Law (2015), we can term this ontology as the 'One-World world' (OWW) which is based on various dualisms and a number of universalist assumptions. Based on this, I will further refer to Development and its ontological politics of inequality as *OWW Development*.

A key element of the OWW is how it strictly separates human and biophysical worlds, ultimately subordinating the latter under the former:

> the natural world and the biosphere have been treated as a dump, as forming the unconsidered, instrumentalised and unimportant *background* to 'civilised' human life; they are merely the setting or stage on which what is really important, the drama of human life and culture, is played out.
>
> (Plumwood 1993: 69; emphasis original)

These ideas correspond to a largely modernist imagination and social construction and not to something natural, objective or inherently 'true' that can be found 'out there', unencumbered by power.

The radical separation of humans and nature is a consequence of the core dualism of Western metaphysics, as expressed in Enlightenment thinking which counts 'mind' and 'world' as ontologically separate entities. 'Hence the former can gain growing objective knowledge of, and control over, the latter' (Pellizzoni 2015: 15), which results – among many other things – in the plundering of nature.

In this liberal Enlightenment ideal, non-human nature becomes diametrically opposed to an extremely narrow definition of the (human/male) mind and (human/male) reason, which constitutes the founding dualism for many other dualisms that ultimately manifest themselves in the OWW's various social practices. As Plumwood (1993: 3) argues,

> the concept of reason provides the unifying and defining contrast for the concept of nature, much as the concept of husband does for that of wife, as master for slave. Reason in the western tradition has been constructed as the privileged domain of the master, who has conceived nature as a wife or subordinate other encompassing and representing the sphere of

materiality, subsistence and the feminine which the master has split off and constructed as beneath him. The continual and cumulative overcoming of the domain of nature by reason engenders the western concept of progress and development.

Val Plumwood's account highlights how the founding dualism of human/reason/ mind/consciousness/culture on the one side, and nature on the other, not only leads to the ontological distinction between humans and nature, and thus to the notion of '*humans outside of nature*', but also to the existence of manifold dualist hierarchies between human beings.

This further demonstrates how the OWW's dualist ontology is related to the presupposition of inequality: 'a dualism is an intense, established and developed cultural expression of ... a hierarchical relationship, constructing central cultural concepts and identities so as to make equality and mutuality literally unthinkable' (Plumwood 1993: 47). In short, a dualist ontology serves to naturalise hierarchy, domination, exploitation and oppression.

It is no wonder, therefore, that OWW Development as hierarchical world-making practice offers many affinities and potentialities to be combined with an equally hierarchical Hindutva ontology and its various social practices. The reason/nature dualism of the OWW, for example, is accompanied by a hierarchical and oppressive inequality between superior (mostly white, male; 'developed') and inferior (mostly female and/or non-white; 'underdeveloped') humans, where the inferior, the *less intelligent humans* are seen as the ones who are 'closer to nature' or 'part of nature' (as opposed to the superior humans).[26]

Looking at Hindutva ontology, we can see how this dualism is further applied to 'rational and virtuous Hindus' and 'Others', particularly Muslims, who are seen as closer to nature:

> the ascetic and paternal elements of 'idealized' Hindutva imaginary also interlink and find their counterpart in the projection of its opposite onto 'the Muslims' who are legitimized as targets of violence by virtue of being seen as meat-eating, sexually aggressive, and overpopulating 'Other'.
>
> (Kaul 2017: 13)

The OWW, having at its core the human/nature dualism which corresponds to the male/female and many other dualisms, then is, in essence, a fundamentally *patriarchal* ontology. It is

> characterized by actions and emotions that value competition, war, hierarchies, power, growth, procreation, the domination of others, and the appropriation of resources, combined with the rational justification of it all in the name of truth. In this culture, which engulfs most modern humans, we live in mistrust and seek certitude through control, including control of the natural world.
>
> (Escobar 2018: 13)

In turn, it is again not hard to identify further affinities between OWW Development and the social practices of an equally patriarchal Hindutva worldview. This is evident, for instance, in

> the conservative patriarchal-pragmatic policy approach to empowerment by the current [Modi] regime [which] seems to assume the economic dependence of female on male members of the family as 'natural' in a 'traditional' society, and the withdrawal of women from the labour market is interpreted as protecting the honour of the family.
>
> (Gudavarthy and Vijay 2020: 476)

Another confluence of both ontologies can be seen in the Indian government's response to the plight of millions of migrant labourers amid what has been dubbed 'the world's strictest lockdown' which began on 24 March 2020 to tackle the coronavirus pandemic. As such, the Indian state as 'father figure', as more equal than its 'children', ignored the desires of migrant labourers to return to their home villages as mere noise rather than reason, as irrational, unintelligent, infantile demands of not yet grown-ups. What was expected from the migrants instead was to stay where they were, show patience, discipline and virtue in the times of crisis, and to heroically make their sacrifices for the sake of Bharat (the nation).[27]

At the same time, the government saw the potential mass exodus of labourers as a threat that would undermine the exploitative neoliberal Development model for which cheap labour in the cities is indispensable, which also explains its strong reluctance to provide transport for the labourers. The BJP-led Karnataka state government, for example, reversed its plans to provide free transportation for migrant labourers after a meeting between Chief Minister B S Yediyurappa and several property developers. According to the news website The Quint, it was decided in the meeting that migrant workers were needed to revive the state's economy.[28] The decision only was revoked after growing public outrage against 'slavery-like practices'.

As Radhika Menon writes,

> the plight of workers is analogous to women's condition in a patriarchal society, wherein the husband's family controls their labour, bodies, and mobility once they leave their native household. The state regards workers as the property of the capitalist and exhibits patriarchal muscle in controlling their mobility even in the face of extreme suffering, thereby denying workers rights as free citizens. This patriarchal logic was extended through the infantilization of workers whose legitimate demands were rejected as irrational, comparable to the treatment received by women attempting to escape exploitative demands and disputes at the marital household.
>
> (Menon 2020)

This shows how OWW Development and Hindutva can combine into a toxic mix especially for the less privileged through the interlocking forces of a market-based social order and a religious, patriarchal, nationalist belief system which assigns to the majority of Indians subordinate, severely marginalised and oppressed roles.

Summation

OWW Development constitutes an ontological politics of inequality by denying the equality of anyone and everyone not abiding by some or all of the beliefs and practices of the hierarchical OWW. They are those people, communities and movements whose ideas, practices, actions, ways of life and lifeworlds exceed in one way or another its ontological limits. OWW Development thus continuously attempts to marginalise, destroy and transform the lives of those who pursue non-OWW-based ways of worlding into lives fitting within its dualist, singular and reductionist worldview. In doing this, it ends up *taking away people's capacity to co-create their own meaningful lives* outside the dualist OWW.

With its ontological blindness for different worlds, OWW Development 'both enables its own questions, answers, and understandings and disables as unnecessary or unreal the questions, answers, and understandings that fall outside of its purview or are excessive to it' (De la Cadena 2015: 13). And this is a huge dilemma. As Santos (2016: 44) puts it, 'we face modern problems for which there are no modern solutions'. Looking at the multiple (economic, social, political, spiritual, environmental, etc.) crises which are indeed the result of OWW Development, we urgently need to start asking these 'excessive questions' and come up with 'excessive answers'.[29]

However, as I have shown in this chapter, the rise of Hindutva ideology in contemporary India does not constitute a shift away from OWW Development but rather its modification and intensification. As such, the dualist, hierarchical OWW ontology shares many affinities and potentialities with Hindutva. As a result, OWW Development's neoliberal programme is rather accelerated, while also utilised in specific ways to further the BJP's communal agenda.

Given the relentless advancement of OWW Development in India and elsewhere, it is an urgent task to identify, analyse and contribute to any possible alternatives to OWW Development that lead to different ideas of what makes meaningful lives beyond Development and can challenge its hegemony and hierarchical logic. The second chapter does exactly this.

Going back to postdevelopment theory as our point of departure, I will establish an anarchistic version of the former as 'the ontological politics of equality' to counter OWW Development's ontological politics of inequality. This will serve as a point of departure for subsequent chapters in order to imagine an education that reflects and practices the ontological politics of equality and therefore equally ventures *beyond Development*.

Notes

1 Parts of this and the following chapter were originally published as Neusiedl, C. (2019) The Ontological Politics of (In-)Equality: A new research approach

for post-development. *Third World Quarterly*, 40 (4), pp. 651–667, DOI: 10.1080/01436597.2019.1573636. Copyright © 2019 Southseries Inc., www.third-worldquarterly.com, reprinted by permission of Informa UK Limited, trading as Taylor & Francis Group, www.tandfonline.com on behalf of Southseries Inc.

2 A recent example for this is how allegedly progressive, socialist governments in Latin America co-opted the radical notion of 'buen vivir', often ending up to be used 'simply as synonymous with modern, capitalist development' (Lang 2019: 178).

3 See also Esteva (2019).

4 See Ziai (2013).

5 Thanks to Manish Jain for suggesting this translation.

6 Gandhi envisioned *nai talim* not as a static, rigid system of education, learning and living, but as always flexible, localised and context-dependent. Accordingly, various individuals inspired by Gandhi's philosophy interpreted *nai talim* in different ways and put their own touch to it. As Manish Jain of unschooling organisation Shikshantar writes, 'Vinoba Bhave poetically articulated the soul of nai talim as *yog* (union of individual with the divine), *sahyog* (collaboration), udyog (meaningful work). He emphasized the importance of humility. Narayanbhai Desai talked about *Preeti* (love), *Mukti* (responsible freedom), *Abhivyakti* (expressions). Satish Kumar talks about soil, soul and society. In our work in Shikshantar, we have added unlearning, gift culture, jugaad ["playful improvisation and resourcefulness"] design thinking as some of the key dimensions of nai talim' (Jain n.d.).

7 According to Gould (2019: 36), in 2015 alone the total volume of public and private Development aid amounted to USD 315 billion.

8 The neoliberal Development model is broadly understood here as a restructuring – rather than rolling-back – of the nation-state to support free trade and capital mobility as well as to promote international competitiveness and the emergence of a market-based society.

9 Hindutva or 'Hindu Nationalism' can be broadly understood as 'Hinduism as (the only) way of life' across India that everyone should follow. It is propagated most heavily by the Rashtriya Swayamsevak Sangh (RSS), a paramilitary organisation and movement that is founder of the Sangh Parivar or family of Hindu-nationalist organisations of which the BJP is part of.

10 See Fischer (2020); Kaul (2017).

11 India's 64-year-old Planning Commission, equipped with the power to allocate funds to ministries and state governments, and with a mandate of working towards poverty reduction, welfare, equity and social justice (although with a very mixed track record on this), was abolished by Prime Minister Modi on 15th August 2014 in his first Independence Day speech and replaced by the National Institution for Transforming India, the NITI Aayog – a think-tank without fund-allocation powers (Sengupta 2015).

12 Gudavarthy and Vijay (2020); Chacko (2019).

13 This would also be similarly applicable to other approaches, where other specific types of equality are distributed by the state, the vanguard, or other elites and elite institutions. In this context of 'passive equality', for Amartya Sen, 'the issue that divides various philosophies of politics is the question of what it is that there should be equality of' (May 2008: 4).

14 Moreover, the slogan of 'Clean India' also serves as a teleological metaphor to break away from a 'dirty, corrupted past' and move towards a 'clean and pure future' (Gudavarthy and Vijay 2020).

15 Chacko (2018b).

16 Gudavarthy and Vijay (2020).

17 Dalits – officially referred to by the Indian state as 'Scheduled Castes' – make up more than one-sixth of India's total population. The term 'Dalit' has been popularised by iconic Dalit leader B.R. Ambedkar and means the 'oppressed', 'exploited' or 'downtrodden'. The term is used to make visible the extreme discrimination, exploitation and oppression that Dalits face on a daily basis up to today. This oppression is based on the

Dalits' low societal status that relegates them literally to 'outcastes', situated outside the four-tiered Hindu caste system. At the apex of this order stand the Brahmins, followed by the Kshatriyas, the Vaishyas and the Shudras. Not even included in this order are the Dalits, referred to also as the Atishudras, Avarnas or Pancham, who are placed outside the caste system and thus considered 'untouchables', carrying out the most menial work.

18 This however is not so dissimilar from the thoughts of Gandhi, who rather than annihilating the caste system strived to abolish 'untouchability' by integrating the Dalits in the fourth (the lowest) varna (caste) and promoted the retention of hereditary professions and the traditional division of labour; see Mahajan (2013); Singh Rathore (2019).

19 Rancière's notion of *police* includes but also far exceeds the idea of a disciplinary 'police state' in the traditional sense: 'the distribution of places and roles that defines a police regime stems as much from the assumed spontaneity of social relations as from the rigidity of state functions' (Rancière 1999: 29). What Rancière refers to, then, is an all-encompassing order in which everyone and anyone has their pre-assigned identities, roles and places. As Biesta (2016: 120; emphasis added) importantly notes, *'this is not to say that everyone is included in the running of the order.* The point simply is that no one is excluded from the order'.

20 See also Ferguson (1994) and Escobar (1995).

21 The United Nations adopted 'The Right to Development' in 1986.

22 After India's independence, Development became an 'ersatz nationalism': 'the crucial years of defining Indian national belonging by the state, in legal and constitutional terms, took place against the backdrop of the formation of Pakistan, allowing Hindu nationalists to argue that the residual Indian state would now be a Hindu state. Those on the left, backed by Jawaharlal Nehru, insisted that national belonging would not be defined by religion, ethnicity, etc. but by virtue of common belonging to India' (Zachariah 2013: 59). Hence it was Development and not ethnicity, culture or religion that would become the common denominator and unifying cause on which to base and legitimise the existence of the independent Indian state.

23 Ruparelia (2015: 755).

24 See Babones (2018).

25 Kaul (2017).

26 As Plumwood (1993: 4) also points out, 'racism, colonialism and sexism have drawn their conceptual strength from casting sexual, racial and ethnic difference as closer to the animal and the body construed as a sphere of inferiority, as a lesser form of humanity lacking the full measure of rationality or culture'.

27 In stark contrast, Prime Minister Modi encouraged middle- and upper-class families, from the secure confines of their homes, to participate in event-like rituals such as clapping, lighting lamps and showering flowers, as their contribution in the fight against coronavirus.

28 The Quint (2018).

29 Philip McMichael (2014) provides a practical account of this dilemma in context of the global food crisis and the competing ontologies of 'land commodification' (as the OWW Development response) and 'land sovereignty' (as alternative to OWW Development which exceeds the latter's ontological limits), each proposing fundamentally (ontologically) different ideas and approaches to how to tackle this issue. Another – and related – case in point is the question of how to tackle climate change, where lunatic ideas of geo-engineering seem to have the edge over plans to substantially reduce carbon emissions by changing the OWW way of life.

References

Abdi, A.A. (2016). 'Globalization, culture and development: Perspectives on Africa'. In Caouette, D. and Kapoor, D. (eds.), *Beyond Colonialism, Development and*

Globalization: Social Movements and Critical Perspectives. London: Zed Books, pp. 223–241.

Babones, S. (2018). *The New Authoritarianism: Trump, Populism, and the Tyranny of Experts.* Cambridge: Polity Press.

Berger, M.T., and Weber, H. (2014). *Rethinking the Third World: International Development and World Politics.* New York: Palgrave Macmillan.

Biesta, G. (2016) *Good Education in an Age of Measurement: Ethics, Politics, Democracy.* London: Routledge.

Blühdorn, I. (2011). 'The sustainability of democracy: On limits to growth, the post-democratic turn and reactionary democrats'. https://www.eurozine.com/the-sustainability-of-democracy/.

Chacko, P. (2018a). 'Marketizing Hindutva: The state, society, and markets in Hindu nationalism'. *Modern Asian Studies*, 53 (2), pp. 377–410.

Chacko, P. (2018b). 'The right turn in India: Authoritarianism, populism and neoliberalisation'. *Journal of Contemporary Asia*, 48 (4), pp. 541–565.

Chacko, P. (2019). 'Emerging regimes of market citizenship: The politics of social policy in contemporary India'. In D'Costa, A.P. and Chakraborty, A. (eds.), *Changing Contexts and Shifting Roles of the Indian State: New Perspectives on Development Dynamics.* Singapore: Springer Nature Singapore, pp. 39–55.

Da Costa, D. (2016). 'Liberating development from the rule of an episteme'. In Caouette, D. and Kapoor, D. (eds.), *Beyond Colonialism, Development and Globalization: Social Movements and Critical Perspectives.* London: Zed Books, pp. 187–204.

De la Cadena, M. (2015). *Earth Beings: Ecologies of Practice across Andean Worlds.* Durham: Duke University Press.

Dhoot, V. (2017). 'Who is Rajiv Kumar'? https://www.thehindu.com/business/Economy/who-is-rajiv-kumar/article19567215.ece.

Escobar, A. (1995). *Encountering Development: The Making and Unmaking of the Third World.* Princeton, NJ: Princeton University Press.

Escobar, A. (2012). *Notes on the Ontology of Design.* Unpublished manuscript. Chapel Hill: UNC.

Escobar, A. (2018) *Designs for the Pluriverse: Radical Interdependence, Autonomy, and the Making of Worlds.* Durham: Duke University Press.

Esteva, G. (2019). 'New political horizons: Beyond the 'democratic' nation-state'. https://www.radicalecologicaldemocracy.org/new-political-horizons-beyond-the-democratic-nation-state/.

Esteva, G., and Escobar, A. (2019). 'Postdevelopment @ 25: On 'being stuck' and moving forward, sideways, backward and otherwise'. In Klein, E., and Morreo, C.E. (eds.), *Postdevelopment in Practice: Alternatives, Economies, Ontologies.* London: Routledge, pp. 21–36.

Ferguson, J. (1994). *The Anti-Politics Machine: 'Development', Depoliticization, and Bureaucratic Power in Lesotho.* Minneapolis: University of Minnesota Press.

Fischer, A.M. (2020). 'The dark sides of social policy: From neoliberalism to resurgent right-wing populism'. *Development and Change*, 51 (2), pp. 371–397.

Gandhi, M. [1946] (2009). 'Every village a republic'. In Gandhi, M., *India of My Dreams.* Delhi: Rajpal & Sons, pp. 96–98.

Gould, J. (2019). 'Development aid'. In Kothari, A., Salleh, A., Escobar, A., Demaria, F., and A. Acosta (eds.), *Pluriverse: A Post-Development Dictionary.* New Delhi: Tulika Books, pp. 34–37.

Gudavarthy, A., and Vijay, G. (2020). 'Social policy and political mobilization in India: Producing hierarchical fraternity and polarized differences'. *Development and Change*, 51 (2), pp. 463–484.

Harmes, A. (2012). 'The rise of neoliberal nationalism'. *Review of International Political Economy*, 19 (1), pp. 59–86.

Jain, M. (n.d.). 'Thoughts on resurrecting nai talim'. http://shikshantar.org/articles/tho ughts-resurrecting-nai-talim.

Jensen, D. (2004). *Walking on Water: Reading, Writing, and Revolution.* White River Junction, Vermont: Chelsea Green Publishing Company.

Karim, L. (2008). 'Demystifying micro-credit: The Grameen bank, NGOs, and neoliberalism in Bangladesh'. *Cultural Dynamics*, 20 (1), pp.5–29.

Kaul, N. (2017). 'Rise of the political right in India: Hindutva-development mix, Modi myth, and dualities'. *Journal of Labor and Society*, 20 (4), pp. 523–548.

Kothari, A., Demaria, F., and A. Acosta (2015). 'Sustainable development is failing but there are alternatives to capitalism'. http://www.theguardian.com/sustainable-business /2015/jul/21/capitalism-alternatives-sustainable-development-failing.

Kumar, R. (2006). *The Crisis of Elementary Education in India.* New Delhi: SAGE Publications.

Lang, M. (2019). 'Plurinationality as a strategy: Transforming local state institutions toward *buen vivir*'. In Klein, E., and Morreo, C.E. (eds.), *Postdevelopment in Practice: Alternatives, Economies, Ontologies.* London: Routledge, pp. 176–189.

Law, J. (2015). 'What's wrong with a one-world World'? *Distinktion: Journal of Social Theory*, 16 (1), pp. 126–139.

Mahajan, G. (2013) *India: Political Ideas and the Making of a Democratic Discourse.* London: Zed Books.

Matthews, S. (2004). 'Post-development theory and the question of alternatives: A view from Africa'. *Third World Quarterly*, 25 (2), pp. 373–384.

May, T. (2008). *The Political Thought of Jacques Rancière: Creating Equality.* Edinburgh: Edinburgh University Press.

May, T. (2009a). 'Democracy is where we make it: The relevance of Jacques Rancière'. Symposium. *Canadian Journal of Continental Philosophy/Revue canadienne de philosophie continentale*, 13 (1), pp. 3–21.

May, T. (2009b). 'Rancière in South Carolina'. In Rockhill, G., and Watts, P. (eds.), *Jacques Rancière: History, Politics, Aesthetics.* London: Duke University Press, pp. 105–119.

May, T. (2010). *Contemporary Political Movements and the Thought of Jacques Rancière: Equality in Action.* Edinburgh: Edinburgh University Press.

May, T. (2016). *A Significant Life: Human Meaning in a Silent Universe.* Chicago: The University of Chicago Press.

McMichael, P. (2014). 'Rethinking land grab ontology'. *Rural Sociology*, 79 (1), pp. 34–55.

Menon, R. (2020). 'Between lockdown and crackdown: Gendered impacts of COVID-19 on the lives of migrant workers in India'. https://www.rosalux.de/en/news/id /42523/between-lockdown-and-crackdown?cHash=81a4c9e5ee817488c09eaad bb441f01e.

Newman, S. (2016). *Postanarchism.* Cambridge: Polity Press.

Oksala, J. (2010). 'Foucault's politicization of ontology'. *Continental Philosophy Review*, 43 (4), pp. 445–466.

Padel, F., and Das, S. (2010). *Out of This Earth: East India Adivasis and the Aluminium Cartel*. New Delhi: Orient Blackswan.

Pathak, A. (2002). *Social Implications of Schooling: Knowledge, Pedagogy and Consciousness*. Delhi: Rainbow Publishers.

Pellizzoni, L. (2015). *Ontological Politics in a Disposable World: The New Mastery of Nature*. Burlington: Ashgate.

Plumwood, V. (1993). *Feminism and the Mastery of Nature*. London: Routledge.

Rancière, J. (1999). *Disagreement: Politics and Philosophy*. Minneapolis: University of Minnesota Press.

Ruparelia, S. (2015). ''Minimum government, maximum governance': The restructuring of power in Modi's India'. *South Asia: Journal of South Asian Studies*, 38 (4), pp. 755–775.

Sachs, W. (1992). *The Development Dictionary: A Guide to Knowledge as Power*. London: Zed Books.

Samaddar, R. (2016). *Neo-liberal Strategies of Governing India*. New York: Routledge.

Santos, B.d.S. (2016). *Epistemologies of the South: Justice against Epistemicide*. New York: Routledge.

Sengupta, M. (2015). 'Modi planning: What the NITI Aayog suggests about the aspirations and practices of the Modi Government'. *South Asia: Journal of South Asian Studies*, 38 (4), pp. 791–806.

Shah, A, and Lerche, J. (2018). 'Tribe, caste and class – New mechanisms of exploitation and oppression'. In Shah, A., Lerche, J., Axelby, R., Benbabaali, D., Donegan, B., Raj, J., and V. Thakur, *Ground Down by Growth: Tribe, Caste, Class, and Inequality in Twenty-First Century India*. New Delhi: Oxford University Press, pp. 1–31.

Shrivastava, A., and Kothari, A. (2012). *Churning the Earth: The Making of Global India*. New Delhi: Penguin.

Singh Rathore, A. (2019). *Indian Political Theory: Laying the Groundwork for Svaraj*. New York: Routledge.

The Quint. (2018). 'Slavery: K'taka order cancelling trains for migrants criticised'. https://www.thequint.com/news/india/karnataka-migrant-workers-trains-cancelled-after-meeting-business-leaders-reactions-slavery.

Ward, C. (1996). *Anarchy in Action*. London: Freedom Press.

Zachariah, B. (2013). 'Developmentalism and its exclusions: Peripheries and unbelonging in independent India'. In Fischer-Tahir A., and Naumann, M. (eds.), *Peripheralization*. Wiesbaden: Springer VS, pp. 55–76.

Ziai, A. (2013). 'The discourse of "development" and why the concept should be abandoned'. *Development in Practice*, 23 (1), pp. 123–136.

Ziai, A. (2016). *Development Discourse and Global History: From Colonialism to the Sustainable Development Goals*. New York: Routledge.

Ziai, A. (2017). 'Post-development 25 years after the development dictionary'. *Third World Quarterly*, 38 (12), pp. 2547–2558.

2   Anarchistic postdevelopment and the ontological politics of equality

Paying heed to the postdevelopmental calls for 'alternatives to Development', this chapter sets out to develop the notion of *anarchistic postdevelopment* as a way to counter OWW Development and its ontological politics of inequality with a vision of how to constitute meaningful lives beyond the straitjacket of Development. As I will show, anarchistic postdevelopment serves both as a new analytical framework that addresses some of the major shortcomings of postdevelopment as well as an emancipatory politics pursued through what we can term *the ontological politics of equality*. Therefore, the chapter lays the foundation to devise an anarchistic postdevelopmental education which not only reflects but indeed actively practices such a politics that can lead us towards alternatives to Development which are based on more egalitarian relations among human beings as well as between humans and nature.

Addressing first some of the concerns and issues with existing postdevelopmental approaches towards alternatives to Development, the chapter turns to anarchist philosophy and its many parallels to postdevelopment as a way to anchor the latter within a sound, yet flexible and open-ended, ethico-political framework.

In order to finally operationalise this theoretical framework, I will return to the philosophy of Jacques Rancière and harness what he calls *the principle of the presupposition of equality* as the basis for a liberatory, anarchistic postdevelopmental politics. This *ontological politics of equality* is a world-making practice which, following contemporary philosopher Todd May, posits that *everyone and anyone is equally capable of creating meaningful lives*. It therefore constitutes a powerful antidote to the OWW's hierarchical social practices such as Development based on the presupposition of inequality and helps us to reimagine meaningful lives beyond Development.

Postdevelopmental alternatives to development

As we have seen in the first chapter, postdevelopment theorists do not oppose 'social change' in general. Instead, they reject a particular, hegemonic notion and ideology of it which is deeply rooted in the OWW ontology and therefore prevents the emergence of other visions, theories and practices of social change.

What postdevelopment scholars and activists then have in common is the vision of 'different futures based on non-capitalist values, communal ownership and a humbler relation of human beings to nature' (Ziai 2017: 2552). Andrew McGregor further describes the requirements and characteristics for an initiative to be considered as postdevelopment as follows:

> it should contribute to the dismantling of the physical and discursive hegemony of development so that new locally grounded futures may be imagined and pursued. This includes freeing bodies, minds and community processes from the pursuit of development and opening up new socio-political spaces in which local imaginaries can be enacted and empowered ... While macro-scale initiatives have many important and empowering outcomes, such as improved health or decentralised governance, the location of decision making is normally far beyond that of the communities affected and so, despite their benefits, will not be considered ... Programmes that are much more likely to share post-development ideals are those that operate at the micro-scale, thus having the potential and flexibility to recognise and support local imaginaries and perspectives.
>
> (McGregor 2007: 161)

Here, McGregor already outlines the contours of what we can call 'constructive postdevelopment', which is not only concerned with a critique of OWW Development that is often coupled with the retreat to a romanticised, rather naïve understanding and valorisation of 'traditional ways of life'. Instead, constructive postdevelopment also looks ahead and contributes to *what lies beyond OWW Development*.

This is most often referred to as *the pluriverse*. The worlds found in the pluriverse are characterised by their post-dualist, *relational ontologies* based on a continuity between the human, natural and supernatural worlds.[1]

> Relational ontologies are those that eschew the divisions between nature and culture, individual and community, and between us and them that are central to the modern ontology. Some of the today's struggles could be seen as reflecting the defense and activation of relational communities and worldview ... and as such they could be read as ontological struggles; they refer to a different way of imagining life, to an other mode of existence.
>
> (Escobar 2011: 139)

Relational worldviews and their emphasis on interdependence therefore go directly against the core idea of the dualist OWW ontology, which makes sense of the natural world as independently existing – as inert matter and not active agent – and subordinate to the anthropocentric OWW.

The concept of the pluriverse thus highlights the shift from the dualist OWW built upon the socially constructed idea of *humans-outside-nature* living in a *human-centred world* towards the relational pluriverse built upon the idea of *humans-in-nature*, living in *more-than-human worlds*, as a central characteristic of postdevelopment alternatives.[2]

Yet, beyond more or less abstract accounts of communities found to pursue relational lifeworlds, postdevelopment still remains rather vague in its analysis. Moreover, the focus on qualitatively different human–nature relations alone is not enough to identify postdevelopmental projects and can also become problematic at times – after all, *cow vigilantes*, for example, should certainly not be considered as embodying anything postdevelopmental.

The vagueness of postdevelopment, or its 'radical openness' in more positive terms, is of course owed in no small part to its rejection of any blueprint solution for social change in order to not repeat the failures and mistakes of Development. As Rist (2006: 241) representatively states the postdevelopmental position, 'there are numerous ways of living a "good life", and it is up to each society to invent its own'.

However, the reluctance to devise any kind of more concrete framework(s) for the pluriverse then risks falling into one of two extremes. On the one hand, postdevelopment risks relativising and downplaying the significance of its own analysis of postdevelopmental projects. By reducing its applicability purely to the analysed case which is found to be so unique in its own right, its lessons, it is argued, cannot serve to inform the analysis of any other postdevelopmental cases or help to come up with a more general framework for the construction or analysis of alternatives to Development.

On the other hand, and at the other extreme of the spectrum, postdevelopment risks falling into OWW Development's dualist trap by identifying everything outside the Development–state–markets nexus as a postdevelopmental alternative. This brings with it the additional danger of slipping into cultural relativism by either eschewing an analysis of power relations on the ground altogether, or by justifying and romanticising any hierarchical, exploitative power relations as a natural part of 'traditional' communities' way of life outside the OWW, and thereby making them immune to any criticism and change.[3]

This highlights that the many failures of OWW Development must not lead to an unqualified glorification of local and 'traditional' ways of life, often marked by equally authoritarian, hierarchical and oppressive social structures. Nevertheless, a tendency to do so surfaces at times across postdevelopment thinking.[4]

As such, postdevelopment often erroneously assumes that power is only exerted *upon* the bottom, but never *at* the bottom, and that power is always suppressive but never productive.[5] Based on this understanding of power, the alternatives to Development that postdevelopmentalists seek are usually found to emerge from local, 'traditional' communities and various social and grassroots movements. Dismantling the oppressive apparatus of Development and seizing power from the bottom is all too often understood and portrayed as an unproblematic way to build 'benign' alternatives to Development, making postdevelopmental analyses at times too simplistic by eschewing any analysis of power relations on the micro-level.[6]

Looking at recent developments in India, it therefore becomes important to differentiate between Hindutva-inspired ideas of the 'pure, traditional community' that consist of both external and internal hierarchies (i.e. valuing the Hindutva 'way of life' above all others and pitting communities against each other, as well as internally justifying the oppression of women, community members of different castes, etc.), and community-based, grassroots initiatives that struggle for their own ideas of what constitutes meaningful lives in relative harmony with others and based on (relative) equality among community members.

As Kalpana Wilson accordingly notes,

> recently we have seen right-wing Hindu nationalist ideologues explicitly mobilising the ideas of post-development theorists like Ashis Nandy in their promotion of an upper caste Hindu supremacist project which, ironically, is not only colonial in origin, but today is inseparable from the corporate-driven predatory neoliberal version of 'development' pursued by the Narendra Modi government.
>
> (Wilson 2017: 2687)

Another, closely related danger of postdevelopment is that of essentialising those movements and their members who are found to pursue post-dualist practices and lifeworlds along a 'postdevelopmental ideal', i.e. portraying them as rejecting each and every practice of modernisation and OWW Development, rather than acknowledging their agency to carefully and selectively appropriate some practices which fit into their ontologies and ways of life. Instead of letting these people and communities speak for themselves, this risks speaking on behalf of them and misrepresents their own ideas and imaginations which are often much more complex and intricate than the simple Development–postdevelopment binary which is employed at times.

This problematic is reflected in how NGOs that implicitly or explicitly build on postdevelopmental positions, such as Survival International, oftentimes essentialise local communities who mobilise against OWW Development as 'authentic natives' that the NGO and its Western audience allegedly need to protect. A recent example of this can be found in the portrayal of the Adivasi-led Dongria Kond movement in Odisha which struggles against the exploitation of the Niyamgiri hills by mining corporation Vedanta:

> the construction of the members of the Dongria Kond community within NGO discourses as pre-modern, innocent and uncorrupted 'noble savages' appears to preclude consideration of their engagement in sustained political organising which has made possible the series of protests, marches and blockades which prevented mining from 2002 onwards; their historic and present relation to political structures such as the various levels and arms of the Indian state and its colonial predecessor; or their articulation of any visions of the future which depart from a narrative of restoration of 'traditional' lifestyles and livelihoods.
>
> (Wilson 2017: 2694)

Overall, we can say that, on the one hand, postdevelopment plays an important role in (re-)assessing, promoting, strengthening and re-valuing alternatives to Development which exhibit post-dualist, more relational ontologies. Thus, it contributes an important part to challenging and tearing down the artificial separations between humans and nature that structure the entire OWW Development discourse.

On the other hand, with its focus on challenging and minimising the hierarchies between humans and nature, postdevelopment risks overlooking the existing hierarchies among and between human beings, or normalising and romanticising them, as well as simply reversing the hierarchical binaries found in OWW Development.

To address these shortcomings, I will establish the concept of *anarchistic postdevelopment*. This not only provides the search for and analysis of postdevelopmental alternatives to Development with an overarching, yet loose and flexible enough framework that does not translate into a Development-like blueprint, but also helps us to transcend a potential OWW-pluriverse dualism and avoid any danger of essentialism.

Towards an anarchistic postdevelopment

Vilified, falsified and misrepresented by mainstream media and politicians alike as a curious mixture of violence and chaos, anarchist philosophy and practice have seen a remarkable revival on the streets in recent history.

Be it the Black Lives Matter movement, the various Occupy and alter-globalisation movements around the world, elements of the French Gilets Jaunes, the Kurdish Rojava Movement or the autonomía movements in Latin America, all of them share some core tenets of anarchist philosophy. Similarly, many groups and movements in India following ideas of radical ecological democracy,[7] Swaraj ('rule over the self') or various approaches towards self-governance[8] share important anarchist ideals.[9]

We can understand the various strands of anarchism as

> a body of political thought that seeks to abolish and challenge rigid hierarchies (like the State), rethink and dismantle capitalist ideological structures, disrupt modes of forced coercion, build a society based on [libertarian] communist aspirations, free people's desires from historically oppressive social norms, and create organic and communal societies based on mutual aid and social justice.
>
> (DeLeon 2008: 123)[10]

As such, anarchism's core principles – reflected to varying degrees in the movements mentioned above – consist of 'anti-hierarchy', 'prefiguration', a 'social view of the self' and 'liberty'.[11]

Anarchism's anti-hierarchical nature is most pronounced in its anti-state and anti-capitalist positions. As Indian anarchist M.P.T. Acharya noted, 'anarchists want freedom, democracy and socialism. But they consider – nay are convinced, these cannot be obtained or maintained under state protection or direction' (Acharya [1948] 2019: 195).

However, the anarchist critique goes much beyond the spheres of the state and the economy and rejects each and every form of *domination*, which May (2007: 21; emphasis added) characterises as '*power that operates deleteriously*'.

> Anarchism, then, should be seen as a critique of domination, rather than as a critique of the state. Unlike Marxism, anarchism does not concern itself with a particular type of oppression – exploitation – that arises in a particular arena – the mode of capitalist production. Rather, it concerns itself with the various dominations that occur throughout the social arena.
>
> (ibid.)

This means that anarchism, especially in its contemporary form, does not recognise a single, Archimedean point of domination that needs to be attacked as an ultimate priority. Likewise, anarchism draws attention to the *intersectionality* of various practices of domination such as racism, sexism, patriarchy, etc., as well as of many of our everyday customs and practices that are often based on (hidden) social hierarchies.

Therefore, anarchism sees all sites and practices of domination as interrelated.[12] Engaging in 'single-issue struggles' is seen indeed at best as leaving other sites and practices of domination unchanged, and at worst as reproducing and intensifying them. Relatedly, there is no 'privileged site of struggle', as all anti-hierarchical struggles are equally important.

This, in turn, is closely related to the anarchist understanding of power, which is especially pronounced in its *postanarchist* variant. Rather than constituting a radical change from 'classical' anarchism, postanarchism is an extension of the former, adding to it a poststructural micro-analysis of ubiquitous power relations.

As Lewis Call remarks, 'broadly speaking, post-anarchists believe that an effective anarchist politics must address not only the modern forms of economic and state power, but also the more pervasive and insidious forms of power which haunt our postmodern world' (Call 2011: 183). This leads us towards an understanding of multiple, potentially infinite and always irreducible axes or rhizomes of power that can exist across all levels, from the global and the national to the local. It therefore serves as an important corrective to postdevelopment's limited understanding of and engagement with power.

As power is ubiquitous – although not all of its forms are necessary *deleterious* – anarchism aims to 'create spaces and relations where domination and oppression are kept to a minimum' (Mueller 2003: 144). To achieve this, any strategies which are based on capturing power first in order to abolish it later are categorically rejected.[13] Anarchists, in turn, believe that power only corrupts and begets more power, therefore *capturing existing power* or creating new forms of power can never be a path to revolution but is always and already doomed to failure.

This further relates to the concept of prefiguration, understood in Gandhian terms as 'being the change you want to see in the world'. Therefore, 'the means used to achieve a goal must foreshadow or embody, albeit perhaps only partially or temporarily, the desired outcome' (Franks 2020: 28).[14] Prefiguration then mostly takes the form of direct action, which according to Gordon (2009: 254–255) is a matter of taking social change into one's own hands, by intervening directly in a situation rather than appealing to an external agent for its rectification.

The notion of the social view of the self, as another key principle, is delineated from anarchism's view of human nature which rejects any essentialised, foundational concept of it. On the one hand, anarchists emphasise the cooperative, mutual aid-based and inherently social capacities of human beings. This serves to counter the narrative of the egoistic, self-interested and purely rational actor or – in its more extreme form – of the inherently brutish, violent and evil nature of human beings that is only constrained through social contracting.

On the other hand, this does not lead anarchists – in contrast to many postdevelopmentalists – to fully embrace an unrestrictedly positive concept of human nature, i.e. the idea of a benign human essence. Instead, Bakunin observes how 'man has two opposed instincts; egoism and sociability. He is both more ferocious in his egoism than the most ferocious beasts and more sociable than the bees and ants' (Bakunin quoted in Maximoff 1953: 136).

Ultimately, then, anarchist philosophy posits that there is no predetermined nature or fixed identity of what it means to be fully human. Instead, humans are 'socially formed … It recognises that the self is partly constructed by its relationship to others, and is indeed dependent on relationships to others' (Franks 2020: 28). This also forecloses a teleological notion of what it means to become fully human, i.e. to strive towards a preordained state of 'human perfection' and to understand history as a linear form of progress towards this perfection.

The 'contextualist view' of human nature then also explains the importance which anarchism gives to education and learning as a social practice – and why an anarchist-influenced postdevelopment theory should do the same in order to weaken the hold of the OWW Development paradigm upon us.

The potential of education as revolutionary means is already stressed in the work of many 19th-century anarchists such as Peter Kropotkin and Voltairine de Cleyre.

> Accepting Rousseau's insight that individuals are products of their environments, he [Kropotkin] called for continuing programmes of non-dominating cultural change to promote life-enhancing ways of living. This is revolution as de Cleyre understood the term, 'some great and subversive change in the social institutions of a people, whether sexual, religious, political, or economic'. Education is a favourite recipe in this anarchist cookbook.
>
> (Kinna 2019: 84)

As Benjamin Franks states, the three anarchist principles of anti-hierarchy, prefiguration and social view of the self then mutually define and reinforce each other. 'Anarchist organisation prefigures anti-hierarchical relations as this is the best way for self-development and it foreshadows liberatory and fulfilling social relations' (Franks 2020: 28).

Together, this leads to a concept of freedom which 'means not just negative freedom, which can legitimise economic inequalities, or modern liberal freedom, with its restricted view of moral agency, but *includes notions of harmonious living and cooperation*' (ibid.: 29–30; emphasis added). The principle of liberty is therefore closely related to notions of mutual aid and equality, i.e. an 'equality of freedom' for everyone and anyone to co-create their own meaningful lives alongside each other (see below).

Looking at the core tenets of anarchist philosophy, we can indeed identify a close yet usually unnoticed affinity between postdevelopment theory and anarchist philosophy.[15] Some of the striking similarities include an outright rejection of the modern nation-state, its hierarchy and its various apparatuses and manifestations (such as Development); an anti-authoritarian ethos and accompanying aversion to 'experts' and other authorities seeking to speak for others; a shared belief in local autonomy, self-determination and the effectiveness of micro-politics;[16] a preference for direct action; as well as a radical openness to how future societies can look instead of following a predetermined blueprint.

Both postdevelopment and anarchism hence clearly seek alternatives to the OWW 'in which people are not told who they are, what they want, and how they shall live, but who will be able to determine these things for themselves' (May 1989: 179).

Introducing anarchist philosophy into the postdevelopment school of thought combines the strengths of both theories and also addresses some of their weaknesses. Left on their own, they tend to focus separately on hierarchies between humans and nature (postdevelopment) and among human beings (anarchism). Through the notion of anarchistic postdevelopment, we bring both aspects more closely together.

As such, anarchistic postdevelopment includes two complementary approaches. One is based on movements, communities and (individuals-coming-together-as) collectives who already and explicitly pursue or strive to pursue lifeworlds characterised by more egalitarian human–nature relations through following – from the beginning or in the process – to a considerable degree the four anarchist key principles of anti-hierarchy, prefiguration, social view of the self and liberty. Such approaches can potentially be found mostly as already existing, or gradually emerging, within the pluriverse of indigenous communities and grassroots movements.[17]

The other approach – which is more commonly found across the OWW and the many struggles to transcend it altogether or at least parts of it – emerges where movements, communities and collectives follow the four anarchist key principles but do not *directly*, or to varying degrees as part of their broader struggles, address any qualitative change in human–nature relations through their actions, practices and projects. They are likewise considered as anarchistic postdevelopment as long as their actions and the consequences of these actions – at a minimum – do not harm nature, while they challenge the hegemony of any parts and practices of the OWW and thereby equally contribute to the emergence of post-dualist practices, projects, livelihoods and lifeworlds.

This together provides us with a flexible yet stable framework to seek, identify and analyse postdevelopmental alternatives to Development. The question then becomes if and how the theoretical framework we have established can be operationalised and turned into an *emancipatory politics* that gives agency to people themselves rather than instructing them what to do. Therefore, we will return to the political philosophy of Jacques Rancière.[18]

Anarchistic postdevelopment and the presupposition of equality

Opposed to the dominant, hierarchical and elitist conceptualisation of equality and Development we have explored in the first chapter, Jacques Rancière establishes *the principle of the presupposition of equality of anyone and everyone* not as a passive political process within a given hierarchical order but as a practical form of direct action taken by the ones who are considered, by the state and its apparatuses, as less equal than others. 'Equality is not given, nor is it claimed; it is practiced, it is verified' (Rancière 1999: 137).

Such a politicised conceptualisation of equality then does not consist in (primarily or only) advancing a demand towards the state or any other authority to be recognised as equals, but it consists of creating a dissensus within the given order by *already acting as equals*. This 'wanting to be the author ... of one's life' (Amsler 2015: 73) – the presupposition of equality – and the dissensus it introduces into a hierarchical society thus constitutes, following Rancière, the basis of all *democratic politics*.

As such, Rancière's conceptualisation of equality is diametrically opposed to the traditional, liberal understanding of equality we have explored in the previous chapter:

> his proposal does not answer the question of how people ought to be treated by the state; it is not a distributive theory of justice. Rather, it concerns how people ought to act if they are to act democratically ... Liberal theory, we might say, is top-down. It starts from the state, and asks how people should be treated by it. Ranciére's approach to democratic politics is bottom-up. It starts from the people who engage in political action, and sees changes in the state (or the economy, or the family, etc.) as resulting from that.
>
> (May 2010: 14)

If the liberal form of equality constitutes a form of productive power that reinforces the hegemonic, hierarchical order, the presupposition of equality simply ignores, negates and transcends this power – it is an example of what Saul Newman terms '*non-power*', or what I refer to below as '*potentiality*'.[19] The idea of equality as a point of departure for all democratic politics hence

> starts not with the desire to change external conditions which might be said to oppress the individual but, rather, with the affirmation of the self over these

conditions, as if to say: power exists but it is not my concern; I refuse to let it constrain me or have any effect on me; I refuse power's power over me.

(Newman 2016: 54)

Within the theoretical framework of anarchistic postdevelopment, this non-power of the presupposition of equality serves as a *standard value*, i.e. an ethical guideline, as well as a concrete strategy to *operationalise* anarchistic postdevelopment.[20]

Applying Rancière's politics in this way is consonant with all four key principles (anti-hierarchy, prefiguration, social view of the self, liberty) of anarchist philosophy': presupposing equality both among each other (within a given group or community) as well as with anyone and everyone else outside the community serves to minimise domination, power and violence. Ultimately, even one's oppressors are considered as equals – not as superior but also not as inferior, thus not simply replacing one dominating power with another. The presupposition of equality also relies, by default, on direct action taken by people themselves and practises a prefigurative politics by assuming that and acting as if anyone and everyone is *already* equal to each other.

Moreover, presupposing equality implies and means that by interacting, communicating and cooperating with our fellow human beings, who are equal to anyone else, we can create meaningful lives alongside each other and improve our lives by supporting and learning from each other, thereby reinforcing a social view of the self. In turn, this leads us towards an anarchistic understanding of freedom embedded in notions of mutual aid, cooperation and harmonious living.

But before we move too quickly, we first need to assess in more detail the nature of equality out of which anyone and everyone is to act. Interestingly and importantly for the further arguments made in this book, Jacques Rancière moves to the realm of education and learning in order to develop his principle of equality.

In *The Ignorant Schoolmaster* (1991), Rancière coins the figure of the 'ignorant schoolmaster' after Joseph Jacotot, a 19th-century teacher from France exiled to Flanders. Faced with the seemingly unsurmountable issue of not knowing the Flemish language, while his students did not speak French, Jacotot made a virtue out of necessity by resorting to a dual-language edition of Fenelon's *Telemaque* as *a thing in common* between himself and his students.

With the help of a translator, Jacotot then asked his students to read and re-read the bilingual book until they could write to him in French what they had understood. To his own surprise, Jacotot's students were indeed able to make sense of what they had read and submitted insightful, high quality work.

the experiment showed that his mastership was not connected to his (superior) intelligence that offers access to knowledge. He had not transferred any knowledge. His mastership lay in the command that he had given ... He had supported his students' will. And he soon applied himself to varying the experiment. He started to teach things he did not know himself. He announced to his students that he had nothing to teach them, that he had no knowledge to transfer to them, but that all intelligences are equal and that they could learn what they want. He only asked them to be attentive to a thing in common and to speak about their intellectual adventures: What do you see? What do you think? What do you say?

(Cornellisen 2011: 17–18)

This ultimately led Jacotot-Rancière[21] to the insight of the *equality of all intelligence*, which, as we will see in later chapters, serves as a key principle for any anarchistic postdevelopmental education.

When he [Rancière] writes of the equality of intelligence, he does not mean that we are equally capable of scoring the same on SAT exams … What he is after is more pedestrian. We can all talk to one another, reason with one another, and construct meaningful lives on the basis of this reasoning and our own reflections. While our specific intellectual skills may differ from one another, we are all equally capable of using those skills to communicate, to discuss, to make decisions, to take account of the world around us, and to act on the basis of all this. The presupposition of the equality of intelligence is the starting point for all politics.

(May 2013: 15)[22]

In short, the presupposition of equal intelligence is the presupposition of equal capacity (not its distribution) – it is '*the presupposition that everyone is capable of building a meaningful life in interaction with others*' (May 2010: 96; emphasis added). What is important here is not the need to rationally, scientifically prove that everyone is equally intelligent, but to start from and experiment with this assumption, to act out of this axiom and see where it leads to:

it is true that we don't know that men are equal. We are saying that they *might* be. This is our opinion, and we are trying, along with those who think as we do, to verify it. But we know that this *might* is the very thing that makes a society of humans possible.

(Rancière 1991: 73; emphasis original)

This shows how the presupposition of equality operates as a *political assumption* on how to structure social relations among and with each other, and not as a foundational claim going back to a notion of a fixed human essence. However, as we will further explore below, it is precisely this radical political assumption which makes the presupposition of equality into a world-making practice and therefore an ontological politics which challenges and goes beyond the limits of the OWW.

Indeed, we can refer to the presupposition of equality also as 'a [political] potentiality: the capacity of ordinary people to discover modes of action to act upon common affairs' (Ross 2009, quoted in Simons and Masschelein 2011: 6). Applying the potentiality or non-power of equality then first and foremost means, as Rancière (1999) continuously emphasises, to reclaim one's capacity to speak for oneself, which has been taken away by 'the part that has a part' in the dominant social order and its institutions from 'the part that has no part' (e.g. the capacity of ordinary people in both the global North and South to determine their own ways of life and pursue their own ideas of what makes meaningful lives alongside each other).[23]

A *democratic politics* in the Rancièrean sense, therefore, starts with the asserting and *acting out of the presupposition of equality* by the part that has no part – common people who are, in the given, dominant police order, *acted upon* based on the presupposition of inequality:

> politics consists in disrupting the police order that excludes or marginalizes them through the assertion, often both in word and in deed, of their equality in that police order. That assertion, that *heterogenous assumption*, disrupts the police order by showing its contingency. There is no reason why those on top are over here and those on the bottom or outside are over there. That arrangement is due to the contingencies of history rather than the necessities of nature. Politics is the assertion of equality among those who presuppose it among themselves.
>
> (May 2010: 10; emphasis original)

The presupposition of equality is verified and realised by the act of speaking for oneself, refusing to be reduced to mere background noise and creating 'an obligation to hear' (May 2008: 72) and be heard as speaking and thinking beings. This leads to a changed *partitioning of the sensible* in the social arena in which the presupposition of equality is enacted.

A partition or distribution of the sensible is understood as 'order of things ... composed of conventions that privilege certain contingencies over and against others' (Lewis 2011: 126) in a given police order. A specific partition of the sensible can be thought of as consisting of various micro-partitions of the sensible which in turn consist of the social and daily practices and actions and manifestations of everyday life that we usually take for granted.

These practices, actions and micro-partitions are then 'bundled together' to form a hegemonic partitioning of the sensible across a specific field, for example, Development. Overall, a partitioning of the sensible then

> makes possible what can be perceived (i.e. what can be seen or heard) and also establishes the different parties that interact within society (i.e. roles, identities, etc.). It determines the modes of being of human beings in a broad ontological sense.
>
> (Jacobs 2015: 4)

By refusing to fit into and fill out the demarcated roles in society that one has been assigned and reduced to by the OWW and its practices such as OWW Development, we therefore move beyond its ontological limits. As such,

> politics consists in reconfiguring the distribution of the sensible which defines the common of a community, to introduce into it new subjects and objects, to

render visible what had not been, and to make heard as speakers those who had been perceived as mere noisy animals.

(Rancière 2004: 25)

This is a clearly anarchistic postdevelopmental position, rejecting the idea that human beings are in need of any superordinate authority that represents and speaks for them in order to live their lives in meaningful ways, be it the modern nation-state in general or the Development apparatus in particular. Instead of accepting their role as mere objects and passive spectators of OWW Development incapable of speech, the people who act out of their own equality 'take up a position as speakers, speakers who have as much right to make sense of the world as any other person' (Bingham 2017: 1999).

If we follow Todd May's assertion that 'for a human life to be meaningful, it must be one in which I am not a spectator but a real participant, and a participant in something that matters to me' (May 2016: 51), we can further see how OWW Development prevents us from becoming an active participant in our own lives by pursuing the ontological politics of *inequality*.

Accordingly, OWW Development 'divides people into those who are politically active and those who are politically passive. And to be politically passive is not to be equal, in the creation of one's own life, to those who are active' (May 2010: 5). As with equality, a meaningful life is not something that can be given or awarded by someone or something from the outside to someone – e.g. by religion (god), the state (politicians), Development (consultants), free markets (consumer goods). Instead, it has to be taken, seized, expressed and lived by oneself in order to become meaningful.[24]

In addition to the 'subjective part' of engagement and participation in one's own life, we can furthermore draw on Todd May's concept of '(objective) narrative values of meaningfulness'. Acting out of the *presupposition of inequality* and persuading people that their lives are less equal, less 'developed' and less 'civilised', 'inferior' and 'backward', OWW Development instead is full of what we can call, following May, '*narrative disvalues*', which often lead the ones who are made into the objects of OWW Development to reflect upon their own life trajectories in negative, hopeless and alienated ways. In other words, 'they withdraw rather than add value to the arc of a person's life' (May 2016: 85).

To provide a brief example, Manish Jain, in the documentary *Schooling The World* (2010), narrates how he encounters elder people in villages across India who talk about themselves in extremely disempowering ways, as 'not knowing anything', not 'understanding anything' and not being able 'to teach anything', seeing themselves as inferior due to their 'lack' of modern school education and Development.

This is despite the abundance of knowledge and wisdom they often possess but which is completely ignored and marginalised by a concept of Development that gauges people's worth, dignity, value and entire lives according to their place within (or outside) the market society. It is just one example of how OWW Development alienates people from their own lives by creating an extremely biased, narrow and distorted set of 'stories' (or maybe even just one main story) of how one's life should look like in order to be meaningful.[25]

Based on this, anarchistic postdevelopmentalists could see one of their roles as being engaged in a form of *narrative therapy*. Narrative therapists can help 'to investigate with people who feel disempowered different and more empowering stories they might tell themselves' (May 2016: 66). In other words, they can help verify the equality of those thought less equal than others. This of course is not based on 'making things up', but on weaving facts together 'in a different way, revealing other sides of people and allowing them to become engaged with their world in a more satisfying way' (ibid.).

Contributing to making people see the world differently – as full of opportunities; as open and yet unwritten and always changeable; or as a world equally (or more) characterised by mutual aid, cooperation and compassion as by individualism and competition – could be one important way of how anarchistic postdevelopmentalists can help animate and motivate people – up to a certain, limited point – to come together through and act out of the presupposition of equality. What these people make out of those new, different stories is of course entirely their choice and does not follow any laid out, natural or organic path.

Nonetheless, Gibson-Graham offers one of many examples on how to approach this task. Carried out as a 'community economies' research project in the Philippines, the typical OWW Development practice of drawing 'need maps' – i.e. what is (economically) lacking within a community – was replaced by the creation of 'asset maps' drawn by the local population.[26]

The outcome showed that there was much more emphasis on the community's already existing capacities and strengths, leading to the emergence of new, innovative ideas of how the community could build on these – which included, but far exceeded market-based solutions. This is in stark contrast to the exercise of drawing need maps, highlighting deficiencies, wants and lacks that usually result in the foregone conclusion that there is too little economic Development, which finally allows the Development practitioner – going through the arduous process of 'community participation' – to devise the foregone solution of *enhancing access to markets* in one form or the other.

Another example can be found in the work of Udaipur-based 'unschooling organisation' Shikshantar. Its project 'Udaipur as a Learning City' (ULC) aims to regenerate 'the local learning ecology … The city is a living organism and people are active co-creators of meaning, relationships, and knowledge' (Jain 2008: 209). Other than similarly titled projects that are usually nothing more than technology-heavy skill and specialised knowledge programmes to cater to current market demands,

> the principles behind ULC lie in paradigms of abundance as opposed to deficit and scarcity-driven frameworks. In practice, this means beginning with an appreciation of what people have and an openness to any and all to join in co-creating. These activities evolve naturally from 'ordinary' peoples' own unique gifts, questions, and dreams, to connect to larger systemic issues and

concerns. This approach actively nurtures peoples' capacities to say 'no' to the institutions/ attitudes/structures that do not serve them, and to instead organically construct spaces and relationships that do serve them.

(ibid.: 213)

Both examples are based on the axiom of equality and therefore involve 'the cultivation of affective orientations and thinking practices that are generative, experimental and hopeful' (Gibson-Graham 2005: 17).

Of course, such initiatives can – and should – never 'guarantee' that people will start to act out of the presupposition of equality, as this is the prerogative of people themselves. However, they can be one way in which anarchistic postdevelopment activists as narrative therapists can attempt to actively contribute to the emergence of 'equality struggles' by countering the narrative disvalues of OWW Development which serve to weaken any tendency towards the radical political assumption of equality.

Ultimately, by acting out of the presupposition of equality, the 'count of the uncounted' – as Rancière often refers to those considered less than equal to others – proves to themselves and others – including their 'opponents' – that the practices, actions, ideas, projects, livelihoods, worldviews and lifeworlds they pursue or strive to pursue are indeed meaningful and equally worthy of respect, and not what OWW Development and its narrative disvalues make of them and reduce them to (i.e. underdeveloped, backward, uncivilised, uneducated, etc.).

The presupposition of equality as ontological politics

It is in this context that we can conceptualise the presupposition of equality, established as a key strategy to operationalise anarchistic postdevelopment, as *the ontological politics of equality*.

The latter then always constitutes a *dissensus* from one or more of the OWW's social practices and (micro-)partitions of the sensible which reinforce social hierarchies. As a result of this dissensus, a redistribution of the sensible can happen which interrupts the attempts to perpetuate or expand the OWW. The ontological politics of equality, thus, opens up the path to ideas, practices, actions, livelihoods and lifeworlds outside the ontological limits of the OWW, and thereby moves us closer towards post-dualist, more relational lifeworlds.

This means that the ontological politics of equality can potentially happen anywhere and everywhere, at any and every time, with any and all people. Whenever and wherever people come together in order to challenge one or more of the OWW's partitions of the sensible by enacting the presupposition of equality, whenever and wherever they refuse to accept some of the pre-assigned roles and pre-determined identities on offer by the dualist OWW, *they engage in the ontological politics of equality*.

As we have also seen in the previous chapter, all the various dualisms that pervade the OWW are interrelated with each other and follow the human–nature core dualism. All the various struggles which pursue the ontological politics of equality then can be likewise seen as interrelated, as mutually reinforcing and strengthening each other by prying open the OWW's various partitions of the sensible, rearranging them and thus challenging the overall hegemony of the OWW ontology.

However, the ontological politics of equality does not suddenly, randomly or coincidentally emerge. People do not wake up one day and tell themselves that they are equal to each other. And even once they start to act out of that presupposition and utilise its (non-)power, they might, most likely, not be aware that it is the principle of the presupposition of equality they follow.

> It's understood that an egalitarian movement is not a movement of people who are constantly preoccupied with the feat of achieving equality. An egalitarian movement is a movement of people who place in common their desire to live a different life – to put it in the most classic terms. I've always said that equality was a dynamic and not an end. You don't come together to achieve equality; you achieve a certain kind of equality by coming together.
>
> (Rancière 2016: 117)

What we can understand as the unfolding of the ontological politics of equality is based on a new count, or re-count, that starts with *negativity and dissensus* towards the given, dominant OWW order, and leads to *positivity and hope* that creates at the same time a *declassification of or dis-identification with* given identities, what Rancière calls *subjectification*, in turn leading to a *repartitioning of the sensible*.

The presupposition of equality originates in the political refusal or ontological dissensus to accept the given count of the OWW as the dominant social reality: 'the people who are considered less than equal in a given police order no longer assent to that order … They may have unity among themselves, but they introduce division into the social order' (May 2007: 25).[27]

Ana Cecilia Dinerstein, drawing on Ernst Bloch's *Principle of Hope* (1986), further describes such processes of negation and dissensus as

> inextricably connected to the possibility to anticipate a new or oppressed reality that is latent in the present … It is very difficult to disentangle negation and creation, for negation makes possible to engage in the new that is already on its way.
>
> (Dinerstein 2015: 62)

Thus, by disagreeing with the hegemonic count and negating dominant social reality, negativity turns into hope, ultimately challenging 'the given demarcation of what is real and what is not, what exists and what does not' (ibid.).

In other words, acting out of the presupposition of equality is 'a form of autonomous action, a way of acting and thinking anarchistically in the here and now, seeking to transform the immediate situation and relationships that one finds oneself in' (Newman 2016: 12). By challenging and disrupting the ontological politics of inequality, the presupposition of equality then replaces 'oppressive

relationships in favor of a participation that starts from the idea that each participant is equal' (May 2010: 24).

This process is referred to by Rancière as 'subjectification', the practice of
collective, direct action under the presupposition of equality that leads to the
emergence of a previously non-existing collective subject. As such, subjectification declassifies people's naturalised, common-sense roles and identities imposed
upon them by the OWW and instead creates something new that exceeds the ontological limits of the OWW.

The new collective subject 'redefines the field of experience that gave to each
their identity with their lot. It decomposes and recomposes the relationships
between the ways of *doing*, of *being* and of *saying* that define the perceptible
organization of the community' (Rancière 1999: 40; emphasis original).

Subjectification, or the creation of new political (dis-)identities which exceed
the ontological limits of the OWW, then at the same is accompanied by a repartitioning of the sensible, 'the production of new ways of seeing, being, hearing,
and interacting within the present' (Lewis 2012). The redistribution of the sensible impacts both the collective subject practicing equality and the experience
and perception of others within the OWW. Ultimately, this leads the people
pursuing the ontological politics of equality to recapture their capacity to create meaningful lives by transcending the boundaries of the OWW both in the
figural (i.e. the broadening of one's 'radical imagination') and the literal (i.e.
the prefigurative, direct actions taken to pursue other ideas, practices, lives and
lifeworlds) sense.

Consequently, dis-identification/subjectification and the accompanying repartitioning of the sensible further create and nurture hope by making the part who –
until their acting out of the presupposition of equality – had no part 'sense the
world differently. This sensibility lends one an aura of empowerment, in which
the world opens itself at the same time that one feels a greater sense of one's own
capacities' (May 2008: 111).

We can then further see how the ontological politics of equality, and its characteristic processes of 'subjectification' and the 'redistribution of the sensible' in
particular, creates positive and empowering narrative values, as opposed to the
ontological politics of inequality which is full of narrative disvalues.

Through the former, therefore, new and meaningful narratives emerge through
which 'people *reproduce* themselves into what they would rather be' (May
2016: 66; emphasis original). They are not internalising anymore the stories and
narrative disvalues that OWW Development tells about them and their limited
capacities.

In sum, dissensus, hope, declassification/subjectification and the repartitioning
of the sensible shape the ontological politics of equality in a way that serves 'not
so much to unify as to declassify, to undo the supposed naturalness of orders and
replace it with the controversial figures of division' (Rancière 1995: 32–33).

As a result of practicing the ontological politics of equality, there emerge not
only new collective subjects beyond Development. The accompanying reconfiguration of the 'developmental field of experience' at the same time enables us to

challenge the dominant understanding of OWW Development and what makes a meaningful life.

What is created instead is something 'new', a radical opening to meanings and horizons that lie beyond the OWW, emphasising an abundance of visions and ideas of how to construct meaningful lives with and alongside each other based on anarchist principles. This is in stark contrast to the ontological politics of inequality which reinforces teleological, liberal notions of Development as 'improvement' and 'progress'.

The dissensus and conflict which is inherent in the ontological politics of equality, therefore, 'is a sign of democratization rather than of problematic obstacles to it' (Tanabe 2007: 570). As such,

> in contrast to liberal theory, equality is not a matter of distributing the same ...
> It is not a matter of coming to consensus. If people are equally intelligent and are to act out of the presupposition of that equal intelligence, it is neither to confirm any particular identity nor to propose one. It is instead to refuse the identities that are on offer, the roles that have been proffered by the current police arrangement. To put the point another way, it is not in the name of an identity or of a sameness that equality is acted out; it is in the name of difference.
>
> (May 2010: 15)

In other words, the ontological politics of equality is not about struggling to become integrated or recognised as equals within the OWW – what Val Plumwood (1993) calls 'uncritical equality' – but about struggling to (re-)create, defend and reassert other ideas, (dis-)identities, practices, actions and ways of life which exceed the ontological limits of the OWW. Accordingly, such a world-making practice opens up new political and social spaces 'outside the ontological order of state sovereignty, even if they [indirectly] impose demands upon the state' (Newman 2016: 14).

As such, the radical political assumption of equality gives power and agency back to people themselves instead of deciding what is allegedly best for them. As Todd May puts it, 'instead of asking what is owed to the demos, it asks what the demos is capable of' (May 2008: 78). This marks a full rupture with the liberal understanding and application of equality which can be found in the various forms and guises of OWW Development.

> I act, we act as if all human beings had an equal intellectual capacity. Emancipation first means the endorsement of the presupposition: I am able, we are able to think and act without masters. But we are able to the extent that we think that all other human beings are endowed with the same capacity ... The presupposition of equal capacity is a principle of shared freedom opposed to the presupposition that the human beings can only act rationally as individuals and cooperate rationally in a community according to a principle of subordination.
>
> (Rancière 2017)

This further demonstrates how the ontological politics of equality is geared towards making visible and tearing down the manifold and irreducible hierarchies that structure the OWW – in other words, it leads to various redistributions of the sensible. Where the manifold hierarchies of the OWW are being challenged and overcome in the name of equality, a new field of experience emerges that exceeds the ontological limits of the OWW and declassifies its pre-given roles and identities:

> hierarchies are imposed by people's coming to see and experience their world in certain ways, ways that sustain and nourish those hierarchies … We live in so many arenas, from our family to our work to hobbies to our civic partici-pation, and each of these arenas participates in a *partage du sensible*. As we intervene politically on each of these, we can make them more democratic, disrupting the police order that maintains oppressive relationships in favor of a participation that starts from the idea that each participant is equal.
>
> (May 2010: 24)

Put differently, true to the anarchist key principles we have explored above, there is no Archimedean point, no single partition of the sensible that is necessarily more important and more worthwhile to struggle against or rearrange than oth-ers. Instead, all of the various struggles under the ontological politics of equality contribute to and reinforce each other and help to make visible, challenge and overcome the various irreducible hierarchies of the OWW.

Summation

By combining the postdevelopment school of thought with anarchist philosophy, we have established both *a theoretical framework* to seek, identify and analyse, as well as an *emancipatory politics* to create, defend and expand *postdevelopmental alternatives to Development* which are *paving the way(s) towards the pluriverse*. While the worlds that make the anarchist postdevelopmental pluriverse may dif-fer in many ways, what they have in common or strive towards is the combined minimising of hierarchical relations between humans and nature as well as among human beings.

The presupposition of equality, which we have further developed into the onto-logical politics of equality, then fundamentally goes against the liberal under-standing of (in-)equality which, as we have seen in the first chapter, constitutes a central part of the OWW and its continuing hegemony.

Moreover, the radical assumption that everyone and anyone is equally capa-ble of co-creating meaningful lives together with others then also is fundamen-tally opposed to more conservative political philosophies. One example for this is the philosophy of Hannah Arendt, who reserves the prerogative of politics for the part that has a part, while the poor are described as being exclusively under the dictate of their physical needs and therefore neither have the time nor the will or capacity to become political actors. Effectively, this means that by virtue of being poor, the part who has no part can never become free and full political actors unless they become integrated into the part who has a part.[28]

This of course constitutes an extremely reactionary idea of politics. On the one hand, it takes away any agency from the part who has no part and reduces 'the poor' to their basic, bodily needs. On the other hand, Arendt makes politics into an exclusive and elevated practice of the ones who already have a part and therefore have a stake in keeping the status quo as it is. Apart from the limited possibility of integrating more people into the part who has a part, this forecloses or at least severely limits the possibilities for any more fundamental change that would exceed the ontological limits of the given, hegemonic world order.

As we have seen, the presupposition of equality is diametrically opposed to such disempowering notions and defines democratic politics instead as a bottom-up process. The ontological politics of equality, therefore, is

> defined by the actions and the understandings of those who struggle, not by the effects upon or actions taken by those the police order supports. Otherwise put, politics lies in the creation of the poor, not in the magnanimity of the rich.
>
> (May 2008: 72)

Taken together, the first two chapters which form the first part of the book have established a framework to make sense of both the continuing dominance of Development as a world-making practice based on the presupposition of inequality, and of ways to counter it through an anarchistic postdevelopment, acted out through the ontological politics of equality. When both encounter and struggle with each other, we can understand this as ontological encounters that advance very different views on 'Development', 'equality' and of what makes meaningful lives.

The second part of the book is going to address the task of how we can further undermine the OWW's intense hold over us that is visible and manifested in the ingrained presupposition of inequality which structures large parts of our daily lives. Here, we will turn to analyse the role of *education* as either a key tool to continuously expand, normalise and legitimise the OWW, or as a means to challenge, change and overcome the latter and move towards the pluriverse.

Chapter 3 starts off the second part of the book by elaborating the strategic importance of education for OWW Development. As we will see, India is indeed a prime example of how the idea of 'modern education' is being strategically utilised by various OWW Development actors in order to advance and further entrench the hierarchical OWW order under the presupposition of inequality in its neoliberal and virtuous neoliberal variant.

Notes

1 Escobar (2015).
2 The notion of people-in-nature builds on the idea of a 'mutual and reciprocal relationship with nature' (Plumwood 1993: 164), in which 'there may be areas of land and life where *humans* are sovereign, as far as they may be without denying dependency, and there may also be a whole fruitful domain where they may undertake together with

earth others "the dance of interaction", being both transforming and transformed, sustaining and sustained' (ibid.; emphasis original).

3 One example for this is how much of postdevelopment research eschews any analysis of existing power relations and hierarchies in movements such as the Zapatistas, which seems to serve as the poster child of 'postdevelopment in practice'. This is by no means to take anything away from the Zapatista movement and its achievements, but to draw attention to the fact that postdevelopment often tends to downplay the internal contradictions and challenges of local communities and social movements.

4 See for example Sachs (1992); Rahnema and Bawtree (1997); Esteva and Prakash (1998).

5 According to Foucault (1991: 194), power produces reality, domains of objects and 'rituals of truth'. Hence, power 'does not repress human subjectivity … – rather it produces it. This denies the possibility of an uncontaminated point of departure outside power, because the human subject who hitherto constituted this "pure" place is contaminated by power' (Newman 2001: 83).

6 One of the few postdevelopment scholars who explicitly addresses this issue is Aram Ziai, contending that 'power does not simply emanate from the state or international institutions, but it is to be found in everyday local and self-evident relations and discourses' (Ziai 2007: 114).

7 See https://www.radicalecologicaldemocracy.org/about/.

8 The Vikalp Sangam platform (http://vikalpsangam.org/), curated by Indian NGO Kalpavriksh, features many case studies and stories on movements striving towards self-governance.

9 While India does not have any notable history of 'anarchism' as such, it has a vivid history and present of anti-hierarchical, horizontal and direct action-based struggles, which, as we will see, form some key elements of anarchist philosophy. The political philosophy of Mohandas Gandhi, who corresponded by letter with Christian anarchist Leo Tolstoy, also represented some central anarchistic elements. As M.P.T. Acharya – a freedom fighter during the Indian independence movement and self-proclaimed Indian anarchist who frequently wrote in the journal *Harijan* founded by Gandhi – noted, 'the only people [in India] who are nearest to anarchism are the Gandhians of the *Harijan* group. They are near-anarchists because they want decentralization (independent village communes), production for use and direct action' (Acharya 1953 quoted in Laursen 2019: 29). Therefore, as Maia Ramnath in her work on decolonising anarchism in India suggests, 'we could locate the Western anarchist tradition as one contextually specific manifestation among a larger – indeed global – tradition of antiauthoritarian, egalitarian thought/praxis … which also occurs in many other forms in many other contexts' (Ramnath 2011: 6).

10 Some parts of this definition are less applicable to the more individualist forms of anarchism such as developed by William Godwin and Max Stirner, instead highlighting the more prominent socialist anarchist strand.

11 Franks (2020).

12 A current example of this can be found in the Black Lives Matter movement which connects various sites of struggle including anti-racism, anti-capitalism, anti-patriarchy and anti-sexism; see CrimethInc (2020) for a detailed account on how the movement reflects anarchist thoughts and practices.

13 This also led to the split between anarchism (represented by Mikhail Bakunin) and Marxism during the First International in 1872, given Marx's insistence on the need for a revolutionary vanguard to capture state power.

14 The congruency of means and ends differentiates anarchism from both neoliberalism and Marxism-Leninism. For the former, free markets as a means to a prosperous society became the ultimate end. For the latter, the existence of a revolutionary party as a means to a class-less, party-less society likewise became the ultimate end in and by itself.

15 The few exceptions here include Nederveen Pieterse (2000: 182) who comments that postdevelopment is permeated by 'an anti-authoritarian sensibility ... an aversion to control and perhaps an anarchist streak'. Wald (2015) further identifies parallels between the anti-hierarchical tendencies and the promotion of equality inherent in both anarchism and postdevelopment.

16 Anarchist Colin Ward (1996: 58) for instance represents a genuine postdevelopmental position when stating that 'the anarchist conclusion is that every kind of human activity should begin from what is local and immediate'.

17 As I have written elsewhere, the Whanganui Iwi Māori and their struggle for the Whanganui River as part of the Iwi's pluriversal, more-than-human lifeworld can be understood as an example of this approach (see Neusiedl 2019).

18 In doing so, I follow Todd May's postanarchist reading/interpretation of Rancière.

19 'Non-power' needs to be distinguished from counter-power which would just replace one arrangement of power with another. As such, Rancière (2009: 41) describes politics based on (the non-power of) the presupposition of equality as 'anarchic "government," one based on nothing other than the absence of every title to govern'.

20 Taking the presupposition of equality as standard value however is not the same as ascribing to it a deep foundation. 'There is no foundation of values that everyone must agree on, but that does not mean that our values are arbitrary. They can be scrutinized, criticized, modified, and defended. In order to do so, however, other values have to be taken as a standard. One can't hold all values up for examination at the same time ... Even if we can't stand outside the web itself and offer it up for an audit, we can, from within it, assess our values and our practices' (May 2016: 156–157). My choice of 'equality' as a standard value and constant 'for the questioning to make sense' (ibid.: 157) then is not just an arbitrary choice. As I argue throughout this book, equality – in one form or another – is always relevant and indeed central to both OWW Development and postdevelopment, to neoliberalism and to anarchism, to liberal democracies and autonomous communities, to modern societies as well as to indigenous communities, and as such serves as the most appropriate standard value within this framework.

21 The book is written in the voice of both Jacotot and Rancière, and the borders between them are often blurred.

22 Rancière (1999: 16) further demonstrates this assumed equal capability of everyone and anyone through the relation between the oppressed and the oppressor: 'there is order in society because some people command and others obey, but in order to obey an order at least two things are required: you must understand that you must obey it. And to do that, you must already be the equal of the person who is ordering you'.

23 Rancière (1999: 29) describes the police order as 'the visible and the sayable that sees that a particular activity is visible and another is not, that this speech is understood as discourse and another as noise'.

24 As May (2016: 139) argues, our lives become more meaningful when 'we are absorbed by the unfolding of our life, when it makes sense to us to continue to do what we do, when we endorse our projects'. This in turn illustrates how OWW Development is detracting from such activities and feelings by acting out of the presupposition of inequality which attempts to convince the vast majority of the world's population that their lives are less worth living than others.

25 This also highlights how the discourse and practice of OWW Development make people into dependent, passive consumers. This is an essential distinction from a position that identifies someone as an 'underdeveloped person' who *needs* Development. Instead, I argue that Development aims to transform a person into an 'underdeveloped' one, unable to live a life without Development.

26 Gibson-Graham (2005).

27 'Dissensus' is not necessarily always a key characteristic of the ontological politics of equality – it is so only in as far as we live in a world (the OWW) pervaded by hierarchical orders.

28 See Arendt [1963] (2016).

References

Acharya, M.P.T. [1948] (2019). 'What is anarchism'? In Laursen, O.B., and Acharya, M.P.T., *We are Anarchists*: *Essays on Anarchism, Pacifism, and the Indian Independence Movement, 1923-1953*. Edinburgh: AK Press, pp. 191–214.

Amsler, S.S. (2015). *The Education of Radical Democracy*. New York: Routledge.

Arendt, H. [1963] (2016). *On Revolution*. London: Faber & Faber.

Bingham, C. (2017). 'Rancière and education'. In Peters, M.A. (ed.), *Encyclopedia of Educational Philosophy and Theory*. Singapore: Springer, pp. 1995–2000.

Bloch, E. (1986). *The Principle of Hope*. Cambridge, MA: The MIT Press.

Call, L. (2011). 'Buffy the post-anarchist vampire slayer'. In Rousselle, D., and Evren, S. (eds.), *Post-Anarchism: A Reader*. London: Pluto Press, pp. 183–194.

Cornelissen, G. (2011). 'The public role of teaching: To keep the door closed'. In Simons, M., and Masschelein, J. (eds.), *Rancière, Public Education and the Taming of Democracy*. Malden: Wiley-Blackwell, pp. 15–30.

CrimethInc. (2020). 'This is anarchy'. https://crimethinc.com/2020/06/09/this-is-anarchy-eight-ways-the-black-lives-matter-and-justice-for-george-floyd-uprisings-reflect-anar chist-ideas-in-action.

DeLeon, A. (2008). 'Oh no, not the "a" word! proposing an "anarchism" for education'. *Educational Studies*, 44 (2), pp. 122–141.

Dinerstein, A.C. (2015). *The Politics of Autonomy in Latin America: The Art of Organising Hope*. New York: Palgrave Macmillan.

Escobar, A. (2011). 'Sustainability: Design for the pluriverse'. *Development*, 54 (2), pp. 137–140.

Escobar, A. (2015). 'Degrowth, Postdevelopment, and transitions: A preliminary conversation'. *Sustainability Science*, 10, pp. 451–462.

Esteva, G., and Prakash, M.S. (1998) *Grassroots Post-Modernism: Remaking the Soil of Cultures*. London: Zed Books.

Foucault, M. (1991). *Discipline and Punish: The Birth of the Prison*. London: Penguin.

Franks, B. (2020). *Anarchisms, Postanarchisms and Ethics*. London: Rowman & Littlefield International.

Gibson-Graham, J.K. (2005). 'Surplus possibilities: Postdevelopment and community economies'. *Singapore Journal of Tropical Geography*, 26 (1), pp. 4–26.

Gordon, U. (2009). 'Dark tidings: Anarchist politics in the age of collapse'. In Amster, R., DeLeon, A., Fernandez, L.A., Nocella, A.J., and D. Shannon (eds.), *Contemporary Anarchist Studies: An Introductory Anthology of Anarchy in the Academy*. New York: Routledge, pp. 249–258.

Jacobs, L.E.D. (2015). 'The ignorant philosopher? On Jacques Rancière's political ontology'. In VIII Congreso Latinoamericano de Ciencia Política, La Asociación Latinoamericana de Ciencia Política (ALACIP), Lima, Perú, pp. 1–15.

Jain, S. (2008). 'Shikshantar: An organic learning community'. In Hern, M. (ed.), *Everywhere All the Time: A New Deschooling Reader*. Oakland: AK Press, pp. 202–213.

Kinna, R. (2019). *The Government of No One: The Theory and Practice of Anarchism*. London: Penguin Random House UK.

Laursen, O.B., and Acharya, M.P.T. (2019). *We are Anarchistst: Essays on Anarchism, Pacifism, and the Indian Independence Movement, 1923–1953*. Edinburgh: AK Press.

Lewis, T.E. (2011). 'Paulo Freire's last laugh: Rethinking critical pedagogy's funny bone through Jacques Rancière'. In Simons, M., and Masschelein, J. (eds.), *Rancière, Public Education and the Taming of Democracy*. Malden, MA: Wiley-Blackwell, pp. 121–133.

Lewis, T.E. (2012). *The Aesthetics of Education: Theatre, Curiosity, and Politics in the Work of Jacques Rancière and Paulo Freire.* New York: Continuum.

Maximoff, G.P. (ed.) (1953). *The Political Philosophy of Bakunin.* New York: Free Press.

May, T. (1989). 'Is post-structuralist political theory anarchist'? *Philosophy and Social Criticism*, 15 (2), pp. 167–182.

May, T. (2007). 'Jacques Rancière and the ethics of equality'. *SubStance*, 36 (2), pp. 20–36.

May, T. (2008). *The Political Thought of Jacques Rancière: Creating equality.* Edinburgh: Edinburgh University Press.

May, T. (2010). *Contemporary Political Movements and the Thought of Jacques Rancière: Equality in Action.* Edinburgh: Edinburgh University Press.

May, T. (2013). 'Humanism and solidarity'. *Parrhesia*, 18, pp. 11–21.

May, T. (2016). *A Significant Life: Human Meaning in a Silent Universe.* Chicago: The University of Chicago Press.

McGregor, A. (2007). 'Development, foreign aid and post-development in Timor-Leste'. *Third World Quarterly*, 28 (1), pp. 155–170.

Mueller, T. (2003). 'Empowering anarchy: Power, hegemony and anarchist strategy'. *Anarchist Studies*, 11 (2), pp. 122–149.

Nederveen Pieterse, J. (2000). 'After post-development'. *Third World Quarterly*, 20 (1), pp. 175–191.

Neusiedl, C. (2019). 'The ontological politics of (in-)equality: A new research approach for post-development'. *Third World Quarterly*, 40 (4), pp. 651–667.

Newman, S. (2001). *From Bakunin to Lacan: Anti-authoritarianism and the Dislocation of Power.* Oxford: Lexington Books.

Newman, S. (2016). *Postanarchism.* Cambridge: Polity Press.

Plumwood, V. (1993). *Feminism and the Mastery of Nature.* London: Routledge.

Rahnema, M., and Bawtree, V. (eds.) (1997). *The Post-Development Reader.* London: Zed Books.

Ramnath, M. (2011). *Decolonizing Anarchism: An Antiauthoritarian History of India's Liberation Struggle.* Oakland, CA: AK Press.

Rancière, J. (1991). *The Ignorant Schoolmaster. Five Lessons in Intellectual Emancipation.* Stanford: Stanford University Press.

Rancière, J. (1995). *On the Shores of Politics.* London: Verso.

Rancière, J. (1999). *Disagreement: Politics and Philosophy.* Minneapolis: University of Minnesota Press.

Ranciere, J. (2004). *Aesthetics and its Discontents.* Cambridge: Polity Press.

Rancière, J. (2009). *Hatred of Democracy.* London: Verso.

Rancière, J. (2016). *The Method of Equality.* Cambridge: Polity Press.

Rancière, J. (2017). 'Democracy, equality, emancipation in a changing world'. https://www.versobooks.com/blogs/3395-democracy-equality-emancipation-in-a-changing-world.

Rist, G. (2006). *The History of Development: From Western Origins to Global Faith.* 2nd ed. London: Zed Books.

Sachs, W. (1992). *The Development Dictionary: A Guide to Knowledge as Power.* London: Zed Books.

Simons, M., and Masschelein, J. (2011). *Rancière, Public Education and the Taming of Democracy.* Malden, MA: Wiley-Blackwell.

Tanabe, A. (2007). 'Toward vernacular democracy: Moral society and post-postcolonial transformation in rural Orissa, India'. *American Ethnologist*, 34 (3), pp. 558–574.

Wald, N. (2015). 'Anarchist participatory development: A possible new framework'? *Development and Change*, 46 (4), pp. 618–643.

Ward, C. (1996). *Anarchy in action*. London: Freedom Press.

Wilson, K. (2017). 'Worlds beyond the political? Post-development approaches in practices of transnational solidarity activism'. *Third World Quarterly*, 38 (12), pp. 2684–2702.

Ziai, A. (2007). 'The ambivalence of post-development'. In Ziai, A. (ed.), *Exploring Post-Development: Theory and Practice, Problems and Perspectives*. New York: Routledge, pp. 111–128.

Ziai, A. (2017). 'Post-development 25 years after the development dictionary'. *Third World Quarterly*, 38 (12), pp. 2547–2558.

3 From OWW Development to OWW Education

As we have seen, the OWW does not constitute 'real reality' that objectively exists out there. Instead, it is a historically and politically contingent worldview that is held together and extended through various practices such as Development. Anarchistic postdevelopment, acted out through the presupposition of equality, then serves as an emancipatory framework to challenge and interrupt the relentless expansion of OWW Development. However, this ontological politics of equality usually takes place on the margins of OWW Development, as a dissensus of the part that has no part against the hegemonic OWW order.

This begs the question of how OWW Development has achieved such an immense hold over most of us. Why is it so hard to transcend the OWW's ontological limits and develop more radical imaginations of how to co-construct meaningful lives with each other?

Modern education, as I will argue in this chapter, plays a key role in both stifling our 'radical imagination' to seek alternatives to Development as well as in recreating, legitimising and normalising the OWW project as the only worthwhile way of life. This becomes evident when we look at how the World Bank – with India being its largest client in education projects – conceptualises education as a means to socialise everyone into a market-based society.[1]

Sarah Amsler, drawing on Marcuse, shows how what we make sense of as OWW Development, especially in today's dominant neoliberal version,

> is an historical and *educative project*, not a mere developmental stage of capitalism. This means that it is not simply a certain way of doing things, but a 'determinate choice, seizure of one among other ways of comprehending, organizing and transforming reality' and one that therefore needs to be continuously accomplished.
>
> (Amsler 2015: 45; emphasis added)

The most important role of modern education, therefore, is to continuously recreate the OWW as 'real reality' and so create the conditions for other, interlocking practices such as OWW Development to unfold. Today, this role of education is often advanced through the promotion of public–private partnerships in education (ePPPs).

EPPPs essentially amount to a creeping privatisation of the public education sector in India and elsewhere through an alliance of what Pasi Sahlberg calls the 'Global Education Reform Movement' (GERM). As we will see, this alliance advances a business agenda of the education system and in the education system while at the same time building a market ecosystem for additional services, thereby fully subjecting the education sector to market relations.

The chapter will conclude with a case study of 'Absolute Return for Kids' (Ark) India which is one of the rising ePPP players in the country, detailing how Ark schools aim to mould students from marginalised backgrounds into 'good consumer citizens' of the OWW order.

OWW Education and the ontological politics of inequality

It is no coincidence that modern education, understood here largely as school-based learning – i.e. 'the age-specific, teacher-related process requiring full-time attendance at an obligatory curriculum' (Illich 1974: 25–26) – is the favourite recipe of nearly all OWW Development actors to 'bring about Development' in the first place. As with Development, it is tied to the OWW ontology and serves to continuously justify, explain, legitimise and normalise its hierarchical, arbitrary order.

It should then come as no surprise that the kind of education which is being promoted and implemented by any and all OWW Development actors today is likewise based on the ontological politics of inequality: '[modern] educators perpetuate a universalist approach to education, which positions progress and development as conformity to the Western canon and which has become synonymous with ideas of what it means to be "modern," "progressive," and "democratic"' (Spoto 2015: 87).

Similarly, Amster et al. (2009: 123) state that

> because traditional schooling has been oppressively linked to the State and capitalism, institutional education has been highly dismissive of non-dominant cultures and has been subtractive and colonial in its attempt to fashion people as workers, managers, and owners. Thus, traditional education has amounted to what Michel Foucault called a colonization of our souls.

This shows how what we can term from here on as *OWW Education* only recognises a certain, subjective kind of knowledge that fits within the ontological limits of the OWW, and at the same time legitimises this knowledge as the one and only, objective truth. It becomes a self-referential entity within what Rose (1999) calls *a hall of mirrors*.

In India, the exclusion of alternative worldviews is particularly visible in the education system's depiction of Adivasis and their lifeworlds: 'the representation of Adivasi in stereotypical negative terms as "backward" people, outside the pale of progress, has meant that elementary education has only reinforced stereotypes and further marked the Adivasi in discriminatory terms' (Veerbhadranaika et al. 2012, quoted in Ramachandran 2018: 102). As Ramachandran (ibid.) further observes, 'another site of alienation is the content of our textbooks, which give primary importance to urban-centred subjects and do not weave in the histories and cultures of the tribal people of India'.

Alvares (2002: 216) moreover notes how on a general level,

> European ideas are considered the only basis for a proper schooling programme and for 'civilized' living. History textbooks in India, for example, still unabashedly hail the arrival of Vasco-da-Gama as a great event. Or repeat themes produced by English historians like James Mill or even Karl Marx. Incorporating the intellectual corpus of Indian or other civilisations into the materials prepared for courses still provokes resistance from some quarters.

Helena Norberg-Hodge similarly observes how the changes that came with the introduction of OWW Education to the erstwhile remote region of Ladakh in the Indian Himalayas

> made children think of themselves and their culture as inferior. Everything in school promoted a highly romanticised Western model in which it appeared that modern technology and money provided a life of constant excitement and glamour. It looked like a life of leisure – one in which there was no need to get your hands dirty, no need for the drudgery of physical effort.
>
> (Norberg-Hodge 2016: 53)

In times of what we have termed virtuous neoliberalism, this pre-selection of educational content is further intensified by the Indian government's direct interventions in the education system. In a recent move and with the justification of 'rationalising the curriculum' in view of the coronavirus pandemic, the Central Board of Secondary Education

> deleted chapters on federalism, citizenship, nationalism, and secularism from the political science curriculum of Class 11 for the academic year 2020-'21 … Sub-sections including 'why do we need local governments?' and 'growth of local government in India' have also been removed from the curriculum … The political science curriculum for Class 10 students was also restructured to remove chapters on democracy and diversity; gender, religion and caste; popular struggles and movement, among other sections.
>
> (Scroll.in 2020)

While it remains to be seen if this suspension will be only temporary or not, it is part of a broader agenda to change the school curriculum, as can be observed across several BJP-ruled states in India. As the neoliberal curriculum – in India and worldwide – already marginalises and ignores the voices and perspectives of people that do not fit into its narrow worldview, recent interventions in India go even further by additionally aiming to revise whole parts of the nation's history.

In the then BJP-led state of Rajasthan, for example, newly introduced textbooks promoted

> the BJP's political program and ideology. They argue for the veracity of Vedic myths, glorify ancient and medieval Hindu rulers, recast the independence movement as a violent battle led largely by Hindu chauvinists, demand loyalty to the state, and praise the policies of the BJP prime minister, Narendra Modi. One book reduces over five centuries of rule by a diverse array of Muslim emperors to a single 'Period of Struggle' and demonizes many of its leading figures.[2] These textbooks are part of the BJP's ongoing campaign to change how Indian history is taught in middle and high schools. Textbooks issued last year by two other states under BJP rule, Gujarat and Maharashtra, resemble the Rajasthan books in their Hindu triumphalism and Islamophobia. So, in a subtler fashion, do updates made in May to federal textbooks.
>
> (Traub 2018)

While this might be seen by some as a 'corrective' to a too Western-centric curriculum, it just replaces the strands of one dominant OWW-narration with another one where the external supremacy of Europeans is complemented by the internal supremacy of Hindus, in effect still oppressing all other (hi)stories.

The new National Education Policy (NEP) by the Indian government, which was introduced in July 2020 and replaces the NEP of 1986, then further is an amalgamation of the state's nationalist agenda and the neoliberal OWW Development agenda.

It seamlessly ties together the need for an education 'to lead the country into the 21st century and the fourth industrial revolution'[3] (Government of India 2020: 37) with a strong and continuous emphasis on Indian values, traditions, culture and philosophy alongside a push for Sanskrit education.[4] It establishes the need for coding classes and vocational training for students while it praises the benefits of ancient and traditional Indian knowledge, and manages to put into a single sentence the proposal for 'substantial investment in *a strong, vibrant public education system* as well as the encouragement and facilitation of *true philanthropic private and community participation*' (ibid.: 6; emphasis added), achieved through 'light but tight' – i.e. less – regulation.

In India as across the globe, therefore,

> education is at the 'front lines' of the contemporary ideological war conducted by corporate media, official organs of the State, and influential economic institutions. Whether that emerges through corporate textbooks that omit subaltern experiences and worldviews, standardised testing that stress rote memorisation, or a curriculum that reproduces Eurocentrism and Western ways of knowing, education is invested in reproducing dominant conceptions of the world.
>
> (DeLeon 2012: 314)

The human capital approach to education

We can find one of the most visible manifestations of the reproduction of dominant conceptions in the World Bank's decades-long stance on education which is based on the idea of 'human capital' and a related understanding of learning as 'a largely technical activity to be managed by skilled people available primarily in the world's richest countries' (Klees et al. 2019: 605).

The *Education Strategy 2020*, adopted in 2011 as one of the most influential education policy-shaping tools across the globe, reflects the Bank's 'obsessive attachment to human capital theory' (Fine and Rose 2003: 156), which appropriates education as a tool for economic growth and increased incomes.

A leading figure at the Delhi-based UNESCO Mahatma Gandhi Institute of Education for Peace and Sustainable Development (MGIEP) sums up the World Bank's human capital approach as follows:

> you acquire skills so that you can enhance the abilities of the human being in improving or *contributing to financial capital*. So *technology, technical skills, which will allow you to make more money*, catering to whatever the different requirements of the world are, is what has been the focus.
>
> (personal interview, October 2017; emphasis added)

This also becomes visible in the below excerpt from the World Bank's Education Strategy 2020:

> investments in quality education lead to more rapid and sustainable economic growth and development. Educated individuals are more employable, able to earn higher wages, cope better with economic shocks, and produce healthier children … Learning for All means ensuring that all children and youth – not just the most privileged or the smartest – not only can go to school but also acquire the knowledge and skills they need to lead healthy, productive lives and secure meaningful employment.
>
> (World Bank 2011: foreword)

We can furthermore see an ideology of Social Darwinism at work where the ones who are better educated and earn more will 'produce healthier children' and lead 'healthy, productive lives', as opposed to the rest whose lives seem to be doomed without the right (OWW) education. Moreover, the presupposition of inequality is clearly visible by indirectly implying that the more privileged children are also the smarter ones, and by generally dividing children into 'smart' and apparently not so smart children.

The World Bank's 'obsessiveness' with human capital finds its continuation in its 'Human Capital Project' (HCP). The discourse of the HCP is, not surprisingly, embedded within the OWW's liberal individual-real-science-markets ensemble, the World Bank's extremely narrow and subjective understanding of Development as economic growth and increased income and the taking-for-granted of the liberal approach towards equality (i.e. the presupposition of inequality):

> scientific and technological advances are transforming lives: they are even helping poorer countries close the gap with rich countries in life expectancy. But, poorer countries still face tremendous challenges … There is a moral case to be made, of course, for investing in the health and education of all people. But there is an economic one as well: to be ready to compete and thrive in a rapidly changing environment. 'Human capital' – the potential of individuals – is going to be the most important long-term investment any country can make for its people's future prosperity and quality of life … The frontier for skills is moving faster than ever before. Countries need to gear up now to prepare their workforces for the tremendous challenges and opportunities that are being driven by technological change … The World Bank Group is committing to help countries prioritize human capital in a sustained way, given the deepening recognition that jobs and skilled workers are key to national progress in countries at all income levels.
>
> (World Bank 2018a)

As we can see, the World Bank understands people's 'future prosperity' and 'quality of life' as the capacity 'to be ready to compete and thrive in a rapidly changing environment' – i.e. to become a full and active part of global market society. This demonstrates again how the human capital approach has a very particular idea of what makes a meaningful life, rooted firmly within the OWW: the more human capital one accumulates, the more one can convert it into financial capital to buy more and more products and contribute to economic growth – this is the Bank's ultimate and only vision of a 'productive life'.

In other words, OWW Education aims to transform independent, capable human beings into incapable, market-dependent consumers. This is no wonder, given the World Bank's 'insistence that society be understood as a market rather than a polity' (Klees et al. 2019: 608–609). At the same time, this proves once more how allegedly neutral, objective expert knowledge is utilised to advance a specific worldview. As Klees et al. argue in their analysis of the World Bank's 2018 World Development Report (WDR) titled '*Learning to Realize Education's Promise*',

> the World Bank prides itself on being evidence- and research-based, but it is not. Its premises and conclusions are based on ideology, not evidence … The ideology behind the 2018 WDR and of the World Bank is neoliberalism, a term World Bank economists barely acknowledge … This neoliberal school of economics hides its ideological recommendations behind a veneer of science. World Bank staff are intelligent and well intentioned – but hopelessly biased. They are hired and retained because their perspectives fit with the narrow neoliberal views that dominate the Bank.
>
> (ibid.: 615–16)

The pursuit of World Bank-recommended education policies in India and else-where then needs to be seen as another form of the ontological politics of inequal-ity which reinforces the hierarchical, market-based OWW order. As a result of this narrow understanding of education, people today are – on one side – more and more deprived of their skills to create and produce anything on their own, while on the other side they are more and more pressured and exploited in the workplace, assigned to complete meaningless, repetitive and often useless tasks.[5]

Consequently,

> the social costs of consumerism as the core educational promise includes not merely a crisis of meaning, the alienation of the individual from the self, from nature, and from others; but it also empties out the political and ethical pos-sibilities of education as the only vision of social improvement becomes the individual promise of consumer commodity acquisition.
>
> (Saltman 2011: 17)

At the centre of mainstream education, then, stands the *belief* that there is only one – the modern, individualist, consumerist, capitalist – way of life that is worth-while and meaningful. Accordingly, in today's common-sense logic of OWW Education, farmers, peasants, manual labourers, so-called 'school dropouts', indigenous people, forest dwellers and anyone and everyone else pursuing other ways of life, most often the ones which are 'closer connected to nature', are seen as 'uneducated' and in need of OWW Education to finally be able to live their lives in meaningful ways as 'good consumer-citizens'.

This is particularly the case in the schooling mode of education which aims to mould students into consumer-citizens from an early age on. Relatedly, recent Indian high school graduate Akshat Tyagi observes how

> those who do more manual jobs are thought to be unfit for children to be friends with, and their interaction with them is kept at lowest possible levels. I have seen schools where they make sure you do not talk or even face the janitors, housekeepers or drivers. They might take you on a class trip to the school gardener for learning about seeds, they will not let you come to the same gardener every day for learning something other than what the cur-riculum prescribes. Such a practice will be termed as a wastage of your time. This is probably what many have described as the 'caste system of modern knowledge', in which these physical laborers are treated as untouchables and the presumed intellectuals are placed at the apex.
>
> (Tyagi 2016: 21)

Ironically, while students are supposed to learn how to become a 'productive part' of global market society, they are strongly discouraged and prevented from find-ing out about what is going on in their own backyard, leading to an ever bigger disconnect with nature and a careless attitude concerning the exploitation of local, natural resources. This becomes also evident in the following account by Helena

Norberg-Hodge, talking about the meaning of 'education' before and after the introduction of OWW Education in Ladakh:

> for generation after generation, Ladakhis grew up learning how to provide themselves with basic needs – food, clothing and shelter … Developing the skills to make shoes out of yak skin and clothes from the wool of sheep or how to build houses out of mud and stone required location-specific knowledge. Education nurtured an intimate relationship with the living world. It gave children a wealth of ecological knowledge that allowed them, as they grew older, to use resources in an effective and sustainable way … This all began to change when Western-style education came to Ladakh in the 1970s. In the modern schools, none of the cultural or ecologically adapted knowledge was provided. Children were instead trained to become specialists in a technological monoculture, rather than in diverse ecologically adapted societies. School was a place to forget traditional skills and, worse, to look down on them.
>
> (Norberg-Hodge 2016: 52)

By (being forced to) focusing on highly specialised tasks instead of understanding entire processes and the causes and effects of and between these, school-going children today merely see final products devoid of any inner value and meaning. As Manish Jain accordingly argues,

> students around the world are actively being de-skilled (particularly those from artisan, healing and farming backgrounds) and are being taught to despise and devalue physical labor – since labor is considered as non-intellectual work … For the first 23 years of their lives, students are not encouraged to be meaningfully involved in productive activities related to their basic needs or their community's needs which would encourage them to understand deep inter-connections or a sense of right relationship/limits vis a vis their natural resources.
>
> (Jain n.d.)

What becomes clear then is that the 'skills' taught across the various OWW Education strands promoted and implemented by OWW Development actors are not intended to serve as the means required for people to create, build, enhance and expand their livelihood options, and thus to build meaningful lives with each other based on the presupposition of equality. Instead, these skills are seen as – and dictated by – current and always changing market demands that 'help' an individual to integrate him- or herself in the highly specialised, exploitative and uneven division of labour of the global economy.

A current example for this is also the new emphasis on *multidisciplinary* higher education in the Indian government's National Education Policy 2020. Multidisciplinarity – not to be confused with interdisciplinarity – aims to provide students with basic knowledge across multiple disciplines while eschewing any kind of depth and critical understanding of different disciplines. The purpose – in line with the overall NEP framework which continuously stresses the need for greater flexibility and talks about the 'quickly changing employment landscape and global ecosystem' (Government of India 2020: 3) – then is, first and fore-most, to create a multi-skilled labour force that can easily adapt to various market demands.

Another example can be found in what is packaged by various OWW Development actors in the euphemism of 'lifelong learning' as part of one's 'self-fulfilment' and 'self-development'. As such, the promotion of lifelong learning (rather than learning for or about life) merely reflects the ever-increasing need for the retraining and redeployment of skills according to global market demands.

Both schooling and lifelong learning as part of OWW Education thus contrib-ute to a further de-skilling of people by making them even more dependent on the market and the acquiring of a range of narrow technical skills which might become obsolete again in no time. Be it through skill and vocational training pro-grammes or schools,

> youth [and adults alike] are not taught independent survival skills, which they might desire (knowledge of local environments, food sources, produc-tion skills). Rather they are left only with the option to work for wages as mediated means to meet some survival needs (and many others geared only toward the survival of the market, such as many consumer goods).
>
> (Shantz 2017)

While OWW Development portrays schooling as 'the great equaliser' in India and elsewhere, this constitutes indeed nothing more than another variant of OWW Development's *Myth of Equality*. Given that especially the most marginalised groups in India have gained unprecedented access to the modern education system over the last decades, we should expect a positive co-relation between increased access to education, decreasing inequality and rising income levels and employ-ment rates. Instead, the opposite holds true with the disparities between the rich and the vast majority of India's population ever, and ever faster, growing.[6]

While India features one of the highest numbers of billionaires in the world, there is a deeply entrenched, persistently high level of informal, insecure work 'creating a highly exploitable labour force … The majority of Indian workers – 92 per cent – are engaged in precarious work … trapped in low wages or vulner-able self-employment and miserable work conditions' (Shah and Lerche 2018: 11). Moreover, 75% of India's large rural population continues to live on less than 33 rupees (equal to 0.44 USD) per day.[7]

Nothing much has changed, then, ever since Bowles and Gintis ([1976] 2012: 8) came to the conclusion that 'education over the years has never been a potent force for economic equality'. As we will further see, OWW Education's many failures and shortcomings – in parallel to what we have explored with the overall OWW Development model – have not led to calls for the abolishment of OWW Education, but to calls for its intensification and acceleration.

Taken together, we can see how OWW Education's ultimate task is to transform social, independent and creative human beings – who have many different and diverging ideas of what makes meaningful lives – into individualist, passive, market-dependent consumer-citizens who seek fulfilment in life through the amassment of status symbols and products.

It is an education which privileges one way of living above any others and indeed looks down upon, marginalises and destroys other ways of life. Being completely empty of any content and ways in which we can co-create meaningful lives with each other based on notions of diversity and harmonious co-living, such an education then can also very easily incorporate a nationalist agenda which further alienates people from each other and adds even more divisions and hierarchies to a worldview already pervaded by the presupposition of inequality.

The GERM-infection of education

In order to further entrench, expand and accelerate the contemporary, neoliberal OWW Education model, an unholy alliance of various OWW Development actors, from the World Bank to so-called philanthrocapitalists, has emerged. This is what Pasi Sahlberg refers to as 'GERM', or the Global Education Reform Movement.

According to Sahlberg, at least five globally common features of education policies and reform principles have been employed since the 1980s to allegedly improve the quality of education and fix the perceived problems in the public education system. These five features include (1) the global standardisation of education (particularly as regards learning outcomes, curriculum and testing);[8] (2) a focus on core subjects (literacy, numeracy, science); (3) low-risk, non-experimental and standardised ways to reach predefined learning goals; (4) the use of corporate management models in both the way schools are operating and how and what they are teaching; and (5) using test-based accountability policies for schools (Sahlberg 2012).[9]

This conforms to a type of education and pedagogy which prevails today across the globe (i.e. OWW Education), based on 'direct instruction, authoritarian classroom discipline, promotion between classes based on grades and testing, clearly defined subjects that are taught separately, and recitation and drill' (Spring 2006: 105–106). Sahlberg (2012) adds that 'tellingly, GERM is often promoted through the interests of international development agencies and private enterprises through their interventions in national education reforms and policy formulation'.

From within an OWW Development perspective, this of course makes sense – in the OWW of neoliberal globalisation, where transnational corporations (TNCs) roam around freely across the globe to momentarily settle in that part of the world which offers the cheapest labour and the least amount of provisions to protect human dignity and nature's sanctity, it is vital for those companies to be able to have recourse to a standardised pool of labour across the globe.

The labourers 'produced' in this way are expected to follow and adhere to the same education in terms of the exploitable 'market skills' they acquire and the 'knowledge' they abide by (not questioning or even challenging any of the exploitative strategies and tactics of the TNCs), as well as the discipline and (docile, submissive) attitude they show.[10] Therefore,

> we are told that standardized testing must be imposed to make sure students meet a set of standardized criteria so they will later be able to fit into a world that is itself increasingly standardized. Never are we asked, of course, whether it's a good thing to standardize children (sorry, I mean students), knowledge, or the larger world. But none of this ... is really the point at all, and to believe so is to fall into the fallacy that school is about learning information, not behaviors.
>
> (Jensen 2004: 5)

The GERM-infection of education, however, not only establishes OWW Education as a standardised consumer product, but – by relatedly making students into standardised customers or clients – it also creates a whole new market and market ecosystem *in*, *for* and *of* OWW Education.

Consequently, OWW Development advances (a) a business agenda *of* the education system (education as creating consumers for the OWW Development model); (b) a business agenda *in* the education system (supporting private education systems to the detriment of public schooling and increasingly advocating for for-profit schools and universities); and (c) a business agenda *for* education-related private companies and service providers (e.g. building of infrastructure; public–private partnerships; providing services including giving loans to schools, data analysis and various IT software to measure performance and control students and teachers; selling new and 'more effective' pedagogies and learning/teaching methods; private tutoring of students, etc.).

In this process, many states including India 'are becoming market makers, commissioners, contractors and regulators rather than being responsible for service delivery' (Ball 2017: 6). However, to shift the state's role from 'service provider' *of* education to 'market maker' *in* education, it was necessary first to delegitimise the public education system. In India, the opportunity to do so arose with the vast budget cuts enforced by the World Bank's infamous structural adjustment programme that was rolled out from July 1991 onwards and ushered in the country's New Economic Policy reforms.[11]

This meant that the Indian state became more dependent on external aid for the education sector, with the World Bank becoming 'the single most important source of aid for education in India, exercising a high degree of serious influence even on other international actors and their policies in the area in India' (Tilak 2008: 36).

Seen together with the adoption of the 1990 Jomtien Declaration at the United Nations and World Bank-sponsored 'World Conference on Education for All: Meeting Basic Learning Needs' which advocated for a massive increase in external funding for education, Anil Sadgopal argues that

> the undeclared but operative strategy in such schemes and projects was to *let the vast government education system (from schools to universities) starve of*

funds and, consequently, deteriorate in quality. As the school quality would decline, resulting in low learning levels, the parents, even the poor among them, would begin to withdraw their children from the [public] system.

(Sadgopal 2009: 12; emphasis original)

As Professor Ravi Kumar, Associate Dean of Faculty of Social Sciences, South Asian University, affirms, this was a conscious strategy to open up the education sector to private actors. Talking about the World Bank's role in the influential District Primary Education Project (DPEP) in the 1990s, he says:

their logic was very simple … They wanted the government expenditure on the education system to go down so that the state keeps withdrawing from it and would rather open up the education system to private capital. That is what happened … The various research projects commissioned by the government, the World Bank and others were conducted to delegitimise the public education system … The concern is not that the poor should study or learn. Their concern is to help private capital get as much profit as possible.

(personal interview, September 2017)

In India, this 'successful' delegitimisation campaign led to a mass exodus from public schools, which have now often become the exclusive spaces for children from the least privileged backgrounds.

In turn, this paved the way for the Indian government to open up the education sector for private capital. The Indian government's 11th Five-Year Plan (2007–2012) for the first time explicitly promoted ePPPs as an important means to reach the 'Education for All' goals adopted at Jomtien and reinforced in the 'Dakar Framework for Action' in 2000. As such, the plan states that

in the liberalized global economy where there is a pursuit for achieving excellence, the legitimate role of private providers of quality education not only needs to be recognized, but also encouraged. Public–Private Partnership (PPP) need not necessarily mean only seeking private investments to supplement governmental efforts, but also encouraging innovation in education that the government schools may lack.

(Government of India 2011: 9)

The NITI Aayog, as the Planning Commission's successor, continues to heavily promote ePPPs. Its Three Years Action Plan published in 2017 suggests privatising a large number of state-run schools, calling

for radical reforms such as handing over the student-challenged schools to private entities under the PPP (public-private partnership) mode and hiving off the education department into a separate autonomous directorate under professional management … Making a strong case for private players, the NITI Aayog said, 'A working group at the Centre should be set up with

participation of the states for bolder experiments, which may include education vouchers and local government led purchasing of education services'.

(Anand 2017)

PPPs have become key tools of OWW Development, being the prototypes of
how it extends capital accumulation and market relations into developing countries while at the same time providing some risk-mitigating (if not to say risk-
free) tools for private actors through the involvement of the state and/or bi- and
multilateral agencies acting as guarantors, providing infrastructure or other key
resources, or contributing to or completely paying the overall costs of a project.

Where PPPs were previously and prevailingly attached to mega-scale infrastructure projects, we can now see a proliferation of ePPPs across both the global
North and South as a tool to introduce the de-facto privatisation of one of the last
market frontiers in a more palatable way to the public.

In an almost schizophrenic move, the World Bank in turn legitimises a growing reliance on ePPPs and the inclusion of private actors through the very budget
cuts in public education that it was advocating for across the last decades, without
mentioning its role in the disastrous structural adjustment programmes and other
policies negatively affecting the public education sector.

Instead, lack of financing for public education is portrayed as consequence of
a natural scarcity of government funds and not a conscious policy decision. As an
'Education Specialist' at the World Bank's India office puts it,

> regardless of their good intentions, governments realise – and India is no
> exception – that there is not enough money for the government to do every-
> thing. Education is connected to other competing demands that the govern-
> ments have to deal with, and for which again there are limited resources. So, in
> other words … governments have unlimited needs and very limited resources.
>
> (personal interview, November 2017)

This is but one example of how OWW Development actors ignore structural
causes and factors while extolling technical, manageable, market-based solutions.
This also finds its continuation in the World Bank's 'Strengthening Teaching-
Learning And Results for States' (STARS) programme for India which has been
approved by the Bank in June 2020 with a USD 500 million loan.

The Project Information Document on STARS seamlessly builds on the Bank's
human capital discourse explored above and promotes increased privatisation and
PPPs in the education sector. Moreover, the programme pushes for more standardised testing and new assessment mechanisms and tools accessible to all educational stakeholders as part of creating a 'performance culture'.[12]

Ultimately, the widespread introduction of ePPPs plays an important role in
the attempts of OWW Development actors to create an increased dependency on
the market in the education sector as well as far beyond:

> educational stakeholders are enlisted by public-private partnerships (PPPs)
> through the refrain of public school failure. Moreover, not only are they

recruited into these market-mediated resolutions, they are simultaneously directed away from making demands of the state for money or support … It involves both a structural reorientation towards the quasi or full privatisation of education, and the simultaneous cultivation of and enlistment of individuals as choice-making subjects.

(Mitchell 2018: 119)

To make educational stakeholders, particularly parents, into consumers and *advocates of* and *believers in* 'market-based choice', they need to have – at least in theory – adequate information to compare and make an 'informed decision'. Therefore, OWW Development actors such as the World Bank alongside most private and ePPP-based schools are obsessed with ideas of competition and the creation of as much measurable, quantifiable data as possible to show how they are providing a 'competitive advantage' for children over other schools. Here, the business language of accountability, effectiveness, quantifiable outcomes and measurable results finds another entry point into the realm of education.

Along with the focus on quantifiable data, other important aspects of schooling outside quantifiable metrics such as exam scores are being mostly if not completely ignored. As Katharyne Mitchell (2018: 120) states,

the assumption of philanthropists and politicians is that if the appropriate expertise is provided for measuring and assessing teachers and schools, the parents will be nudged not just to make the right school choices for their children, but also to become believers in choice and in neoliberal reforms more generally.

The irony with this mantra of choice is of course that the increased commercialisation of education is a consequence of the structural destruction of the public education system which actually has decreased and taken away – whatever limited – choice. As such, the shiny world of free markets and consumption which seems to offer freedom, free choice and equality to the passive consumer conforms to the 'liberal version' of equality based on the presupposition of inequality. In the words of Todd May, being a consumer

is much like being a voter. There are large, powerful, well-funded interests that decide what choices will be offered to people, who then cast ballots or dollars for one or another of those choices. In both cases, the whole thing is presented as though it were up to the voters or consumers. But … by the time the choices arrive before us they have been vetted by their respective elites.

(May 2010: 117)

Another example for this is the introduction of school voucher systems to promote 'parental choice'. Such schemes are also currently pushed in the World Bank's STARS project for India. The rationale for voucher systems, not surprisingly,

is a neoliberal one. It is assumed that by giving parents the freedom to choose where their child is enrolled – and by diversifying the menu of options available – schools will increase their performance in the face of competition from other institutions.

(Mitchell 2018: 131)

While this overlooks other important factors such as mobility and class, it again actually decreases choice by making schools compete against each other according to quantifiable, standardised outcomes which in turn shapes what and how everything is taught. Looking at the impact of high-stakes testing in the United States, Mitchell (2018: 109) notes how 'teachers desperately spent increasing amounts of time preparing students for taking tests and devoted less time to discussion, critical analysis, creative classroom pursuits, and more social assessments of student learning and success'.

Moreover, it is mostly public schools which are losing in this competition – and among them overwhelmingly those in so-called 'deprived areas' – which are then often closed down or taken over by private actors. A recent example for this is how in 2017 the Rajasthan government – following the recommendations of the NITI Aayog's Three Years Action Agenda – shared its plans to hand over 300 schools with 'poor test results' to private actors under the ePPP model.[13] The state of Odisha recently announced plans to close down 11,500 schools with less than 40 students as part of the NITI Aayog's 'Sustainable Action for Transforming Human Capital' (SATH) programme supported by the World Bank.[14]

This trend is set to accelerate and increase, as a look at the National Education Policy 2020 reveals. Instead of providing adequate funding and support to resource-strained schools with low enrolment rates, it suggests closing them down altogether. In turn, the NEP endorses the establishment of school clusters or school complexes which are expected to result in 'greater resource efficiency and more effective functioning, coordination, leadership, governance, and management of schools in the cluster' (Government of India 2020: 29).

The increasing pressure on schools to 'perform' thus leads to an ever-increasing competition between schools. This further means that schools have to find ever new ways to attract students (and their parents) by highlighting their competitive edge and showing how they produce surplus value by helping students to secure their place in the market economy. Some school chains such as 'Absolute Return for Kids' (Ark) India, which we will analyse in more detail below, then capitalise on how they dedicate even '*more time for learning*' as their unique selling point. After all,

> as business knowledge and market competition become core elements of education, institutional and individual 'success' become defined by what produces surplus value. Value, in this case, concerns the improvement of individual life chances and the creation of advantage over others.

(Mitchell 2018: 134)

In Ark's case, this includes to 'run a longer school day'; to 'open at weekends and during school holidays, offering masterclasses and revision sessions' – 'in every school, no time is wasted – every hour of every day is devoted to children learn-ing' (Ark 2017).

Here we can see how OWW Education equates 'learning' with being in a class-room and 'education' with the formal school system. In turn, this model does not provide any space for children to learn and explore on their own. Schooling thus 'reduces the spaces and opportunities for "valid" human learning by demanding that they all be funneled through a centrally-controlled institution. It creates artificial divisions between learning and home, work, play, spirituality' (Jain and Jain n.d.).

This also highlights how OWW Education negatively impacts the development of social relations within the family and the broader community. By keeping chil-dren in their most formative years locked in separate and enclosed concrete build-ings and rooms for a good part of the day, five to six days a week, grouped together only with children of their same age, and most often of a similar socio-economic background, against which they need to compete for grades and other rewards,

> school disconnects, as it was charged to do … Children are divided from their families, their traditions, their communities, their religions, their natu-ral allies – other children – their interests and on ad infinitum. They are … disconnected from the experiences of risk-taking and adventure in which the grand discoveries of history have been fashioned; young men and women emerge from school unable to do much of anything.
>
> (Gatto 2012: 149)

Not even included in this is the time children spend for exam preparations, private tuition classes, extra work and assignments, detention, homework and – increasingly for the middle classes – on extracurricular activities. This goes hand in hand with the pervasive OWW ideology of competition and the need to ensure one's own compet-itive advantage in a dog-eats-dog world. As such, parents will (and ostensibly have to) make sure that from a very young age on, their children will spend their time in 'conducive, enabling learning environments' pursuing 'productive tasks' that are said to help them in the future in order to secure a superior position in the OWW.

This trend is also reflected in the NEP 2020 which introduces the concept of 'Early Childhood Care and Education' (ECCE) for 0–8-year-olds as the 'founda-tion of learning'. As such, pre-schooling is now brought into the ambit of con-trolled, formal education, 'ensuring that all children entering Grade 1 are school ready' (Government of India 2020: 7). In other words, children will be increas-ingly drilled from the birth bed onwards to become 'good students' and therefore good, virtuous consumer-citizens.

On aggregate, this means that more and more children will have ever less time to create their own spaces, spend time playing freely and unstructured, or to just go out and connect with nature – resulting in what Louv (2005) calls 'nature deficit disorder' – as all this is seen as 'unproductive' and therefore unnecessary:

> infants and children are no longer expected to just play; they must also learn and be productive in terms of their own lifelong learning and portfolio

development ... The persistent valuation of a child's free time as productive or unproductive is a relatively new phenomenon, one clearly associated with the increasingly competitive drive to create high-performance adults and workers. In order to 'succeed' in the market spaces of the global economy, children are now primed in countless ways ... to the extent that many children experience no unscheduled time whatsoever and declining amounts of family time overall.

(Mitchell 2018: 34–36)

This also holds increasingly true for students from less privileged backgrounds who in India spend hours after school in private tuition centres, often for seven days a week. This has made the private coaching business into an estimated seven billion USD industry (Nanda 2019).

Taken together, parents are indeed forced to become consumers of and in the education market: on the one hand, parents seem to have no choice but to prepare their offspring for the rat race out there, while on the other, if kids and their parents become 'smart consumers' and choose the right, pre-packaged educational experiences and approaches, they will allegedly have a head start in the race.

The final section now looks at the emergence of philanthropic organisations such as 'Absolute Return for Kids' (Ark) as some of the most influential institutions involved in advancing the OWW Education model. As Mitchell (2018: 135) emphasises,

philanthropy foundations are the most important of these new institutions, forming partnerships with governments as well as for-profit and non-for-profit organisations. The rise of PPPs between all of these players is the key story for the new millennium, affecting many areas of development, but with particularly strong ramifications in health and education.

Between competition and 'choice': A case study of Absolute Return for Kids India[15]

Over the last number of years, philanthropic organisations have become some of the biggest promoters of and actors in ePPPs. According to Mitchell (2018: 101), they are

the new rich of the twenty-first century who now wish to disperse their vast fortunes. They are the wealthiest of the wealthy, men and women (though mostly men) who made money primarily from postindustrial activities: computers, patents, telecommunications, insurance, finance, and real estate. How and where they made their wealth is relevant because the foundations they establish themselves are oriented towards the same kind of business logic that was effective to their founders. This includes considerations of intellectual copyright, targeted and short-term financial investment and leveraging, pilot trials, quick exits, and rapid returns on investment.

Antonio Olmedo further refers to these actors as 'philanthrocapitalists', inspired by what poster boy philanthropist Bill Gates has termed 'creative capitalism', or 'doing well by doing good'. As such, creative capitalism aims

> to extend neoliberal sensitivities into places and spaces where they had not had access before. Indeed, the argument is now being made that the disciplines of competition and profit are what is needed to reform and re-energize the provision of public sector services.
>
> (Olmedo 2016: 45)

One important player among the numerous philanthropic organisations active in the Indian education sector is Ark, a British 'education charity' founded by two hedge fund managers, with operations in the UK, US, Uganda and India.

In India, Ark is also a founding member of 'The Education Alliance' (TEA). TEA is an ePPP advocacy platform/lobby group funded by Ark, Dell Foundation and Omidyar Network, three of the most influential ePPP actors in India and worldwide.[16] The way in which organisations such as Ark and TEA talk about the goals and objectives of education then clearly shows how business logics and language are creeping into the education sector. As a project manager at TEA puts it: 'we are approaching this [education] from a cost-per-child perspective. The cost-per-child is a number, and we want to add a very minimal delta to that and still show the outside world of significant growth in terms of learning outcomes' (personal interview, October 2017).[17]

The overall concept of bringing in private actors into the public education system is being portrayed under the typical neoliberal narrative of the bureaucratic, inflexible state and the creative, innovative private sector that can team up together to create a win-win situation. As the TEA project manager describes it,

> The Education Alliance started in 2014 with the intention [of] how do we set-up great government schools through partnerships. We felt that the government has something going really well for them which is infrastructure, policy, scale, reach. And the private sector in itself has a bit of innovation in terms of curriculum, in terms of pedagogy, and the sort of nimbleness you can associate because it's a smaller unit to turn around rather than a government, which the government schools could also benefit from … The government schools are primarily serving the lower socio-economic classes … Most often this is the last option a parent would choose for their child. That is the mindset we also want to change because we want to say good quality education can be provided even in a government setting … What we are trying to establish through Government-Partnership Schools – we refrain from using PPP because it has very controversial connotations in other industries unfortunately, so we call our schools as Government-Partnership Schools – these become a new set of schools in the system. So you have a private school, a public school, and now you have a Government-Partnership School which we want to establish.

Another notable development is that lobby groups such as TEA have started to take over the 'watchdog role' from the state in terms of defining and assessing the educational quality of schools and setting standards. As in the case of TEA, the organisation monitors and evaluates – according to their own set criteria – the very schools that are operated by its own founders and funders, such as Ark, and on whose behalf it lobbies the government. According to the TEA project manager,

> the role of TEA is as a programme monitoring and evaluation person. So we ensure that the right partners are chosen for the programme, so we do it with due diligence, we analyse their programme, we visit their schools, we speak to their children. Once that is done we connect these potential partners for potential options for funding, external funding so that they can support themselves here, and then we also liaise with the government in two ways: as a common voice for the partners in order to raise issues at the systemic level for the project, and also on behalf of the SDMC [South Delhi Municipal Corporation] to do a lot of monitoring, saying that you had set enrolment targets, set attendance targets, are you able to meet that. We also conduct external, standardised annual assessments to check if their [students] learning in English, Hindi and Maths is adequate … So we make a solid case that an intervention is actually making a positive impact and here are the numbers to prove it. Rather than measuring inputs, we are measuring the actual effect of those inputs as well in order to make our decision more data-driven … We ensure government review meetings where those reports are discussed on a quarterly basis. We are right in between the government and the partners, equally assisting them both while also looking for potential partners who can be a part of the programme and also looking for potential schools who can be a part of the programme, with also the aspect of monitoring, research and evaluation where we are studying the assessment results and also sort of monitoring what inputs lead to what kind of outcomes.

What we can further identify in this interview excerpt is the strong focus on measuring data-driven, quantifiable outcomes based on standardised testing with a focus on basic literacy and numeracy, in line with the World Bank's human capital ideology and the Indian government's NEP 2020.[18] OWW Education is reified as evidence-based practice in which the outcomes are already given at the outset, while the only question is how to reach these outcomes most effectively from a 'cost-per-child' perspective.

This is also strongly reflected in the three Delhi-based schools which are fully operated and run by Ark India (now 'Peepul') under the ePPP model. These were former public schools singled out as 'failing schools' and offer pre-school and primary school till grade five. The schools are specifically targeted towards children from low-income communities and have an exclusive focus on Hindi, English and Maths, demonstrating the further reduction of education, even within the OWW model, to what is now proudly referred to as 'minimum learning outcomes' – a term we would presumably not hear being used too much in middle- and upper-class schools.

As Paul Marshall, one of Ark's founders, patronisingly explains, 'at ARK, we demonstrate that if you set high expectations, robust discipline and focus relentlessly on literacy and numeracy, poor children can achieve as well as prosperous ones' (quoted in Ball and Junemann 2012: 108). This implies that there need to be schools only for the poor and that poor children need more 'discipline' than 'prosperous' children, that they are not able to learn on their own nor possess any knowledge, skills and education yet.

In sum, it posits poor children as less intelligent than others. The alleged inferior intelligence of poor children then justifies schools for the poor where they learn only the basic skills they need in order to serve as cheap labour for the OWW – this all under the smoke screen of philanthropy, charity and giving back to society.[19]

In the process, it is not only the poor children who are seen as less intelligent, but also their 'uneducated' parents who are apparently unable to raise their children without the help of enlightened educationists. Talking about the close cooperation between school and parents, the then Ark India Head of Schools explains how

> in the course over the last two years, you can see how their ability to support their children has improved, because we have given them concrete skills and techniques they can use at home. Just because they didn't go to school themselves doesn't mean they can't be great parents. They can be good parents, if they are taught parenting in a systematised manner, if they are given simple techniques to do at home and simple resources to use at home, they would be getting better.
>
> (personal interview, October 2017)[20]

Not attending school is equated with being less intelligent and uneducated, which in turn is equated with the notion that the uneducated lead 'unproductive lives' and therefore cannot even raise their own children adequately to become productive consumer-citizens.

'Schools for the poor' and allegedly less intelligent then not only come with a special curriculum for the poor, but also with a special pedagogy for the poor. As Ark Founder Marshall stated above, what the poor allegedly need the most is 'discipline'.

In India, this 'discipline' is being instilled by what Ark proudly calls its Behaviour Management System. On its website, Ark celebrates as 'transformation in behaviour' that, thanks to the introduction of the Behaviour Management System in its Delhi model school, children 'line up, wait for their turn, follow class rules and engage in collaborative study and play' (Ark 2015). One cannot but wonder if such a statement would have been published about an Ark school in the United Kingdom.

As Junemann and Ball (2013: 431) further state, the Ark Academies in the United Kingdom, after which the Ark India schools are modelled, have a strong

> emphasis on discipline and behaviour management … One of ARK's co-founders and trustees, Paul Marshall, said in an interview that the only way for headteachers to reverse underperforming schools is if they 'first of all sort behaviour'.
>
> (Evening Standard, 7 March 2011)

This betrays a latent racism and class bias that sees poor children in need of military- and corporate-style 'strong leadership'.

Another important element of Ark India is how business- and entrepreneurship-like norms and behaviours following the market-mantra of 'choice' are embedded in the school pedagogy by applying forms of productive power to achieve desired outcomes. This becomes evident in the following account by Ark India's head of school:

> what we train our teachers to do is to use something called positive reinforcement. So as an organisation we believe in behaviour for learning, not behaviour for disciplining. That is a big difference. I'm not going to ask you to do this, just because I'm ten times bigger than you, and I'm the adult and you shouldn't follow me just because I'm the adult. You should want to do that. You should see the merit in doing that. And you should understand that your choices have consequences. So that's the premise we believe in … Everything is choice-based in our school. The behaviour tracker [a tool used in every class] is really simple. It has four phases going from a star to a smiley face to a neutral face to a sad face. All kids when they come in the morning, they are stars … All their names are stuck at the top. Now at the beginning of the day the teacher reminds them that all are stars. And then it's up to you – if you make smart choices, you stay a star. If you make not so smart choices, you will be coming down.

Based on my observation of one first grade class for about an hour, the tracking tool was used very frequently by the teacher. Already after a few minutes, some children would be 'graded down', with two or three children reaching the lowest phase (the 'sad face') within the first hour of the class, which means a reduction of their 'playtime', which is generously allowed by the school to take place from 12:25 to 12:55 pm every day.[21]

The teacher would furthermore continuously stress how it is each child's own choice where they would 'end up' on the tracking tool. This demonstrates how OWW Education is a fundamentally liberal approach that assumes natural self-interest and sees this as a positive aspect that should be nurtured. It also clearly assumes unequal endowments of intelligence and expects that there are penalties for bad choices on the part of the student-consumers.[22]

The strong emphasis on 'choice' in Ark's pedagogy then further reflects OWW Development's move

> from the individual as citizen (in the liberal conception of the term) to the individual as omni-consumer/customer, who is expected to act in all settings and circumstances according to the principles of rational choice theory and/ or is cajoled by behavioural economic incentives.
>
> (Olmedo 2014: 578)

According to Mitchell (2018: 26), choice is a key component of neoliberalism because it rests on ideas of both individual freedom and individual responsibility, i.e. the freedom to choose one thing over another, and to be held accountable for that choice. This is seen as promoting entrepreneurial character traits by promoting (narrow) cost-benefit calculations and strategic investments based on informed decision-making.

Other forms of productive power employed in Ark schools essentially boil down to the introduction of individual competition across all spheres of the school life. In the words of Ark India's head of schools, Ark provides

> a tremendous amount of opportunities in the class to appreciate kids. There are teams, each team gets points, each student has a pouch in the class, they collect coupons, we have themes for all our classrooms. So for example this class is the 'Amazing Ants' … As ants love sugar, they get coupons that look like sugar cubes for every time they are doing well and at the end of the day we count who has the most and they are the student of the day. At the end of the week we count who has the most and they become student of the week. We put their picture outside the classroom. We also have a 'best class' trophy. So in the corridors, there is a tracker, which is a simple bar graph. Your class can earn stickers for walking down to playtime quietly, coming back very smartly without disturbing anyone else. So if principal sir or mam sees you, they will give your class a sticker. At the end of the month, whosoever's bar graph is the tallest, they get the 'best class' trophy in front of the whole school and that trophy sits in your class for one month … We have school values. We use an acronym called 'REACH'. Respect, Exploration, Achievement, Courage and Honesty. At the end of each month, we pick three students from each class that have shown these values and we appreciate them in front of the whole school by giving them certificates.

All this is intended to make students feel as if they are in a race against each other where there are only a few winners and many losers. It therefore incentivises children to become individualistic, hyper-competitive human beings in a hyper-competitive, unequal world. It is again not hard to imagine how a nationalist agenda can further exploit and thrive in such an environment.

Ark India also introduces questionable learning approaches in its schools, for example by using the Jolly Phonics programme by British for-profit company Jolly Learning for its English language classes. This might be seen as an effective, technical tool to achieve minimum learning outcomes, but certainly is far away from any notion of critical literacy. As Cohen (2017) writes on the promotion of synthetic phonics programmes in the Australian government's 'back to basics education approach',

> synthetic phonics … is made up of a rigidly presented, one-size-fits-all, instruction in letter-sound relationships. There are countless commercially marketed synthetic phonics programs, such as Jolly Phonics, for which the [Australian] government's agenda promises a profit bonanza. They typically present one letter-sound per day or per week instruction for the whole

class … and use commercially-produced phonics texts ('the fat cat sat on the mat') instead of engaging books written by genuine authors to entertain and enlighten the children. In attempting to reduce the learning of reading to a mindless set of mechanical skills, the government is promoting synthetic phonics as another means of narrowing the school curriculum and suppressing creative and critical thought among young people in the public school system.

In sum, we can see how newly emerging actors in the education sector such as Ark India – now operating as 'Peepul' – construct the breeding ground for the OWW Development ontology to thrive. This is achieved by attempting to mould students into individualist consumer-citizens equipped with basic numeracy and literacy skills to eke out a living in the competitive OWW, while at the same time creating a whole new market ecosystem of, in and for education.

Key OWW Development actors such as the World Bank play a crucial role in advancing this agenda through their interventions in the public education system. The STARS programme in India explicitly promotes 'fashioning schools on the charter school model where the government buys the services of a service provider and the latter gets paid for the quality service delivery at the school level through a per child cost reimbursement basis' (World Bank 2018b: 9).

Most recently, the National Education Policy 2020 further pushed for an increase in ePPPs and an acceleration of the privatisation of education through what it euphemistically calls models of 'public-spirited private/philanthropic schools' (Government of India 2020: 30).

Organisations such as Ark, with their questionable understanding of education rooted in quantifiable, minimum learning outcomes and a likewise questionable pedagogy embedded in neoliberal values underpinned by racist and classist assumptions, stand to benefit the most from this.

However, despite all the – justified – limelight that we have put on ePPPs and the privatisation of education, what we need to keep in mind is that although state-led, public education may at times be the lesser of two evils, it still forms an essential part of the hierarchical, inherently unequal OWW Development model based on the presupposition of inequality.

Normalising hierarchy and discrimination

From the perspective of anarchistic postdevelopment, calls for increased funding of public schools or demands for equal access to 'quality education' within the given structure of the modern education system do not provide a very promising path to follow. At best, such reforms can lead to what Rancière would call *a better police order*.

This is because modern schooling, from its very beginning, has been designed according to an authoritarian, disciplinary structure rooted in the presupposition of inequality.[23] What we can observe today is merely a shift in the role of schools from creating 'good citizens of the nation-state' towards creating good 'consumer-citizens' situated within the state-market nexus. With the arrival of virtuous neoliberalism in India, this might likewise increasingly shift in the future towards the creation of hyper-nationalist, 'virtuous consumer-citizens'.

As with OWW Development, OWW Education in its contemporary, mainly neoliberal, form offers many opportunities to incorporate a nationalist and divisive, hierarchical agenda in its ontological politics of inequality. As much as OWW Education is concerned with the dissemination of a certain type of subjective and selective knowledge and experience, it is concerned with the imposition of a certain kind of behaviour and 'discipline' on its students, designed to relegate everyone to his or her appropriate, (pre-)assigned role within the hierarchical OWW. This is achieved by moulding 'us' into 'good citizens, good boys and girls … We won't question country, God, capitalism, science, economics, history, the rule of law, but in all those areas will defer – and continue to defer – to experts, just as we were taught' (Jensen 2004: 6).

This essential aspect of OWW Education is highlighted in Meenakshi Thapan's analysis of civic education in Indian secondary schools which not only naturalises the construct of the nation-state but

> rarely encourages questioning or challenging authority or taking issue with the practices of the state … The idea of the 'good' citizen instead serves to dwell on … developing certain socially desirable behavioural traits and practices. This is done through developing a respect for authority, the rule, the law, socially constituted and legitimised norms for good behaviour that are rewarded and reproduced, and through rituals and ceremonies in school, a reiteration of national ideals, a celebration of collective life and the value of an ideal community. The obedience that is sought to be inculcated reflects a concern with developing a particular kind of subjectivity that recognises the necessity of compliance and agrees to submit, rather than question.
>
> (Thapan 2014b: 160)

This 'authoritarian ethos' is a key characteristic of the modern education system as a whole. The disciplinary, oppressive regime upheld in many schools serves as a gradual adaptation and normalisation process for students to accept, internalise and even embrace the hierarchical, unequal, unjust norms that constitute the OWW in any of its forms.

As John M. Elmore (2017) argues, the authoritarian school environment attempts to mould children into 'authoritarian personalities'. On one side, they are submissive and obedient, accepting that there is no alternative to the hierarchical OWW they are literally 'born into'. On the other side, they develop authoritarian traits themselves by trying to compete against others and control and command others below them in a dog-eats-dog world. As Thapan (2014a: 343–344) accordingly observes in schools across India,

> students themselves are trained to become disciplinarians as they get through school by aiding teachers and school administrators in the task of enforcing

'the rules'. They are assigned the role of 'monitors', 'captains', 'group leaders' and the like. These roles are played out with some seriousness by senior
students while at school and often result in the bullying and 'ragging' of
younger students. It results in the creation of a student culture that is closely
modelled on the school culture of control and domination. The insidiousness
with which power is sought to be exercised by using older students against
younger ones breeds a culture of fear, distrust and sycophancy in the student
body.

It is no wonder, then, that schools often become breeding grounds of discrimination, abuse and bullying. In Indian schools, this takes especially egregious forms
with regards to Dalits. A 2017 study by the National Dalit Movement for Justice
documents a whole range of psychological and physical torture including practices of segregation, permanent humiliation, violence and sexual abuse.[24]

With a rise of Islamophobia across the country, Muslim students are also
increasingly affected by discrimination and hostilities in the classroom and beyond.
Nazia Erum – who spoke to 145 families in 12 cities as well as 100 children
studying in 25 elite schools across Delhi – says it is increasingly common that
'in playgrounds, schools, classrooms and school buses, a Muslim child is singled
out, pushed into a corner, called a Pakistani, IS, Bagdadi and terrorist' (quoted in
Pandey 2018).

Another important element which accompanies modern schooling's authoritarian ethos and the consequent emergence of the *equally subservient and authoritarian character traits* found among students is the idea that '*we*' are all merely
small, insignificant cogs within a big, inexorable machine; or, 'we' are part of a
project of inexorable progress which is 'bigger than us'.

This results in a lack of confidence in one's own abilities to create a meaningful life outside this inexorable machine, or even forecloses the imagination to
do so, or to see this as desirable. Erich Fromm (1957, quoted in Elmore 2017)
describes the authoritarian personality as characterised by 'the inability to rely on
one's self, to be independent, to put it in other words: to endure freedom'. Elmore
(2017), further drawing on the work of Fromm, concludes that

> from the lack of confidence in oneself a lack of confidence in others naturally
> follows, which serves as fertile ground for condemning anyone who is differ-
> ent from what has been deemed ideal by those in power. Such a negative view
> of others leads to the conclusion that harsh laws and a strong police or army
> are necessary. Also, it leads people to the pessimistic certainty that humans
> would devolve into narcissistic debauchery and be totally immoral if they
> were left to govern themselves free of external control.

Once again, it is not hard to see how the institutionalised authoritarianism of
schools undermines the presupposition of equality, reinforces the hierarchy of the
OWW in all of its forms and provides fertile ground for the inculcation of further
oppressive and divisive agendas.

Summation

OWW Education is the potentially most important and influential instrument of OWW Development. It practices the ontological politics of inequality by negating and marginalising ideas, practices, actions, ways of life and entire lifeworlds outside the OWW. In turn, it is promoting and disseminating a knowledge and pedagogy that takes away people's capacity to create meaningful lives outside the OWW and instead makes them more dependent on and compete against each other within the OWW.

Looking at recent trends and developments in OWW Education, I have shown how the Global Education Reform Movement, in collusion with the Indian nation-state, contributes to and accelerates the demise of public schooling in favour of increased private sector participation, which today often takes the form of ePPPs. As I have argued, these ePPPs further serve to entrench a 'business-friendly' language, mentality and ideology in society by extolling the virtues of free markets and a consumer society based on the illusion of choice. As Katharyne Mitchell observes, this spread of business language and mentality

> has become a dominant motif, not just in education, but also in many other PPP realms. More and more frequently one hears terms in everyday life that used to resonate primarily in the business world. In addition to '24/7', 'quick fix', and 'return on investment', these include language such as 'benchmarking', 'best practices', and 'evidence-based policy'. Additionally, because of the interlinkages and connections between public and private realms, PPPs are ultimately dependent on market-friendly policies in the arena of contracts, intellectual copyright, and labor management.
>
> (Mitchell 2018: 102)

Drawing on the case of Ark India, we have further analysed how philanthropic foundations are wielding an increasingly strong influence that shapes the OWW Education agenda towards a full acceptance and embracement of business logics and language. The emphasis on discipline coupled with a pedagogic approach that sees students as competing consumers in a dog-eats-dog world shows how one of OWW Education's central tasks is to instil the 'right behaviour' and create 'good consumer-citizens' that make the right, pre-vetted choices.

However, we should not be tricked into thinking that the public school system serves as *the* solution to address many of the issues that are accompanying the commercialisation of the education sector. Instead, I have argued that both private-led and state-led schooling are rooted in an authoritarian ethos that justifies and normalises hierarchy, competition and discrimination.

Therefore it is important to emphasise that 'while neoliberal reforms have undoubtedly intensified the traditional patterns of schooling ... we delude ourselves if we frame those reforms as somehow undermining the democratic foundations of those institutions, for such foundations have never existed' (Gabbard 2017).

Adding to this line of thought, the next chapter lays out how indeed each and every form of modern education – no matter if it is disseminated through public or private or ePPP-based schools – perpetuates the presupposition of inequality by analysing in more detail the structure of teacher–student relations and the role of explanation. Following this, we will establish the idea of *anarchistic postdevelopmental education* as alternative practice to OWW Education.

Notes

1 The World Bank's involvement in India ranges from basic and primary education up to higher education.
2 Across the border in Pakistan, this narrative is, not surprisingly, reversed: 'The Pakistani education system has at its core the narrative of a centuries-long Hindu-Muslim conflict … Certain Muslim Kings have been given particular significance in the Pakistani state's educational retelling of this "historical conflict", with the 11th-century Afghan king, Mahmud Ghazanvi, being one of the most important components of this "national story". The tales of Ghazanvi's frequent raids on the Somnath Temple in India are presented to Pakistani children in a way that equates temple destruction with religious and national duty. Through these tales, lessons and stories, the Hindu becomes the other against which the Pakistani national identity is constructed. Interestingly in India, Ghazanvi plays the role of the villain against which the national self is defined' (Khalid 2020).
3 The Fourth Industrial Revolution or 4IR is a neoliberal key concept coined by Klaus Schwab, founder and executive chairman of the World Economic Forum. It is an umbrella term for artificial intelligence, the Industrial Internet of Things, robotics and 3D printing (see Sutherland 2020).
4 See also Shrivastava (2020).
5 The latter are what anthropologist David Graeber calls 'bullshit jobs', 'where the person doing them secretly believes that if the job (or even sometimes the entire industry) were to disappear, it would make no difference – or perhaps, as in the case of say telemarketers, lobbyists, or many corporate law firms, the world would be a better place. And that's not all: think of all the people doing real work in support of bullshit jobs, cleaning their office buildings, doing security or pest control for them, looking after the psychological and social damage done to human beings by people all working too hard on nothing. I'm sure we could easily eliminate half the work we're doing and that would have major positive effects on everything from art and culture to climate change' (Graeber 2018).
6 See BBC (2011); Dang, H.-A.H. and Lanjouw, P. (2018); Oxfam (2020).
7 Tewari (2015). The daily income is based on an average household size of five.
8 As part of the commitment to global standardisation, the World Bank has successfully lobbied India to re-join the global Pisa examination system.
9 Test-based accountability policies refer to the 'tying of school performance – especially raising student achievement – to processes of accrediting, promoting, inspecting and, ultimately, rewarding or disciplining schools and teachers' (Ball 2017: 3).
10 It is again instructive to look at the research of Bowles and Gintis who observe how 'the structure of the educational experience is admirably suited to nurturing attitudes and behavior consonant with participation in the labor force. Particularly dramatic is the statistically verifiable congruence between the personality traits conducive to proper work performance on the job and those which are rewarded with high grades in the classroom … As long as one does not question the structure of the economy itself, the current structure of schools seems eminently rational' (Bowles and Gintis [1976] 2012: 9).

11 As Smith (2008: 18) points out, these reforms were not only an external imposition on an unwilling Indian state, but 'in fact, the ruling castes and classes in India embraced the reforms and neoliberalism. Chopra, for example, maintains that neoliberalism was embraced both by the Indian state and much of Indian capital, establishing neoliberalism "as a dominant discourse across India social space" (2003, p. 421)'.

12 World Bank (2018b).

13 Due to public pressure after the plans were announced and a later shift in government from the BJP to the Congress, the plans have not materialised thus far.

14 Hindustan Times (2020).

15 Ark India has recently been spun off as independent entity and re-branded as 'Peepul' (registered as 'Absolute Return for Kids') with an initial one year of funding from Ark UK.

16 As of 2017, TEA worked together with 12 partners across 30 PPP-based schools that are home to 6000 students in India.

17 All further quotes in this chapter by the TEA project manager are taken from this personal interview.

18 The World Bank's 2018 World Development Report on Education, for instance, defines learning as consisting almost exclusively of reading and mathematics. The renewed focus on learning outcomes in the Indian government's NEP 2020 moreover goes hand in hand with what neoliberal ideology promotes as 'the creation of more enabling environments', i.e. less regulation and control of private education actors. As the NEP accordingly states: 'to make it easier for both governments as well as non-governmental philanthropic organizations to build schools, to encourage local variations on account of culture, geography, and demographics, and to allow alternative models of education, the requirements for schools will be made less restrictive. The focus will be to have less emphasis on input and greater emphasis on output potential concerning desired learning outcomes. Regulations on inputs will be limited to certain areas ... Other models for schools will also be piloted, such as public-philanthropic partnerships' (Government of India 2020: 11).

19 Here we can see a parallel to the inherent racism of 'old school philanthropists' such as Carnegie and Rockefeller, following deliberate strategies 'to keep African-Americans tied to agricultural and factory forms of labor' (Mitchell 2018: 104).

20 All further quotes in this chapter by the then Ark India Head of Schools are taken from this personal interview.

21 The use of the tracking tool was less frequent however in the second and third grades I observed for roughly the same time.

22 As I could further observe especially in grade one, wrong answers given by students were rebuked with a firm, reproachful-sounding 'no' by the teacher, while right answers were celebrated with a 'very good' remark and a handshake or high five between student and teacher. The teacher would further loudly announce to everyone in the class that based on some good work, 'someone is getting a stamp'. I felt that this created a very competitive and indeed tense atmosphere in the classroom where students were encouraged and indeed incentivised to compete against each other for the teacher's appreciation and where too much questioning and giving wrong answers would be punished.

23 See Ward (1996); Jensen (2004); Suissa (2010); Haworth and Elmore (2017).

24 Manikanta, P., and Lal, J.A. (2017).

References

Alvares, C. (2002). 'Launching the multiversity'. In Jain, M., and Jain, S. (eds.), *Unfolding Learning Societies: Experiencing the Possibilities*. Udaipur: Shikshantar, pp. 210–225.

Amsler, S.S. (2015). *The Education of Radical Democracy*. New York: Routledge.

Amster, R., DeLeon, A., Fernandez, L.A., Nocella II, A.J., and D. Shannon. (2009). 'Section three: Pedagogy'. In Amster, R., DeLeon, A., Fernandez, L.A., Nocella II, A.J., and D. Shannon (eds.), *Contemporary Anarchist Studies: An Introductory Anthology of Anarchy in the Academy*. New York: Routledge, pp. 123–124.

Anand, M. (2017). 'Government schools to take private route: Niti Aayog'. https://www.newindianexpress.com/thesundaystandard/2017/may/07/government-schools-to-take-private-route-niti-aayog-1601869.html.

Ark. (2015). 'New school model in South Delhi could transform education'. http://arkonline.org/news/new-school-model-south-delhi-could-transform-education.

Ark. (2017). 'About us'. http://arkonline.org/about-us/what-we-do.

Ball, S. (2017). *Edu.net: Globalisation and Education Policy Mobility*. New York: Routledge.

Ball, S., and Junemann, C. (2012). *Networks, New Governance and Education*. Bristol: The Policy Press.

British Broadcasting Corporation. (2011). 'India income inequality doubles in 20 years, says OECD'. https://www.bbc.com/news/world-asia-india-16064321.

Bowles, S., and Gintis, H. [1976] (2012). *Schooling in Capitalist America: Educational Reform and the Contradictions of Economic Life*. Chicago: Haymarket Books.

Chopra, R. (2003). Neoliberalism as Doxa: Bourdieu's theory of the state and the contemporary Indian discourse on globalization and liberalization, Cultural Studies, 17 (3–4), pp. 419–444.

Cohen, D. (2017). 'Australian government imposes phonics test on six-year-olds'. https://www.wsws.org/en/articles/2017/03/15/phon-m15.html.

Dang, H.-A.H., and Lanjouw, P. (2018). 'Inequality in India on the rise'. *WIDER Policy Brief 2018/6*. Helsinki: UNU-WIDER.

DeLeon, A. (2012). 'Against the grain of the status quo: Anarchism behind enemy lines'. In Haworth, R. H. (ed.), *Anarchist Pedagogies: Collective Actions, Theories, and Critical Reflections on Education*. Oakland, CA: PM Press, pp. 312–325.

Elmore, J.M. (2017). 'Miseducation and the authoritarian mind'. In Haworth, R., and Elmore, J.M. (eds.), *Out of the Ruins: The Emergence of Radical Informal Learning Spaces*. Adobe Digital Editions Version, Chapter 1. Oakland, CA: PM Press.

Fine, B., and Rose, P. (2003). 'Education and the post-Washington consensus'. In Fine, B., Lapavitsas, C., and J. Pincus (eds.), *Development Policy in the Twenty-First Century: Beyond the Post-Washington Consensus*. London: Routledge, pp. 155–181.

Gabbard, D. (2017). 'Don't act, just think'! In Haworth, R., and Elmore, J.M. (eds.), *Out of the Ruins: The Emergence of Radical Informal Learning Spaces*. Adobe Digital Editions Version, Chapter 2. Oakland, CA: PM Press.

Gatto, J.T. (2012). *Weapons of Mass Instruction*. Indore: Banyan Tree.

Government of India. (2011). *Eleventh Five Year Plan*. New Delhi: Planning Commission.

Government of India. (2020). *National Education Policy 2020*. New Delhi: Ministry of Human Resource Development.

Graeber, D. (2018). 'Imagining a world with no bullshit jobs'. https://roarmag.org/essays/graeber-bullshit-jobs-interview/.

Hindustan Times. (2020). 'Odisha to close down 11500- odd schools for better learning outcome'. https://www.hindustantimes.com/education/odisha-to-close-down-11500-odd-schools-for-better-learning-outcome/story-zCaQifPc9IBfLcbQN5DWUL.html.

Jain, M. (n.d.). 'Seven deadly sins of schooling'. http://www.shikshantar.org/articles/seven-deadly-sins-schooling.

Jain, M., and Jain, S. (n.d.). 'Towards an organic learning community'. http://www.swaraj.org/shikshantar/shikshantar_aboutlearningcommunity.htm.

Jensen, D. (2004). *Walking on Water: Reading, Writing, and Revolution.* White River Junction, Vermont: Chelsea Green Publishing Company.

Junemann, C., and Ball, S.J. (2013). 'ARK and the revolution of state education in England'. *Education Inquiry*, 4 (3), pp. 423–441.

Illich, I. (1974). *Deschooling Society.* London: Marion Boyars.

Khalid, H. (2020). 'Putting the attacks on Islamabad's first Hindu temple in context'. https ://www.aljazeera.com/indepth/opinion/putting-attacks-islamabad-hindu-temple-cont ext-200723100958702.html.

Klees, S.J., Stromquist, N.P., Samoff, J. and S. Vally. (2019). 'The 2018 world development report on education: A critical analysis'. *Development and Change*, 50 (2), pp. 603–620.

Louv, R. (2005). *Last Child in the Woods: Why Children Need Nature, How It Was Taken from Them, and How to Get It Back.* Chapel Hill, NC: Algonquin Books of Chapel Hill.

Manikanta, P., and Lal, J.A. (2017). *Exclusion in Schools: A Study on Practice of Discrimination and Violence.* Delhi: National Dalit Movement for Justice – NCDHR.

May, T. (2010). *Contemporary Political Movements and the Thought of Jacques Rancière: Equality in Action.* Edinburgh: Edinburgh University Press.

Mitchell, K. (2018). *Making Workers.* London: Pluto Press.

Nanda, P.K. (2019). 'Searching for jobs: India's tuition trapdoor'. https://www.livemint .com/politics/policy/searching-for-jobs-india-s-tuition-trapdoor-1548787140226.html.

Norberg-Hodge, H. (2016). 'Practitioner perspective: Learning for life'. In Skinner, A., Smith, M.B., Brown, E., and T. Troll (eds.), *Education, Learning and the Transformation of Development.* New York: Routledge, pp. 50–57.

Olmedo, A. (2014). 'From England with love … ARK, heterarchies and global 'philanthropic governance''. *Journal of Education Policy*, 29 (5), pp. 575–597.

Olmedo, A. (2016). 'Philanthropic governance: Charitable companies, the commercialization of education and *that thing* called 'democracy''. In Verger, A., Lubiensky, C., and G. Steiner-Khamsi (eds.), *World Yearbook of Education 2016*: *The Global Education Industry.* London: Routledge, pp. 44–62.

Oxfam. (2020). 'India: Extreme inequality in numbers'. https://www.oxfam.org/en/india -extreme-inequality-numbers.

Pandey, G. (2018). 'The Indian schoolchildren who are bullied for being Muslim'. https:// www.bbc.com/news/world-asia-india-42650106.

Ramachandran, V. (2018). *Inside Indian Schools: The Enigma of Equity and Quality.* New Delhi: Social Science Press.

Rose, D. (1999). 'Indigenous ecologies and an ethic of connection'. In Low, N. (ed.), *Global Ethics and Environment.* London: Routledge. pp. 175–187.

Sadgopal, A. (2009). 'India's educational policy: A historical overview'. https://parisar.file s.wordpress.com/2009/08/combatlaw:anil-sadgopal_historical-betrayal_aug09_final.pdf.

Sahlberg, P. (2012). 'Global educational reform movement is here'! https://pasisahlberg .com/global-educational-reform-movement-is-here/.

Saltman, K.J. (2011). 'From Carnegie to Gates: The Bill and Melinda Gates foundation and the venture philanthropy agenda for public education'. In Kovacs, P.E. (ed.), *The Gates Foundation and the Future of U.S. "Public" Schools.* New York: Routledge, pp. 1–20.

Scroll.In. (2020). 'Coronavirus: CBSE scraps chapters on citizenship, nationalism, secularism from Class 11 curriculum'. https://scroll.in/latest/966810/coronavirus-cbse -scraps-chapters-on-citizenship-nationalism-secularism-from-class-11-curriculum.

Shah, A, and Lerche, J. (2018). 'Tribe, caste and class – New mechanisms of exploitation and oppression'. In Shah, A., Lerche, J., Axelby, R., Benbabaali, D., Donegan, B., Raj,

J., and V. Thakur. *Ground Down by Growth: Tribe, Caste, Class, and Inequality in Twenty-First Century India*. New Delhi: Oxford University Press, pp. 1–31.

Shantz, J. (2017). 'Theory meet practice: Evolving ideas and actions in anarchist free schools'. In Haworth, R., and Elmore, J.M. (eds.), *Out of the Ruins: The Emergence of Radical Informal Learning Spaces*. Adobe Digital Editions Version. Oakland, CA: PM Press.

Shrivastava, R. (2020). 'The RSS impact on new education policy'. https://www.indiatod ay.in/india/story/new-education-policy-rss-sangh-parivar-impact-sanskrit-1706340 -2020-07-31.

Smith, P. (2008). 'Going global: The transnational politics of the Dalit movement'. *Globalizations*, 5 (1), pp. 13–33.

Spoto, S. (2015). 'Teaching against hierarchies: An anarchist approach'. *Journal of Feminist Scholarship*, 7/8, pp. 78–92.

Spring, J. (2006). 'Pedagogies of globalisation'. *Pedagogies*, 1 (2), pp. 105–122.

Suissa, J. (2010). *Anarchism and Education: A philosophical perspective* (2nd ed). Oakland, CA: PM Press.

Sutherland, E. (2020). 'The fourth industrial revolution – The case of South Africa'. *Politikon*, 47 (2), pp. 233–252.

Tewari, S. (2015). '75 percent of rural India survives on Rs 33 per day'. https://www.ind iatoday.in/india/story/india-rural-household-650-millions-live-on-rs-33-per-day-28219 5-2015-07-13.

Thapan, M. (2014a). 'School experience: An autobiographical approach'. In Thapan, M. (ed.), *Ethnographies of Schooling in Contemporary India*. New Delhi: SAGE Publications, pp. 333–357.

Thapan, M. (2014b). 'Schooling, identity and citizenship education'. In Thapan, M. (ed.), *Ethnographies of Schooling in Contemporary India*. New Delhi: SAGE Publications, pp. 154–181.

Tilak, J.B.G. (2008). 'Political economy of external aid for education in India'. *Journal of Asian Public Policy*, 1 (1), pp. 32–51.

Traub, A. (2018). 'India's dangerous new curriculum'. http://southasiajournal.net/indias-dangerous-new-curriculum/.

Tyagi, A. (2016). *Naked Emperor of Education: A Product Review of the Education System*. Chennai: Notion Press.

Ward, C. (1996). *Anarchy in Action*. London: Freedom Press.

World Bank. (2011). *Learning for All: Investing in People's Knowledge and Skills to Promote Development. World Bank Group Education Strategy 2020 Executive Summary*. Washington: The World Bank.

World Bank. (2018a). 'Investing in people to build human capital'. https://www.worldbank .org/en/news/immersive-story/2018/08/03/investing-in-people-to-build-human-capital.

World Bank. (2018b). 'Strengthening teaching-learning and results for states (P166868)'. http://documents1.worldbank.org/curated/en/120151539242179436/pdf/Concept-P roject-Information-Document-Integrated-Safeguards-Data-Sheet-Strengthening-Teach ing-Learning-And-Results-for-States-P166868.pdf.

4   The axiom of (in-)equality

Towards an anarchistic postdevelopmental education (ANPED)

The school-based learning system in India goes back to the era of colonisation where the British ushered in modern education as means to enlighten a selected few about what was deemed worthwhile knowledge by the British and, at the same time, served British interests. Education, thus, became another tool to normalise, justify and even nourish British domination of India by producing the 'good colonial-citizen'.

However, while the British colonisers officially left in 1947, the basic structure and vision of the modern education system remained intact even after independence. The role of enlightened elites who know what is best for the rest merely has shifted from British elites to Indian elites who would now determine what is taught, how it is taught and to whom it is taught as part of the Indian nation-building process following a Western role model of Development.[1] This likewise relegated and still relegates much of indigenous and local, context-based and situated knowledge to the margins.[2]

From here on – as we have seen across the previous chapter – education would continue to be based on the presupposition of inequality and lay the foundations for the then-prevailing Development paradigm by disseminating only a certain kind of knowledge that would normalise, legitimise and reinforce its hierarchical order.

However, as we have also started to explore in the previous chapter, it is not only the dissemination of a certain knowledge that is quintessential to OWW Education, but also *how* this knowledge is disseminated. The latter is part of what critical theorists refer to as 'the hidden curriculum' of schooling. This hidden curriculum consists not of

> blatant indoctrination but insidious influences that emanate from the everyday climate and structures of the school; the relationship between teacher and pupil, the layout of the classroom, the way the school is managed, the system of rewards and punishments, and so on. Added to this are the unexamined and unspoken assumptions of the teachers who send messages out daily: only certain kinds of achievements count, bookish learning is more valuable than practical skills, middle-class values are more worthwhile than working-class ones, obedience to law is good, disobedience is bad, certain career choices

are more worthy than others, contributing to society is honored, criticizing is discouraged.

(Fremeaux and Jordan 2012: 111)

The first part of this chapter will look at a key element of the hidden curriculum which is part and parcel of any form of OWW Education, no matter what kind of knowledge is being disseminated: the role of '*explanation*' within the OWW Education system, leading to the 'institutionalisation of life' which aims to make everyone dependent on consuming expert knowledge and following expert advice across all areas of life. This will demonstrate how each and every form of OWW Education is based on the presupposition of inequality, and how only by leaving the '*explicative order*' of schooling we will be able to transcend the OWW ontology which it reifies.

Based on these insights, the second part of the chapter is going to conceptualise *anarchistic postdevelopmental education (ANPED)* as a practice that leaves the explicative order of schooling and practices the ontological politics of equality, embodied in the assumption that anyone and everyone can learn anything and everything. As such, ANPED *tests and verifies equality* not as an outcome to be reached, but takes it as its point of departure, thereby 'making it true' in the present. This constitutes a radical departure from OWW Education as well as all alternative models of mainstream education that can only ever perpetuate different degrees of inequality.

A case study of Creativity Adda, a self-learning or 'unschooling' initiative for children in Delhi, then concludes this chapter by outlining how this space constitutes a contemporary form of ANPED in practice.

OWW Education and the pedagogicisation of society

In his influential work *Pedagogy of the Oppressed*, Paulo Freire introduces a central characteristic of the modern education system as what he calls the 'banking model':

> knowledge is a gift bestowed by those who consider themselves knowledgeable upon those whom they consider to know nothing. Projecting an absolute ignorance onto others, a characteristic of the ideology of oppression, negates education and knowledge as process of inquiry. The teacher presents himself to his students as their necessary opposite; by considering their ignorance absolute, he justifies his own existence. The students … accept their ignorance as justifying the teacher's existence.

(Freire 2013: 72)

This draws attention to how teacher–student relations across OWW Education function as a hierarchical model in which the student becomes the passive, ignorant consumer of knowledge distributed and explained to him by the teacher as master-explicator.

To bridge the gap of inequality between the (inferior) student-consumer as not knowing anything and the (superior) master-explicator as knowing everything, the latter engages in the business of explanation.[3] As if there is always some hidden meaning or an opacity to whatever matter the allegedly less intelligent students attend to, only the teacher can reveal to the students 'how things really are' *by means of explanation*. A book, for instance, which explains to students a certain kind of knowledge, is never sufficient in and by itself – the teacher is needed to give an explanation of the explanation, and so forth:

> explanations are needed so that the one who is ignorant might understand the explanation that enables his or her understanding. The regress would be in principle infinite if the teacher's authority did not in fact stop it by acting as sole arbiter of the endpoint where explanations are no longer needed … If explanation is in principle infinite, it is because its primary function is to infinitize the very distance it proposes to reduce. The practice of explanation is something completely different from a practical means of reaching some end. It is an end in itself, the infinite verification of a fundamental axiom: the axiom of inequality.
>
> (Bingham and Biesta 2010)

Put differently, OWW Education conditions us to keep on consuming expert advice about why the world is as unequal and unjust as it is, and why we are unequal and incapable – and in this process justifies and perpetuates our very own inequality. By contrast, '*equality means precisely this: that there is no reason or explanation for inequality*' (Pelletier 2012: 112; emphasis added). This is why Jacques Rancière refers to the act of teaching as 'stultification':

> to explain something to someone is first of all to show him he cannot understand it by himself. Before being the act of the pedagogue, explication is the myth of pedagogy, the parable of a world divided into knowing minds and ignorant ones, ripe minds and immature ones, the capable and the incapable, the intelligent and the stupid. The explicator's special trick consists of this double inaugural gesture. On the one hand, he decrees the absolute beginning: it is only now that the act of learning will begin. On the other, having thrown a veil of ignorance over everything that is to be learned, he appoints himself to the task of lifting it … The pedagogical myth … divides intelligence into two. It says that there is an inferior intelligence and a superior one.
>
> (Rancière 1991: 6–7)

Consequently, OWW Education – in parallel to OWW Development – takes the form of a productive power which manifests itself 'as the belief that one is unable to learn, think and act for oneself' (Biesta 2017: 64). In other words, OWW Education practises an ontological politics of inequality which takes away peoples' capacities to create meaningful lives alongside each other: 'the more completely they [student-consumers] accept the passive role imposed on them, the more they tend simply to adapt to the world as it is and to the fragmented view of reality deposited in them' (Freire 2013: 73).

Therefore, through its very design and structure, OWW Education makes us dependent on expert knowledge and lets us buy in the myth that only certain people can know about certain topics and issues, and that there is always some hidden meaning we cannot understand on our own without expert explanations. As Ivan Illich puts it,

> schools are designed on the assumption that there is a secret to everything in life ... that secrets can be known only in orderly successions; and that only teachers can properly reveal these secrets. An individual with a schooled mind conceives of the world as a pyramid of classified packages accessible only to those who carry the proper tags.
>
> (Illich 1974: 76)

The upshot is what Illich calls 'the institutionalisation of life' and what Rancière refers to as '*the pedagogicisation of society*' which teaches us to become reliant and dependent on experts and authorities not only in school, but across all areas of life, as the presupposition of inequality – the idea that we are not capable of creating meaningful lives on our own – is so deeply ingrained in us.

The modern education system, with its enormous influence and power to shape children and the adults they become over some of their most formative years, then extends the presupposition of inequality across all spheres of life: 'once we have learned to need school, all our activities tend to take the shape of client relationships to other specialized institutions' (Illich 1974: 39). OWW Education, in other words, is

> *teaching the need to be taught.* Once this lesson is learned, people lose their incentive to grow in independence; they no longer find relatedness attractive, and close themselves off to the surprises which life offers when it is not predetermined by institutional definition. (ibid.: 47; emphasis added)

OWW Education, therefore, plays a pivotal role in ensuring the hegemony of the OWW. It first aims to mould independent human beings into passive, obedient and anxious consumer-citizens who consume a very subjective kind of knowledge serving the part that has a part. Therefore, the emergence of critical questions, of potential unrest and of direct attempts by people to change the status quo is already made less likely.

Additionally, OWW Education – through the pedagogicisation of society – conditions us to seek (complicated) explanations and consume pre-vetted expert advice that keeps answers and solutions firmly within the orbit of the OWW, instead of enabling us to finding our own – and often indeed simple – answers, and thereby often preventing us from challenging and changing anything more fundamentally on our own. As a result, 'this dependency creates a form of alienation which destroys people's ability to act. Activity no longer belongs to the individual but to the expert and the institution' (Spring 1998, quoted in Shantz 2012: 136).

If there is always an 'objective' and 'true' explanation for the existing ine-qualities given to us by experts and enlightened leaders, then inequality becomes normalised, becomes a *natural part* of our society and of our lives that has to be accepted, because it can be rationally explained. There is not just – simply – ine-quality which needs to be eradicated as a screaming, intolerable injustice, but there is *inequality explained* as naturally occurring phenomenon in the process of being eliminated, while at the same time it is ever perpetuated with (sometimes new or revised, and sometimes the ever-same) explanations for its recurring existence.

In sum, 'equality (in the future) is precisely that which legitimises the presup-position of inequality (in the present). The notion of social progress ... is that which is used to make inequality appear utterly apparent and obvious' (Pelletier 2009: 145).

Ironically, the expert explanations for existing inequalities then frequently refer back to the modern education system itself:

> inequality is no longer the arbitrary distribution of wealth and power, but a supposedly 'rationalised' order, which puts people in their 'proper' place; in other words, it is an explanation for inequality. A progressive social order calls for the justified distribution of ranks. *In a democratic society in which all men are equal, it is therefore the role of public education to justify ine-quality whilst promising to perpetually reduce it.* The idea of social progress in effect is the idea of pedagogy applied to the whole of society; it is the idea of those who give themselves the authority of reducing the inequality of oth-ers with respect to themselves.
>
> (Pelletier 2009: 144; emphasis original)

This means that OWW Education serves as the perfect scapegoat for the continu-ous failures of OWW Development to bring about equality.[4] Any responsibility for existing inequalities is blamed on the modern education system itself – either on some shortcomings within the system which can be addressed through some reforms here and there, or on the individual, failing student who did not use her chances and choices adequately, or on the individual, incompetent teacher as an exceptional figure.

At a maximum, all that needs to be improved is the efficiency of the distribu-tion of modern knowledge within the given OWW Education system. This can be achieved through the introduction of new or improved pedagogies, sending teachers for 'leadership training' and giving them (monetary) incentives (or, in turn, threatening to fire them if their students don't 'perform'); focusing on narrow 'learning outcomes', instilling 'market discipline' or introducing new technologies.

Through this process, most existing inequalities can conveniently be explained through the shortcomings in and of the OWW Education system itself – hence any proposed solutions do not exceed the ontological limits of the OWW:

> social problems redefined as learning deficits are simultaneously excluded from more responsible political agendas. For instance, defining unemployment

in terms of personal employability, and therefore as a lack of 'proper' education adequate to current trends in the job market, masks the fact that it is a structural phenomenon the alleviation of which requires changes in the operation of [the] global economy.

(Szkudlarek 2013: 2)

Paradoxically, then, the OWW Education system must be perpetually in crisis and fail almost by default. This exactly is its *raison d'être* – the very design and purpose of OWW Education serve to make sure that failure is inevitable and in-built in the system in order to justify the larger inequalities across society. At the same time, this very inequality can be, ostensibly, *explained* and improved within and through the modern education system. Accordingly,

> inequality is made innocent: it is simply an ordering of capacity. The state or economic power which follows from academic achievements is consequently framed as properly assigned, a justified difference, a justified inequality. Claims about the redistributive power of education serve therefore to justify hierarchy – to *explain* inequality. The presumption of inequality which underpins the setting of equality as the goal of the education system is the very means by which the actualization of equality is infinitely deferred.
>
> (Pelletier 2009: 147–148; emphasis original)

The 'problem' with OWW Education then concerns not only *what* is being taught and *how* something is being taught – the issue is, specifically, *that something is being taught and explained*, which always leads us back to the presupposition of inequality.

Put differently, equality cannot be taught, explained or given. It is not a matter of merely changing the subjects taught in class, replacing traditional pedagogies with more 'student-centred' ones, trying to raise a 'critical consciousness' among the part that has no part or 'moulding' children according to some more desirable traits and characteristics, as many Marxist and critical pedagogues would have it. Instead, the discourse and practice of OWW Education are always and at all times deeply rooted in the presupposition of inequality and thus cannot be 'reformed', 'improved' or 'changed' beyond a certain, very limited extent.[5]

Towards an anarchistic postdevelopmental education

This position clearly differentiates our anarchistic postdevelopmental philosophy of education from socialist and Marxist positions which advocate a strong role for the state in education. It also demarcates the anarchist stance from neoliberal and market-libertarian notions of education which advocate against any direct role of the state in education and as such seem to espouse, on the surface, a similar critique against the state as advanced by anarchist philosophy. However, while neoliberals

> may on the face of it seem to be stating a position akin to that of the social anarchists, this is far from the truth. They may indeed be undermining the institutional power of the state, yet they are not doing so out of a commitment

to a positive vision of an alternative social arrangement based on justice, equality and mutual aid, but rather out of the rather vague – and potentially dangerous – notion that people should be allowed to run their own affairs as far as possible.

(Suissa 2010: 133)

A closer examination of anarchist and market-libertarian positions of course reveals more differences, for instance in the neoliberal efforts to replace the state's role of service-provider with the role of market-maker. This is far away from any anarchist and postdevelopmental positions and indeed constitutes not the withering away of the state but merely a change in its strategy of capturing state power. An anarchist-inflected education instead expresses 'the desire to remove authority from the public or private definition of education and recover a third option to pursue more autonomous learning experiences, overcoming public and private rhetoric' (Todd 2012: 83).

Moving from anarchistic postdevelopment in general to anarchistic postdevelopmental education (ANPED) in particular, it is then also important to briefly lay out the differences between the latter and the influential 'critical pedagogy' school of thought which is most known for its outspoken criticism of the neoliberalisation of education.[6]

Over the last decades, critical pedagogy has become the most popular and influential approach towards radical alternative education. Strongly inspired by (neo-)Marxist thought, it aims to transform education into a tool for emancipation and liberation, as against the oppressive, conservative tool it contemporarily constitutes. As such, it highlights how

the contemporary education system conditions the child for a career of exploitation, inequality and differentials, conformity and passivity; it lowers expectations and confines and fragments a holistic outlook into myriad specialist skills that block the attainment of the bigger life picture.

(Hill, Greaves, and Maisuria 2017: 230)

For critical pedagogy, the Marxist concept of 'false consciousness' plays a key role. It posits that the oppressed and marginalised are usually ignorant about their own predicament. Left to their own devices, they are not able to make sense of the intricate workings of power. Consequently, a key task of critical pedagogy lies in revealing the concealed power mechanisms that oppress the oppressed. Only through this process of demystification will the oppressed then finally be able to liberate themselves.

Therefore, this presupposes that the oppressed need someone, an enlightened teacher, who is situated outside the oppressive power structures and can reveal the latter to the oppressed. Once more, this leads us back to the presupposition of inequality, which

installs dependency at the very heart of the act of emancipation … The modern 'logic' of emancipation starts from a distrust in the experiences of the one to be emancipated, suggesting that we cannot really trust what we see or feel but need someone else to tell us what is really going on. Whereas in classical Marxism the Marxist philosopher was supposed to be able to occupy this position, in our times we often find psychology and sociology in this position, asserting that they can reveal to us what is really going on in our heads – or more often nowadays: our brains – and in our social lives.

(Biesta 2017: 55–56)

Furthermore, while critical pedagogy clearly rejects OWW Education's approach of moulding students into their pre-given roles within the OWW, its proponents do not completely distance themselves from the idea of moulding as such. Rather,

they either reject the dominant *methods* of moulding or the desirable *model* into which students are to be moulded. In short, most critical approaches assume the framework of modern schooling – mass-scale compulsory institutions in which children are segregated, so as to be exposed to content or activities selected by others, and higher education institutions building on schooling in similarly segregated spaces – but seek to modify either the content of these institutions (e.g., more social critique, media awareness, ecology, ethics, challenging privilege) or the methods used once students are in place (e.g., holistic, dialogical, participatory, or student-centered methods).

(Firth and Robinson 2017; emphasis original)

This shows that ultimately, critical pedagogists are upholding a certain type of hierarchy within the education system. Consequently, they likewise – and alongside virtually all philosophers of education – uphold a certain kind of hierarchy across society.[7] As such, they

tend to phrase their critique in terms of making existing society 'more democratic', 'more participatory', 'more caring' and so on. The basic structural relations between the kind of society we live in and the kind of education we have are, more often than not, taken for granted.

(Suissa 2010: 3)[8]

This is an important distinction between critical pedagogy and anarchistic postdevelopmental education (ANPED) which aims to question, challenge and ultimately transcend the OWW ontology and its various material and immaterial manifestations. This includes, particularly but not exclusively, the construct of the modern nation-state, whose role and existence are left unchallenged in both Marxist and liberal philosophies of education.[9]

Likewise, as we have seen now, both liberal as well as Marxist philosophies of education still believe in the necessity of 'enlightened vanguards' in their various forms and guises to lead and then keep the (less intelligent) masses out of their own predicament. This demonstrates at the same time how these philosophies of education are based on the axiom of inequality. In contrast to this, ANPED posits equality as its starting point.

Anarchistic postdevelopmental education and the axiom of equality

In assuming that everyone is already and always equally intelligent, ANPED becomes a performative practice which merely *verifies* equality. For Jacques Rancière, the act of verification is performed through the figure of 'the ignorant schoolmaster'[10] who presupposes and hence verifies equality:

> inequality is no more a given to be transformed by knowledge than equality is an end to be transmitted through knowledge. Equality and inequality are not two states. They are two 'opinions', that is to say two distinct axioms, by which educational training can operate, two axioms that have nothing in common. All that one can do is verify the axiom one is given. The schoolmaster's explanatory logic presents inequality axiomatically ... The ignorant schoolmaster's logic poses equality as an axiom to be verified. It relates the state of inequality in the teacher-student relation not to the promise of an equality-to-come that will never come, but to the reality of a basic equality.
>
> (Rancière 2010)

Here, the central task of the ignorant schoolmaster is not to 'enlighten' the student and teach her what she doesn't know so she can become a good consumer-citizen. Instead, it is to assume her equal intelligence and see where it leads to. This, in turn, provides radical new possibilities by refusing to accept the hierarchical distribution of pre-assigned roles within the OWW. In other words, education and learning become a world-making practice that is able to challenge the OWW's various distributions of the sensible.

The hierarchical relationship between teacher and student in the OWW Education paradigm as one of more and less intelligence, what Rancière calls 'stultification', hence is reconfigured as a relationship between *equal intelligences* of the ignorant schoolmaster and the learner.[11] The verification of equality then is a process of making the student-turned-learner aware (if and when needed) of her equal intelligence, and (if and when needed) of *encouraging her* to use her equal intelligence accordingly. In other words, it is a matter of *the will*:

> There is stultification whenever one intelligence is subordinated to one another. A person – and a child in particular – may need a master when his own will is not strong enough to set him on track and keep him there. But that subjection is purely one of will over will. It becomes stultification when it links an intelligence to another intelligence. In the act of teaching and learning there are two wills and two intelligences. We will call their coincidence *stultification* ... We will call the known and maintained difference of the two

relations – the act of an intelligence obeying only itself while the will obeys
another will – *emancipation*.

(Rancière 1991: 13; emphasis original)

In this lies the ultimate importance of Rancière's philosophy for the ontological politics of equality. By summoning and strengthening the will of learners so
they 'use' their equal intelligence, we leave the explicative order and abandon
the pedagogicisation of society that structures the hierarchical OWW through the
axiom of inequality. As a result,

> Rancière's classroom mirrors the power structures that would be desirable
> in a future society, and … radical pedagogy should reflect its political goals
> … When the 'ignorant' schoolmaster takes part in a mutually transformative
> dissensual dialogue, he not only challenges the power structure of the class-
> room, but makes way for a new organisation of power in society in general.

(Wanggren and Sellberg 2012: 547–548)

At the root of this process of emancipation lies a strikingly simple principle: all
we need to do is summon, utilise and apply the will of both the ignorant schoolmaster and the learner. The ignorant schoolmaster's will is needed to transcend
the common-sense assumptions of unequal intelligences between him and the
learner, as well as to convince the learner of her equal intelligence. The learner,
in turn, must have – or develop in the process – the will to act on her equal intelligence accordingly and make use of it.

As such,

> the problem is not to create scholars. It is to raise up those that believe them-
> selves inferior in intelligence, to make them leave the swamp where they are
> stagnating – not the swamp of ignorance, but the swamp of self-contempt,
> of contempt *in and of itself* for the reasonable creature. It is to make emanci-
> pated and emancipating men.

(Rancière 1991: 101–102; emphasis original)

This highlights again how, seen through the lens of the ontological politics of
equality, it is not the case that some (most) people are less equal than others, but
that they are being made to *feel* less equal and then often accept and embrace
this situation of inequality rather than struggling against it.[12] This refers to what
Saul Newman – drawing on Étienne de La Boétie – calls *voluntary servitude*, i.e.
a certain affinity towards 'a kind of authoritarianism and desire for one's own
repression that permeates the social body, infiltrating everyday habits, behaviours
and practices' (Newman 2016: 93), and which is nurtured by OWW Education
and other hierarchical social practices.

The ignorant schoolmaster's first and foremost task then is to encourage and
nurture the *will* of her learners: to get them out of lethargy, out of the *belief* that

they are inferior, out of 'the swamp of self-contempt' that leads them to think about themselves as less equal and hence prevents any kind of direct action and active participation in the construction of their own lives.[13]

Consequently, the ignorant schoolmaster wants her students merely to 'recall their own power or, rather, to recognize that they had the power [of equal intelligence] all along, they just didn't know it' (Newman 2016: 104). In verifying the equality of his students, the ignorant schoolmaster 'offers us no revolutionary programmes to follow – none are needed. He simply wants us to emancipate ourselves, to emancipate ourselves from our own servitude' (ibid.).[14]

The question, then, becomes how the ignorant schoolmaster verifies equality by imposing her will upon students in concrete situations – is it simply by 'telling' students about their equal intelligence and demanding them to use their equal intelligence accordingly? In a way it is, and in a way it isn't.

As we have seen, we cannot empower or emancipate others simply by telling them they are equal or demanding they act as equals. Rather, the ones who are considered less equal than others need to practically experience their equality. This can be achieved by *co-creating with learners the spaces and platforms in which they can apply their equal intelligence to concrete learning projects that matter to them*. This, indeed, lies at the heart of anarchistic postdevelopmental education.

The key task of the ignorant schoolmaster then lies in (a) co-creating and holding these spaces together with the learners and (b) in encouraging and supporting the learners to become interested in something and put their full attention and efforts to it. This is all there is to emancipation.

The thus 'emancipated students' then can equally turn into 'ignorant schoolmasters' and verify the equality of others. Indeed, we can say that in this very process of emancipation, there lies an inherent and powerful ethos for a *politics of solidarity* that helps us to struggle with and alongside others. In this context, Rancière (1991: 39) states that

> what an emancipated person can do is to be an emancipator: to give, not the key to knowledge but the consciousness what an intelligence can do when it considers itself equal to any other and considers any other equal to itself.

The role of the ignorant schoolmaster thus clearly resembles the one of the narrative therapist. The ignorant schoolmaster imposes her will upon her learners to draw their attention to 'something that matters' in order to verify their equality against a system of OWW Education that is based on the axiom of inequality. The narrative therapist, as we have explored in the second chapter, likewise imposes his will upon 'Development beneficiaries' to co-create new, more empowering stories the part that has no part might tell about themselves in order to verify their equality against a OWW system full of narrative disvalues.

Hence, both the ignorant schoolmaster and the narrative therapist help students (till then passive consumer-citizens of the school and the nation-state at large) and 'Development beneficiaries' (till then passive consumer-citizens of the OWW

Development industry and the nation-state at large) to become subjects rather than objects of and in their own lives. In other words, they both help formerly passive consumer-citizens (re-)discover their capacities to construct meaningful lives alongside others.

This is of course what we have explored earlier through the concept of subjectification, a process which is accompanied by the repartitioning of the sensible. From an educational perspective, 'the subjectification function might perhaps be best understood as the opposite of the socialisation function. It is precisely *not* about the insertion of "newcomers" into existing orders, but about ways of being that hint at independence from such orders' (Biesta 2016: 21; emphasis original).

As we have also discussed, the narrative therapist has no control over what the former 'Development beneficiaries' he or she is working with make out of the new, different stories they co-create together. In the same vein, the ignorant schoolmaster

> doesn't have to worry about what the emancipated person learns. He will learn what he wants, nothing maybe. He will know he can learn because the same intelligence is at work in all the productions of the human mind, and a man can always understand another man's words.
>
> (Rancière 1991: 18)

This points out that the most important aspect of ANPED does not concern *what* is learned or even *how* it is learned – instead, it is about '*learning how to learn*' – i.e. realising that everyone is capable to learn whatever (s)he wants to learn and thus leaving the explicative order and escaping the pedagogicisation of society. Ultimately, 'anyone can learn anything by starting from any point, and therefore the educational content we choose to study is totally irrelevant: whatever we choose to practice is just a means to demonstrate to ourselves that we are capable beings' (Vlieghe 2018: 923).

In this sense, ANPED is 'non-moulding in that there is no transcendent vision towards which participants are transformed' (Firth and Robinson 2017). However, while there exists no transcendent vision, what we can legitimately hope and strive for is that by an education which is based on the axiom of equality, new subjects emerge who follow the anarchist key principles embedded in the presupposition of equality. The emergence of these new subjects, and their refusal to take on their pre-assigned roles in the OWW, ultimately can and already do lead to more egalitarian, post-dualist practices, actions, ways of life and life-worlds beyond Development.

This follows from the nature of ANPED as a prefigurative politics based on the presupposition of equality. Rather than 'teaching' and 'imposing' values and practices such as mutual aid, collaboration, solidarity, emancipation, freedom and equality (which would then most likely turn into its opposite), these are practised, lived and embodied through the educational model that anarchistic postdevelopment espouses.

Therefore, instead of parading around a transcendent vision to be fulfilled at some point in the future, ANPED

> should ideally function as *the focus of intrinsic value*, that is, as the living center and clearest model of what is ultimately desirable in human relations. In other words, education is not a mere training ground for some future community nor is its foremost aim that of producing a supply of well-trained and dedicated anarchist revolutionaries. On the contrary, education must itself manifest, indeed consist of, libertarian relations and activities. Education does not simply lay the groundwork for subsequent achievements; at its best it constitutes the most complete and most feasible paradigm of those achievements.
>
> (Krimerman and Perry 1966: 404; emphasis original)

Having established the framework of an education that practices the ontological politics of equality, the final section of the chapter will provide a case study of the Creativity Adda *unschooling* initiative in Delhi as an example for ANPED in practice.

Unschooling in a school: Creativity Adda Delhi

Being true to its term and connotation, the idea of 'unschooling' is difficult if not impossible to precisely define, given its uniqueness and often subjective understanding and application among different people and groups.[15] As Carlo Ricci, unschooler and founder of the *Journal of Unschooling and Alternative Learning*, puts it, at a general level, we can conceptualise unschooling as 'a learner-centered democratic approach to education, putting the learner's passions and interests first' (Ricci, Laricchia and Desmarais 2011: 141).

A key element of unschooling is its rejection of fixed, predefined ways of what it means to 'educate' and 'learn'. This is tied to a direct challenge against the pillars of the modern education system: 'unschoolers claim that schooling ignores the ways children learn best and often hinders meaningful learning experiences. Unschoolers reject the structured learning of schooling, formal curricula, and testing' (Jones, Robinson and Vaughan 2015: 392).

Alongside the critique of how something is taught, unschooling also fundamentally challenges what is being taught in schools. As Ivan Illich argues in his book *Deschooling Society*, relevant knowledge often comes 'from friendship or love, while viewing TV, or while reading, from examples of peers or the challenge of a street encounter', as well as, for example, from 'the apprenticeship ritual for admission to a street gang or the initiation to a hospital, newspaper city room, plumber's shop, or insurance office' (Illich 1974: 72).

This shows how the whole idea of what knowledge constitutes and how to 'obtain' it radically exceeds the ontological limits of OWW Education. As such, unschooling (or what Illich refers to as deschooling) 'is the creation of a new style of educational relationship between man and his environment' (ibid.).

Given that there are many, indeed infinite, learning sources and possibilities, there are also infinite ways of how unschoolers can learn. Therefore, the concept of self-designed learning (SDL), which is also often referred to as self-determined learning or self-learning, plays a pivotal role in unschooling. Essentially, this means that learners themselves decide how they learn anything that matters to them. They combine various existing or even create new learning approaches according to what suits them best, while no one approach is seen as superior to others.

While the next chapter will provide a more detailed account of the concept and key practices of unschooling through the eyes of families who are unschooling with their children, the remainder of this chapter will introduce the Creativity Adda in Delhi as one among many potential ways of how unschooling is currently practised in India.

Creativity Adda (CA) – run by Udaipur-based unschooling organisation Shikshantar – is an unschooling project within, paradoxically, a government school.[16] Catering to a socio-economically marginalised, dominantly Muslim community in North Delhi, the CA runs for four hours every afternoon, six days a week, for the students of the Mukherjee Nagar Government Boys Senior Secondary School.

Free of cost for the children, 80 to 100 learners come to the space on a daily basis after school, situated in an old, otherwise no longer utilised building on the school campus. As Manish Jain states,

> it's not an add-on to the school, but rather seeks to challenge the entire culture of competition, labelling, stress, text-centricness and examinations. It is a system driven by and towards monoculture. It actually tries to undermine all of those things and let kids have time and space to just be themselves … Kids need real time and space to be free and experiment and explore. So at least 3, 4 hours a day to freely explore, engage, use their hands, connect, collaborate. Even time to unplug and just do nothing. Do that kind of thing, without any kind of constant intervention from any kind of professional teacher or anything.
>
> (quoted in Hopkins 2018)

The CA is a space free from any school pressure, any expectations to 'perform well' and any need to permanently prove one's (OWW-)knowledge and engage in competition with other students. It is free from any teachers and masters who tell the children what to do, and how to do it. Instead, the CA's philosophy is based on the principles of SDL and peer-to-peer learning in which there are no teachers and no students, but only learners who co-create, explore and work together.

Ashish Tiwari, co-founder and coordinator of the Creativity Adda, stresses that the CA serves first and foremost as a platform for the children to explore and co-create new possibilities.

> At Creativity Adda, we are trying to restore power back to the learner that was stripped away by institutionalisation. The learner has a choice what he wants to learn, how and for how long. Nobody is going to force them … We

allow students to design their own learning. When we started the place we were also learning. Because creating a space which we call self-designed learning means that the child has his own power to co-create it. But at some point you have to start. You have to begin with something. So we decided to start with music, dance, theatre ... Then we talked to the kids more and more. We started making personal connections, relations ... At Adda, what we are trying to do is to create a personal bonding so they feel that this is their space. We don't want them to treat us as another teacher ... Overall, we create a platform where children can find their passion. They can decide what they want to learn, and what they want to do with their lives.

(personal interview, September 2017)[17]

As Tiwari further says, many of the students coming to the CA face difficulties in mainstream schooling. As such, their lives are being considered as less equal by OWW Education's ontological politics of inequality:

often, they are neglected by the teachers in their regular schools, designated as 'failures'. The teachers feel that they don't know anything, they are use-less, they won't achieve anything in their lives, and they are basically left alone without any support till they fail in school or drop out. At Adda, they get their freedom with community – there is no restriction, no compulsion, no exam, no homework, and they do things they really like. In schools they do things they are forced to do.

Starting in June 2017 at its current location, the CA now has five 'hubs' which are the Slow Food Junior Chef's Academy; the Community Media Lab; the Design Studio & Makerspace; the Art, Music & Dance Studio; and the Sports & Fitness Academy.

One overarching theme of the CA is to help the alternative learners reconnect with nature. This takes place, for example, through frequent nature excursions in and outside Delhi that are often connected to the different hubs (e.g. wildlife pho-tography and film-making on environmental awareness in the Community Media lab). The Junior Chef's Academy is based on cooking organic food and gives the children an experience and practice of the entire food chain process from farm to plate. Other examples include the Design & Makerspace which emphasises hands-on work using recycled and upcycled materials, as well as the set-up of an urban garden and farm to which all learners contribute.

The children can choose to join any of the hubs and they can change between them at any time. Many focus on one or two hubs and engage in week-long or longer projects. This gives the children the time to explore their interests and pas-sion in more detail and to learn according to their own pace. There is also consid-erable cross-pollination between the hubs and common projects between two or more hubs that combine each other's strengths and help each group to learn from the other. As one of the children shares, 'at the end of the day we all come together and discuss together what we have learned' (focus group discussion, July 2018).[18]

Beyond the hubs, there are numerous workshops and activities offered on a regular basis that are catered to the interests of the children and often organised as per their own ideas and suggestions.[19] If some of the learners are particularly interested in a workshop topic, the CA team together with the learners will organise follow-up workshops, help the learners to keep in touch with the workshop facilitators or identify similar resource persons in the Delhi area, and explore other ways to deepen the newly acquired skills, for example by using freely available online resources.

Additionally, many outside guests from diverse backgrounds are invited to share their life stories and journeys with the children. This gives the learners much more exposure to the outside world and provides them with an opportunity to interact with many inspiring people who often craft their own meaningful lives outside the OWW boundaries. This also includes regular visits by 'full-time unschoolers' – i.e. children and young adults who never went to school or stopped going to school at an early age – who share their skills and unschooling journeys with the learners.

Another level of exposure is created through the organisation of regular learning journeys across India. This includes the participation in various unschooling and alternative education events – such as the annual Learning Societies UnConference (LSUC) or the International Democratic Education Conference (IDEC) – as well as regular visits to some of the other project sites and initiatives in the vast Shikshantar network or outside of it.

Each of the five hubs is supported by a facilitator who co-hosts the space and shares his experiences and journey with the children. The facilitators do not decide what the children should learn or follow a pre-given curriculum or plan. Instead, the learners themselves mostly discuss among each other and with the facilitators about their interests and then engage in various hands-on projects that follow their interests. Neither the children nor the facilitators need to be 'experts' in these learning projects but explore and pursue these together as a *community of learners*.

Therefore, all five hub facilitators – all in their early 20s and some of them 'school walkouts' themselves – are not seen as 'teachers'. Children rather perceive and describe them as good friends. One boy accordingly remarks how 'whatever we learn at Adda is done with lots of love and affection. There is a lot of harmony, a sense of brotherhood here'.

In Rancièrean terms, the CA facilitators are ignorant schoolmasters that support the students' will, as we can see from Ashish Tiwari's account:

> at Adda, we feel everybody is a student and everybody is a teacher. But in the Indian context, a 10-year old child, if you ask him what he knows, before the kid can even reply, his parents, his teachers, elders, they will answer: 'he's still a child, he doesn't know anything'. At Adda, we are throwing this notion out. We are trying to encourage the qualities everybody already has. How can we utilise these qualities and make a better society or better space? … We are saying, you have a special intelligence, skills, you have something, but no

one sees it. At Creativity Adda, we are trying to create a space where they can explore themselves and their interests. This is not a vocational training center but a space where each learner can explore their whole, multi-dimensional selves in the world.

Accordingly, one learner shares how 'over here I get to learn and move ahead, and people support me here. In school, people are always scolding me or beating me'. Relatedly, most children I spoke to emphasised that they learn much more – and much more useful things – at the CA than at school. As another boy eloquently puts it, 'the teachers will only teach us, but the facilitators here will actually make us learn'.

Some children also mentioned that because of this, they want the CA to be open for more than four hours only. One learner noted how although school days are much longer, they learn so much more in the four hours at the CA. Another learner sums it up by saying 'we are having lots of fun and at the same time we are learning many new things'.

In all this, we can see the presupposition of equality at work. As such, the CA introduces a strong dissensus into the dominant OWW order and its count of what constitutes 'education' as well as in its classification of students within the OWW hierarchy. The CA thus is conceptualised as

> a parallel disruptive virus within the general school paradigm. There is a strong attempt to challenge the dominant school monoculture of competition, compulsion, fragmented knowledge, I.Q. labeling, textbooks, reward-punishment, and certification. *At the Creativity Adda, every child is seen as 'intelligent'.*
>
> (Jain and Singh n.d.; emphasis added)

The learners and facilitators of the CA then practise the ontological politics of equality by (re-)asserting their capabilities to create meaningful lives in interaction with others. As Ashish Tiwari says,

> in 9th grade, there is a board exam, before that schools have no right to fail children, so everyone will pass, and then in 9th grade many people fail and they have to leave school. So what will they do? A child who is around 14, 15, and school is saying you have to go, how will they sustain themselves? That situation is a big problem. We thought of creating something to ignite passion and interest in a child at a young age … So we are preparing them. If you're not good in your studies, you are a zero, you are a nothing, for Indian society. You don't know anything. So how can we make these children independent?

It is important to emphasise here that the CA has nothing in common with the kind of vocational skill programmes offered by OWW Development actors. Skill programmes, as we have seen, contribute to a further de-skilling of people by making them even more dependent on the market and thus further reinforce inequality. Whereas skill programmes are ways to reinforce the hierarchical OWW order of exploiters and exploited, the CA engages in rethinking, challenging and ultimately replacing the very core assumptions and ideas of OWW Development and OWW Education.[20]

The CA, consequently, nurtures the ability of its learners to co-create meaningful lives alongside each other. This is done without pre-determining exactly what such lives should look like in detail, but letting the learners explore and decide on their own (and thus not repeating the mistakes of OWW Development and Education). The envisioned lifeworlds potentially resulting out of this initiative thus clearly exceed the ontological limits of the OWW. Overall,

> the objective of this 'unschool' is to give a daily space for kids to nurture intrinsic motivation, creativity, self-awareness, self-discipline, teamwork, confidence, and to explore a range of practical skills and new career options. To help them connect with their real selves, rather than losing their originality, core talents, dreams, and connections to their community and nature ... The emphasis is actually on helping them see the full cycle of how they can take their learning to another level by bringing out a product or providing some service in the community.
>
> (Jain and Singh n.d.)

In other words, the CA provides the space, time, platform and resources to verify the children's equality. Instead of accepting their pre-given roles, the learners work on their own skills, strengths, interests and passions and can pursue them on a daily basis rather than as an occasional hobby.

The ability to choose and design their own education, and the practice of 'learning how to learn' that this entails then makes unschoolers much more confident and gives them a more positive outlook towards their lives and the wider world. As I could observe myself through various visits, the children at the CA show a level of self-awareness, self-confidence, knowledge and practical skills, curiosity, joy and happiness that I could not find among most 'schooled' children in India I met in their classrooms.[21]

The confidence, curiosity and joy 'at work' at the CA can also be observed through the fact that during all my visits none of the learners would ever wait for the instructions of the facilitators to do something. Indeed, the children would organise their own activities even when the hub facilitator was absent.

Remarkably, there is no judgement whatsoever of other learners' skills and talents and no atmosphere of competition whatsoever. As such, new learners do not need to be already skilled or experienced in an activity to join – every activity, workshop, project, etc., is open to anyone who wants to participate, and the more experienced learners will happily introduce and support the newcomers in every hub rather than this being the role of the facilitators.[22]

An important element in creating this atmosphere of freedom, equality and camaraderie is how the facilitators at the CA engage in a politics of solidarity with the children that is based, first and foremost, on *trust*. As one learner says, 'in Adda there is no hierarchy, so everybody is equal. But in school there are so many rules, regulations and restrictions we have to follow'. This is also visible in the following account by Chiara Bockstahler, an intern at Creativity Adda, who talks about a conversation she had with two children at the CA:

> one of the kids shared … [that] 'the teachers don't ask us what we want to do. Instead we have to respect them a lot and only listen to them. In school, they do not trust us. Not like in Creativity Adda where we can easily use all the facilities and tools'. Another boy said, 'I was so confused when I first entered the DesignStudio/MakerSpace of Creativity Adda. The learning guide asked me what I would like to make. He told me that I can use all the tools that are there and if I need anything else I should tell it to him. He trusted me directly, even though he did not even know me'.
>
> (Bockstahler 2018)

This trust in the children is also reflected in how the CA is run on a day-to-day and long-term basis. Weekly meetings of the alternative learners among themselves and with facilitators, followed through by democratic decision-making, make sure that the children – as many of them would also tell me in their own words – 'own the space'. This includes decisions about what activities to conduct, regular clean-ups and repairs on the children's own initiative, the daily cooking and distribution of food completely managed by the children and the monthly organisation of the Dariya Dil community café organised on a gift culture basis. As the March 2018 Newsletter of the CA highlights,

> at the heart of Creativity Adda is the strong belief that everyone of us is equal and that whatever we do is not only for, and not on behalf of, but always *with* and *alongside* our alternative learners. In fact, Creativity Adda is *their* space. As such, we continuously strive for new and more direct democratic ways so our alternative learners can increasingly run the Adda on their own and for themselves. Moving forward in this direction, this month we had a first, very intense and fruitful brainstorming session with our music hub members. We hope that through this initiative, the Adda kids will not only feel increasingly that they are the 'owners' of the Adda, but that they will also learn for life about how to take responsibility as well as how to manage and run an organization. This learning is already taking place across our hubs and will intensify in the future.
>
> (Tiwari 2018)

Another key part of this is the recent establishment of a children's council. Every three to six months, the learners will elect among themselves two members from each hub who will be part of the council on a rotating basis. The council members are responsible for organising discussions and debates in their respective hubs and representing the hub in the council. They will decide, for example, how to spend the allocated monthly budget of 5000 rupees (around 67 USD) and develop new ideas and proposals for the space. As Ashish Tiwari further says, the council members take up more and more 'management responsibilities' and play an important role in organising activities and events. This is a key part of the CA's strategy to let children not only participate in but indeed *own the space.*

The feeling of belonging and ownership is also expressed, as I could observe, in the fact that even on holidays and other occasions when there is no school, many of the regular learners still come to the Creativity Adda. A few of the learners also don't go to 'regular school' and only come to the CA, while some others regularly try to sneak out of class earlier in order to spend more time at the CA.

Many of the children indeed come to the CA regularly for at least four to five days a week. This is despite their tough workload which includes six days of school from morning till 1 pm, spending time at the CA till 5 pm, going for tuition classes afterwards (often on a daily basis including Sundays), going to the mosque for daily prayers, having dinner and doing homework. As one child puts it, 'Adda is very important for me, even more important than attending school'.

While some of the parents do not want their children to go to the CA as they see it as 'waste of (productive) time', many other parents – while also initially reluctant – came around after seeing the positive changes in their children.

Mostly, parents expressed how happy they were to see their kids developing serious interest, passion and commitment to something.[23] They also found their children to show a more positive attitude in general while levels of frustration and anger were said to have remarkably decreased. This is also similarly expressed by many of the young learners themselves. As one boy says:

> Adda is very important for me because after I started going there, I felt various positive changes in me … The mindset of my parents has also changed a lot. Initially my parents used to think that I'm not learning anything at Adda and just go there to avoid learning and have fun. Now their mindset has changed, they see my talents and realise that I can do a lot more things.

Two other children who regularly attend the CA further say that 'before I attended the Adda I was quite mischievous. But right now I have improved and became a much better version of myself' and, respectively, that 'when I did not go to Adda I used to just wander around aimlessly but now I have become much better'.

In more and more understanding and experiencing the philosophy of unschooling and SDL first-hand, the children also often turn into facilitators and hold workshops or informally share their knowledge with other children. Sharing their skills indeed is seen as extremely positive, important and valuable among the learners themselves. Chiara Bockstahler shares one such example:

> Faiz came up with the idea to reuse the wheels of old skates to build his own, self-designed skateboard. Many other kids were impressed by this idea and they asked Faiz to hold a workshop on 'how to make your own skateboard'. Faiz felt honoured by this request. Explaining the others how it worked also helped him to further evolve his design.

> (Bockstahler 2018)

In another example of inter-generational, collaborative learning, Bockstahler narrates how

> Manoj (Class 7) was explaining the functioning of solar lights to all his older friends. Manoj was exploring how solar lights work completely on his own, just by experimenting with it. Several students got interested in it and asked him to share.
>
> (ibid.)

Moreover, these vignettes also show how the CA enables children to become producers and creators rather than consumers. One boy for example shares how 'in Adda, we have learned to make and repair things which we otherwise would have to buy in the shops'.

Learning, sharing of skills, playing games or having conversations with others at the CA completely ignores the typical age barriers imposed by class-based, mainstream schooling. I could frequently observe how younger children learn together with elders and often take the lead, or how elder children play with younger ones and vice versa without any hesitation.

Indeed, there seems to be a high level of solidarity and caring for each other among the children, no matter their age differences. As one boy expresses this, 'here all of us come together and we do things together. But in schools, we are mostly fighting among ourselves'. This succinctly summarises the difference between the OWW Education system in which individual learners compete against each other and ANPED based on the presupposition of equality in which, as in the case of the CA, there emerges a community of learners.

The latter indeed leads to the collapse of various levels of hierarchy that are found across most mainstream schools. Dance Hub facilitator Prakash Chand for instance highlights how caste discrimination among the children completely vanished after the first few months in the CA: 'we are all human beings. We can live together. Now the kids sit together and share their food with each other. It makes me feel good' (personal interview, July 2018).

Another example of this is how in a normal and natural way the learners would include and interact with a homeless child with behavioural difficulties who regularly visited the space. Over the months I regularly revisited the CA, I could clearly see how his confidence level increased and his interactions with the other learners improved.

The sense of solidarity among the children and indeed all members of the CA then also regularly spills over into the broader community. This is the case when the boys of the cooking hub decide to serve food to people in the local community; when the music hub members go out for jamming sessions into the community; when the media lab team engages in dialogue with community members in order to give a voice to them, hear about some pressing issues and concerns as well as to document their experiences, skills and talents; when the Design and Makerspace hub members host their monthly repair café open to anyone in the community, or when any of the learners participate in various volunteering activities. As another learners says, 'I want to do something for others, that is the importance of Adda for me'.

One challenge for the CA is to support the children in continuously developing their potential and skills. At times, it seemed that some of the hubs would rather repeat the same activities all over again which left some of the more experienced children unchallenged and bored. Recently, however, the CA coordinator and facilitators alongside the children have been consciously trying to provide new opportunities and create more exposure.

This is achieved, for example, through an increased participation in outside sports events and food fairs; by reaching out to top restaurant chefs in Delhi to participate in cooking workshops for the children and local community members; through the formation of a professional dance group and music band that perform at outside events; the hosting of public workshops and community events; or the setting-up of an organic, urban farming space at the CA planned and run entirely by the learners.

The hosting of various festivals around sports, food, dance and community short films are also another effort by the CA learners to connect with the local and wider community and create new platforms and networks. Additionally, the CA started to organise various learning events such as the 'Community Learning Mela' that are held in public spaces such as parks to exchange skills and knowledge with community members. Moreover, the CA also regularly organises skill exchange workshops to connect with children from other parts of Delhi.

Overall, the learners of the CA emerge as a collective subject that contributes to a repartitioning of the sensible. In engaging in fields as diverse as dancing, music, organic cooking, film-making and photography and many others, in going on trips to visit the theatre, museum or attend conferences, in giving back to the community, in sharing and caring rather than competing and fighting, they defy societal expectations of what 'school students' from a marginalised community should do with their time, and how they should behave and fit in their pre-assigned roles.

In identifying and then indeed pursuing on a regular, daily basis their own interests and passions, the children do not accept their pre-given roles within the OWW but aim to craft their own meaningful lives while, at the same time, as part of these meaningful lives, they take on leadership roles in the community. As Manish Jain stresses, 'we hope that kids can see that there are many ways to earn a livelihood and contribute to the well-being of their community' (Jain 2015).

The very fact that the CA is taking place in – shaky and at times tense – cooperation with a government school, and indeed on the very premises of a government school, then makes this into a very unique case where we can see how OWW Education and ANPED closely encounter, interact and clash with each other.

Especially during the initial phase of the CA, there was a rather hostile environment created by the then principal and some teachers who would blame the CA for taking away the children's time to study and for failing in their exams. Some teachers would also see how the CA would cut into the children's time for paid tuition given by the teachers and therefore opposed it.

However, with the arrival of the current principal, the situation improved remarkably, as Ashish Tiwari says. Cooperation between the school and the CA for festivals, functions and extracurricular activities has taken off, and teachers are asked to send their children to the CA for exposure visits and potential enrolment – which for all learners is free of charge – from time to time.

While cooperation between the CA and the Mukherjee Nagar school has increased and benefits both sides, it would be wrong to assume that the CA, and Shikshantar as its founding organisation, would have established this model with any ambition in mind to create spill-over effects onto the school and therefore attempt to reform the schooling system from within. As ANPED does in general, so Shikshantar as an unschooling organisation in particular rejects the OWW Education model in its entirety, seeing it as *beyond repair*.

Therefore, there are no illusions within Shikshantar that the project would have a deeper influence on the school's pedagogy. Rather, the CA is set up, as we have also heard above, as a parallel system or virus in the school to dismantle the culture of schooling from within. Having the space within the school and in some way as an extension of the school then makes it easier to reach out to the potential alternative learners – who are already in the school – and also increases the legitimacy and credibility of the space in the eyes of the parents, while the existing infrastructure and resources of the school can be utilised.

As such, we can further understand the CA and its ontological politics of equality as a form of *system hacking*, which

> involves creating spaces within the system, using its resources, where people can be educated about the violences of the system and have their desires re-oriented away from it. This requires 'playing the game' of institutions at the same time that rules are bent to generate alternative outcomes.
>
> (Andreotti et al. 2015: 27)

As one learner at the CA then perhaps aptly summarises it: 'in school they tell us to follow all the rules and regulations. But over here at Adda I'm encouraged to break those rules and regulations'.

Summation

In this chapter, we have established the cornerstones of anarchistic postdevelopmental education, based on co-creating spaces in which learners can apply their equal intelligence to something that matters to them.

This shows how ANPED is practicing the ontological politics of equality by assuming equality from the outset as something that merely needs to be tested and therefore verified. In transcending the hierarchical teacher–student relation and turning passive student-consumers into capable and curious learners, ANPED leaves the explicative order of OWW Education which, as we have seen, leads to the pedagogicisation of society.

Whereas OWW Education socialises students into the OWW and therefore lays the foundations for the OWW Development paradigm to unfold, ANPED rejects the distribution of pre-given roles in the OWW. Instead, it is a world-making practice which leads to the subjectification of learners and an accompanying repartitioning of the sensible.

Ultimately, ANPED as a prefigurative politics challenges many of the established, common-sense hierarchies of the OWW and lets us pave new paths towards the pluriverse. By acting out of the presupposition of equality, it provides one possible approach of 'how we might cultivate ourselves as subjects who desire non-capitalist, non-liberal and non-modern forms of life' (Esteva and Escobar 2019: 32), clearing the way for 'more autonomous, convivial and communal' (ibid.) practices and lifeworlds.

The Creativity Adda unschooling and self-designed learning space is one current example of ANPED in action and hints at how 'other forms of re-existence' (ibid.) can be constructed through a different mode of education. As we have seen, children who are usually seen as less equal by OWW Education – and therefore also by broader society – have started to pursue their own interests and passions and defy the roles and identities otherwise imposed on them.

The presupposition of equality among learners then also increasingly takes hold in the wider Mukherjee Nagar community where parents, family members and friends start to see, understand and support the various hidden skills and talents of their children. This leads to a broader repartitioning of the sensible and the emergence of a more radical imagination of what people from so-called low-income and marginalised communities can do with their lives. As one of the alternative learners says, 'since I'm at the Adda, I realised that I can achieve so many things'.

While the Creativity Adda in Delhi can be described as a rather *structured* unschooling approach catering to school-going children, there are many different ways of practicing ANPED. As such, the next chapter will introduce another variant of it which takes place mostly outside of formal, designated unschooling spaces.

Notes

1 Hence, while they differed in their analysis of causes, both the British occupying forces as well as the Indian national – mostly Brahman and other upper caste – elites had no doubt that India was 'underdeveloped'. Both assumed that the majority of Indians were less intelligent than themselves – in the case of the British it was the Indian population overall that was thought to be incapable of building meaningful lives on their own, and in the case of the Indian elites it was the lower-caste and non-elite Indians who needed a strong, independent Indian state in order to pursue meaningful lives. In both cases, modern education has become one of the key tools of the state to educate and, more importantly, discipline the ones thought less than equal.

2 See also Kumar (2005).

3 Rancière 1991.

4 A case in point for this is also given by Ghosh (2013: 196), referring to the increasing economic, social and political tensions emerging in the India of the late 1990s: 'for

most of the developments like corruption and disintegrity, violence and lawlessness, communal passion and tension in these years, education was singled out, as in the past, as the whipping boy needing a dose of reforms at the hands of its political masters'.

5 This stance, which rejects the entire model of schooling in all its forms and guises, also explains why anarchist approaches to education are largely silenced and made invisible in the mainstream academic discourse. As Gabbard (2017) states, the anarchist position on education violates 'the messianic rule of discursive inclusion. This rule stipulates that in order to speak or write about education, we must present the school as either an inherently benevolent institution – or at the very least, with the proper reforms, a potentially benevolent institution – capable of delivering the individual and/or society into some condition of secular salvation'.

6 See Giroux (2011); McLaren (1995), (2015); Kumar (2016); Hill (2017).

7 Some observers extend this criticism also to the work of Paulo Freire (see Kahn 2009; Haworth 2012; Biesta 2017; Meyerhoff 2019). As Esteva, Prakash and Stuchul (2008: 95) argue: 'Freire wrote for critical educators, revolutionary leaders, social workers, organic intellectuals, a motley crowd of characters who in his view could and would dedicate themselves to the liberation of the oppressed … They become a substitute for a revolutionary party or for guerrilla activities. Once liberated, they become, for Freire, the new enlightened vanguard that would make possible the desirable change'.

8 This is also what differentiates anarchistic postdevelopmental education (ANPED) from other educational philosophies such as the one of Hannah Arendt. Whereas I will conceptualise ANPED as a prefigurative and ontological *politics* to cultivate new ways of being in the here and now, Arendt's view on education relegates it to the social sphere that exists somewhat oddly between the private and the public realms, and thereby is situated at a place outside politics. In Arendt's understanding, the school becomes a place where children are and should be introduced and socialised into the hegemonic world as it is, thereby cementing the status quo and taking away any agency from the child in the same way she takes away agency from the 'poor' as part who has no part (see Chapter 2). This also led Arendt to take up some extremely reactionary positions, such as defending the school segregation policies in the United States (see Arendt 1959).

9 As Saul Newman emphasises, 'it is this implacable hostility to state authority that places anarchism at odds not only with more conservative doctrines but also with liberalism – which sees the state as a necessary evil – with socialism and even with revolutionary Marxism – which sees the state as an instrument, at least in the 'transitional' period, for building socialism, whether through social democratic reforms or through the revolutionary seizure and control of state power' (Newman 2016: 2).

10 See Chapter 2.

11 I consciously use the term 'learner' instead of 'student' from here on as the latter is typically associated with and constituted through the OWW Education system and its axiom of inequality.

12 Rancière's emphasis on the role of explanation in perpetuating inequality does not essentialise the part that has no part as less intelligent based on their pre-given OWW identities. Instead, Rancière demonstrates how the process of explanation works as a self-fulfilling prophecy by inventing the role of the student as being less intelligent and perpetually in need of explanation in the first place.

13 Indeed, we can say that it is the student's *unwillingness* to think otherwise about herself and the world (other than what the OWW tells her to think and how to think) upon which the ignorant schoolmaster intervenes and imposes his will. As such, 'the only forms of coercion, authority, control, interference, and leadership which, for a [anarchist] libertarian, can count as legitimate in the larger community are those that a teacher may rightfully utilize in his endeavor to wean the young away from any further dependence on external regulation' (Krimerman and Perry 1966: 405).

14 The ignorant schoolmaster does not impose her will upon students based on some foundational truth. What the ignorant schoolmaster merely does is to verify – to make true – equality as a performative act or a prefigurative politics by *assuming* the equal intelligence of her students: 'equality is not a given that politics then presses into service, an essence embodied in the law or a goal politics sets itself the task of attaining. It is a mere assumption that needs to be discerned within the practices implementing it' (Rancière 1999: 33).

15 As one unschooling parent says: 'unschooling, it's a very non-standardised way of looking at learning. So it also doesn't believe in standardising the term and defining the term' (personal interview, May 2019).

16 The project was able to take off thanks to the strong support by Pankaj Pushkar, a former member of the Delhi legislative assembly, who is also a close personal friend of Shikshantar founder Manish Jain. Creativity Adda is funded mainly through the Corporate Social Responsibility budget of DS Group, an Indian conglomerate that comprises of a vast portfolio including tobacco, spices, beverages, hospitality, packaging and agro forestry. Jain again has close personal connections with one of the directors of the company. This enabled the collaboration between these various actors, which Jain himself calls 'a strange unholy alliance' (quoted in Hopkins 2018).

17 Unless otherwise stated, all further quotes by Ashish Tiwari in this chapter are taken from this personal interview.

18 Unless otherwise stated, all further quotes by children from the Creativity Adda in this chapter are taken from this focus group discussion.

19 Examples of workshops include clowning, storytelling, poetry, gender awareness, mime theatre, animation, comic art, citizen journalism, publication design and layout, wall painting, film-making, toy-making, ultimate frisbee, drone-making, website design and much more.

20 However, this does not happen without its own challenges and contradictions. Some of the children in the focus group discussion mentioned for example that for whatever skills they acquired at the CA, they would like to get certificates so they can prove their skills to others. As one kid puts it: 'if I have acquired a certain skill, people might ask me for proof, especially because I'm so young. So the certificate is important' (focus group discussion, July 2018). This stands in some tension with the goal of Shikshantar to get rid of the pervasive school culture (which includes the importance that formal certificates and degrees hold) altogether and pursues campaigns such as 'healing ourselves from the diploma disease'.

21 Notably, these are all things which are not (and potentially could not be) 'measured' in and through the outcome-obsessed, quantifiable OWW Education practices.

22 I could experience this myself when joining in various activities from dancing to skating, and cooking to playing cricket – all activities where I more or less (rather more) suck.

23 Parents often added to this description by referring to their children as being 'much more disciplined' than before.

References

Andreotti, V., Stein, S., Ahenakew, C., and D. Hunt (2015). 'Mapping interpretations of decolonization in the context of higher education'. *Decolonization: Indigeneity, Education & Society*, 4 (1), pp. 21–40.

Arendt, H. (1959). 'Reflections on little rock'. https://www.normfriesen.info/forgotten/l ittle_rock1.pdf.

Biesta, G. (2016). *Good Education in an Age of Measurement: Ethics, Politics, Democracy*. London: Routledge.

Biesta, G. (2017). 'Don't be fooled by ignorant schoolmasters: On the role of the teacher in emancipatory education'. *Policy Futures in Education*, 15 (1), pp. 52–73.

Bingham, C., and Biesta, G. (2010). *Jacques Rancière: Education, Truth, Emancipation*. Kindle ed. London: Continuum.

Bockstahler, C. (2018). 'We are here to complete each other: Peer to peer learning in creativity adda'. https://medium.com/swapathgami-walkout-walkon-network/we-are-here-to-complete-each-other-peer-to-peer-learning-in-creativity-adda-9746023da13c.

Esteva, G., and Escobar, A. (2019). 'Postdevelopment @ 25: On "being stuck" and moving forward, sideways, backward and otherwise'. In Klein, E., and Morreo, C.E. (eds.), *Postdevelopment in Practice: Alternatives, Economies, Ontologies*. London: Routledge, pp. 21–36.

Esteva, G., Prakash, M. S., and D.L. Stuchul (2008). 'From a pedagogy for liberation to liberation from pedagogy'. In Hern, M. (ed.), *Everywhere All the Time: A New Deschooling Reader*. Oakland: AK Press, pp. 91–111.

Firth, R., and Robinson, A. (2017). 'From the unlearned un-man to a pedagogy without moulding: Stirner, consciousness-raising and the production of difference'. In Haworth, R., and Elmore, J.M. (eds.), *Out of the Ruins: The Emergence of Radical Informal Learning Spaces*. Adobe Digital Editions Version, Chapter 3. Oakland, CA: PM Press.

Freire, P. (2013). *Pedagogy of the Oppressed*. London: Bloomsbury Academic.

Fremeaux, I., and Jordan, J. (2012). 'Anarchist pedagogy in action: Paideia, Escuela libre'. In Haworth, R.H. (ed.), *Anarchist Pedagogies: Collective Actions, Theories, and Critical Reflections on Education*. Oakland, CA: PM Press, pp. 107–123.

Gabbard, D. (2017). 'Don't act, just think'! In Haworth, R., and Elmore, J.M. (eds.), *Out of the Ruins: The Emergence of Radical Informal Learning Spaces*. Adobe Digital Editions Version, Chapter 2. Oakland, CA: PM Press.

Ghosh, S.C. (2013). *The History of Education in Modern India 1757–2012*. 4th ed. Hyderabad: Orient Blackswan.

Giroux, H. (2011). *On Critical Pedagogy*. New York: Continuum.

Haworth, R. (ed.) (2012). *Anarchist Pedagogies: Collective Actions, Theories, and Critical Reflections on Education*. Oakland, CA: PM Press.

Hill, D. (2017). *Class, Race and Education under Neoliberal Capitalism*. Delhi: Aakar Books.

Hill, D., Greaves, N.M., and A. Maisuria (2017). 'Embourgeoisment, immiseration, commodification – Marxism revisited: A critique of education in capitalist systems'. In Hill, D. (ed.), *Class, Race and Education under Neoliberal Capitalism*. Delhi: Aakar Books, pp. 210–237.

Hopkins, R. (2018). 'Manish Jain: "Our work is to recover wisdom and imagination"'. https://www.robhopkins.net/2018/01/31/manish-jain-our-work-is-to-recover-wisdom-and-imagination/.

Illich, I. (1974). *Deschooling Society*. London: Marion Boyars.

Jain, M. (2015). 'A philosophy of learning and living'. http://www.teacherplus.org/wp-content/uploads/2015/12/A-philosophy-of-learning-and-living.pdf.

Jain, M., and Singh, G. (n.d.). 'Creativity adda'. http://shikshantar.org/innovations-shiksha/creativity-adda/creativity-adda.

Jones, K., Robinson, C. and K. Vaughan. (2015). 'Deschooling, homeschooling, and unschooling in the alternative school milieu'. In He, M., Schultz, B. and W. Schubert (eds.), *The SAGE Guide to Curriculum in Education*. Thousand Oaks, CA: SAGE Publications, pp. 391–399.

Kahn, R. (2009). 'Anarchic epimetheanism: The pedagogy of Ivan Illich'. In Amster, R., DeLeon, A., Fernandez, L.A., Nocella II, A.J., and D. Shannon (eds.), *Contemporary Anarchist Studies: An Introductory Anthology of Anarchy in the Academy*. New York: Routledge, pp. 125–135.

Krimerman, L.I., and Perry, L. (1966). *Patterns of Anarchy: A Collection of Writings on the Anarchist Tradition*. New York: Doubleday.

Kumar, K. (2005). *Political Agenda of Education: A Study of Colonialist and Nationalist Ideas*. 2nd ed. Delhi: SAGE Publications.

Kumar, R. (ed). (2016). *Neoliberalism, Critical Pedagogy and Education*. New York: Routledge.

McLaren, P. (1995). *Critical Pedagogy and Predatory Culture: Oppositional Politics in a Postmodern Era*. London: Routledge.

McLaren, P. (2015). *Pedagogy of Insurrection: From Resurrection to Revolution*. New York: Peter Lang Publishing.

Meyerhoff, E. (2019). *Beyond Education: Radical Studying for Another World*. Minneapolis: University of Minnesota Press.

Newman, S. (2016). *Postanarchism*. Cambridge: Polity Press.

Pelletier, C. (2009). 'Emancipation, equality and education: Rancière's critique of Bourdieu and the question of performativity'. *Discourse: Studies in the Cultural Politics of Education*, 30 (2), pp. 137–150.

Pelletier, C. (2012). 'No time or place for universal teaching: The ignorant schoolmaster and contemporary work on pedagogy'. In Deranty, J.-P., and Ross, A. (eds.), *Jacques Rancière and the Contemporary Scene: The Philosophy of Radical Equality*. London: Continuum, pp. 99–116.

Rancière, J. (1991). *The Ignorant Schoolmaster. Five Lessons in Intellectual Emancipation*. Stanford: Stanford University Press.

Rancière, J. (1999). *Disagreement: Politics and Philosophy*. Minneapolis: University of Minnesota Press.

Rancière, J. (2010). 'On ignorant schoolmasters'. In Bingham, C., and Biesta, G., *Jacques Rancière: Education, Truth, Emancipation.* Kindle ed. London: Continuum.

Ricci, C., Laricchia, P., and I. Desmarais. (2011). 'What unschooling is and what it means to us'. *Our Schools, Our Selves*, 20 (2), pp. 141–151.

Shantz, J. (2012). 'Spaces of learning: The anarchist free skool'. In Haworth, R.H. (ed.), *Anarchist Pedagogies: Collective Actions, Theories, and Critical Reflections on Education*. Oakland, CA: PM Press, pp. 124–144.

Suissa, J. (2010). *Anarchism and Education: A Philosophical Perspective*. (2nd ed). Oakland, CA: PM Press.

Szkudlarek, T. (2013). 'Introduction: Education and the political'. In Szkudlarek, T. (ed.), *Education and the Political: New Theoretical Articulations*. Rotterdam: Sense Publishers, pp. 1–14.

Tiwari, A. (2018). 'Direct democracy!!'. *Creativity Adda Newsletter*, March 2018.

Todd, J. (2012) 'From deschooling to unschooling: Rethinking anarchopedagogy after Ivan Illich'. In Haworth, R.H. (ed.), *Anarchist Pedagogies: Collective Actions, Theories, and Critical Reflections on Education*. Oakland, CA: PM Press, pp. 69–87.

Vlieghe, J. (2018). 'Rethinking emancipation with Freire and Rancière: A plea for a thing-centred pedagogy'. *Educational Philosophy and Theory*, 50 (10), pp. 917–927.

Wanggren, L., and Sellberg, K. (2012). 'Intersectionality and dissensus: A negotiation of the feminist classroom'. *Equality, Diversity and Inclusion: An International Journal*, 31 (5/6), pp. 542–555.

5   ANPED in practice

Radical unschooling among families

In this chapter, we will explore the concept and practice of 'radical unschooling' as a family-based approach in which children, teenagers and young adults consciously choose to not attend school but co-create their own, self-determined learning paths with and alongside their family members and the larger community.

As such, radical unschooling presupposes that there exists – in the first place – a choice between schooling and unschooling, and that there has been *a conscious, voluntary choice* made by the children together with their parents against school-based education and for self-designed learning (SDL) as a key element of unschooling.

This is applicable then to an estimated 10,000 urban, middle-class families across India (who are the focus of this chapter). These families constitute, to various degrees, the part who has a part in the OWW and undergo a process of subjectification in which they refuse to stick to their pre-assigned roles and identities in the OWW. Radical unschooling can be further practised by families in villages and the countryside who want to continue or start re-creating more communal ways of life through a mode of study which is more relevant to their own lives; and by indigenous families who reject OWW Education as a colonial tool and utilise SDL as a continuous, foundational practice to co-construct and recreate their relational lifeworlds outside the ontological limits of the OWW.

As Manish Jain stresses, unschooling indeed is a possibility for everyone, no matter the socio-economic background:

> we still have so many living learning spaces. In villages and even in most towns and cities, you can still find opportunities for apprenticeship learning, you can easily get to a forest, you can experience life in a joint family (full of rich relationships of all ages). We luckily do not have [to] go to a zoo to see animals; we can interact with them on the roads and in the fields. One can learn yoga without going to a yoga center. Everywhere, you can find a million forms of *kabaad* (so-called waste) to *jugaad* with,[1] to make something useful, beautiful and durable. The best part about these opportunities in India is that most have not yet been commodified. One quite fortunately does *not* have to pay a lot of money to access them.
>
> (Jain n.d.; emphasis original)

What all of the unschooling families – no matter their various backgrounds – have in common is that they refuse to accept the hierarchy of knowledge of the modern education system which places everything that helps us to become a 'good consumer-citizen' at the top of the pyramid and marginalises, ignores or ridicules everything else. Instead, they clamber out from underneath the pyramid and leave the building to pursue their own ideas of what makes meaningful lives by acquiring relevant skills and knowledge.

In doing this, unschooling radically goes against the OWW's insistence 'that learning is divorced from the ordinary, from play, from indigeneity, from the world – so that we have to meet special conditions like building sterilized "factories" and classrooms to teach the universal ideals of moustachioed Caucasians' (Akomolafe and Jain 2016), as well as against 'the material and discursive practice of denying the abundance around us in order to make the case for our scarcity-ridden economic and anorexic politic systems' (ibid.). By practicing the ontological politics of equality, radical unschooling therefore is a way of 'learning with and for life' that not only challenges and changes pre-conceived notions of education, but also helps us to move beyond Development.

Instead of providing an exhaustive definition of radical unschooling in the following, I will draw on some key characteristics of what it is and what it is not. In describing and discussing some of its key aspects across this chapter, I build mostly on field research among the unschoolers' movement in India which includes conversations of and together with practicing unschoolers and unschooler parents as well as in-depth surveys with 16 unschooling parents. This is complemented by drawing on some key literature, especially from the Udaipur-based unschooling organisation and movement Shikshantar and its co-founder Manish Jain.

Against the hierarchisation of knowledge

Most unschooler parents who participated in the survey I conducted in February 2019 relate the practice of unschooling to the idea of challenging the modern education system with its hierarchisation of knowledge and its standardised practices of disseminating knowledge.

As one parent says, 'unschooling is learning from the whole universe and there is no time limit to it', while another shares how 'education doesn't mean grades, it is about the continuous exploration of nature and thus enjoying life as a whole'. Other parents further state that 'unschooling is learning to love what you like in your own terms, with the freedom for the child to choose', or describe how

> life is learning and one is constantly learning. It cannot be boxed or compartmentalised. It's wholesome and best experienced and lived. I do not believe in the concept of teaching or being taught. I believe that everyone just learns. This led me to just let my child learn and be and live and experience.

Proponents of unschooling then clearly follow the anarchist postdevelopmental position which emphasises that OWW Education serves, first and foremost, as a tool to discipline students and make them into conformist consumer-citizens. Accordingly, one unschooling parent characterises schooling as a process in which 'children do things not because they believe in it or want to, but because they are asked to. At school they are taught to comply and not question. Without questioning they won't know what they believe in'.

This illustrates how unschoolers introduce a clear and strong dissensus into the OWW by challenging its world-making practice of OWW Education. As philosopher, activist and unschooler parent Bayo Akomolafe puts it,

> who decides that children go to school? Where did we get the idea that children ought to go to school? ... Who came up with the idea that children should be outsourced to an institution? ... Generations of power and movement have created this decision. It's not even parents that have decided to send their children to school. It's beyond parents. It's a whole network, a whole ecosystem, that says the child ought to go to school. And it's the same resistance that we are using that is saying, why do we have to take that course. There ought to be something different.
>
> (reimagining education workshop, May 2018)[2]

Unschooling also draws attention to the artificial separation between manual and intellectual labour which is characteristic of OWW Education, and the negative consequences thereof. Instead of such a strong division, unschooling – according to Manish Jain – stresses that 'it is important to re-look at the link between using our hands/body, meaningful work and the growth of our mind, spirit and emotional well-being' (Jain n.d.).

Indeed, what I have observed among the Indian unschoolers' movement is a strong tendency to value practical work and manual labour over and above strictly 'intellectual' or rather academic activities. For example, one survey participant argues that

> schools focus more on literacy and information ... My belief is that real education should focus on becoming a better human being. Gandhiji said the three important components of education are hand, heart, and head. Schools nowadays only focus on head. This creates a vast difference between what kind of society we want to build and what we have.

Unschoolers therefore acquire many practical skills and pursue many learning projects which are usually relegated to an inferior place in the OWW Education hierarchy of knowledge, if considered at all. These often include (but far exceed) fields and areas such as food and cooking; urban gardening and organic farming; arts and crafts; photography and film-making; singing and dancing; painting and drawing; poetry, storytelling and writing; recycling and upcycling; as well as learning how to create and produce many items themselves using a variety of tools and materials.

Ultimately, as a logical consequence of the wholesale rejection of any hierarchies of knowledges, for unschoolers

> there can be no standardized curriculum for unlearning since the process of unlearning is not a linear, mechanistic, predetermined one. Each of us makes our own path as we go along, and the many small choices (or mistakes) we make along the way can, at any point in time, catapult us into crazy beautiful new directions.
>
> (Jain 2003: 2)

This further translates into the rejection of the widespread belief that there is a certain age to acquire a certain knowledge, and that all same-aged children should learn the same and have the same learning standards against which they are measured and compared.

Instead, unschoolers – if they did not attend school for a significant period of time – will learn even what in the OWW would be designated as 'basic knowledge' such as numeracy and literacy only when they are ready for it – driven by their own curiosity and interest, or when they realise for themselves that this 'basic knowledge' is indeed needed in and useful for their daily life.

As Vidhi Jain, co-founder of Shikshantar, tells about unschooling with her daughter Kanku:

> 'how can Kanku not know how to read and write at the age of 12?' Ironically, that is one of [the] things that Manish and I are least bothered about. We know that this will come naturally and we need not put pressure on her for that. And what if she learns how to read and write at the age of 15 or later? She is learning so many more things that are meaningful to her. We are certain that her undying quest for learning sewing, make-up, cooking, dancing, loving animals, filmmaking, trekking are going to be the doorway for her to learn so many more skills like reading and writing.
>
> (Jain 2016)

Unschooler parent Dola Dasgupta provides an example of how her son gradually and naturally acquired maths skills as follows:

> the interesting thing about math is that it is a life skill to start with, which has been made out to be a feared subject in schools. As I see it, math is all around us … While looking at buildings my son would ask 'how many floors'. So we counted. When he wanted to know about the famous skyscrapers of the world, we looked up the number of floors, how many feet, etc. He then started making comparative charts of these buildings. He would sketch them and place them according to their heights and year of construction. He figured out units of measurement through his passion for architecture. I have

a kitchen weighing scale, which he uses often to weight random things. He takes my mother's tailoring tape to measure random objects in the house. His interest in space and Star Wars fuels his interest in space time travel. How many light years? How many KM apart are planets? How far is Pluto and how close is Mercury? That is enough Math for me for a 11-year-old.

(Dasgupta n.d.)

Radical unschooling as anarchic, self-designed learning

Instead of following a formal and structured curriculum,[3] rooted in a certain kind of pre-selected knowledge, unschooling is based on the autonomous process of SDL. This means first and foremost that any unschooler or unlearner[4] decides her- or himself what they want to learn and why they want to learn something, based on their own needs, interests and aspirations; how they want to learn it,[5] how long they want to learn about it, when they want to learn something, with whom they want to learn and how and in which ways they are using and applying their learning.

This shows that there is a strong emphasis on freedom and autonomy inherent in SDL and consequently in the idea of what 'education' means in an unschooling context. As Vinoba Bhave, a spiritual successor of Gandhi who is often mentioned among the Indian unschoolers' movement, puts it:

in matters of knowledge, no orders can be given. Education does not 'discipline' students, it gives them complete freedom. Whether or not society free from government is ever built in the larger world, such a society must be found in the world of students.

(Bhave 2008: 10)

The freedom to decide what to learn and how to learn, as opposed to the coercion and limitations of schooling, is also highlighted by a 15-year-old unschooler who attended the Shikshantar Unschoolers' Winter Camp in Udaipur, Rajasthan, where about 25 children spent 2 months with each other to learn and unlearn together:

I honestly love unschooling. It gives me the freedom to learn things, to do things that I would never have been able to learn or experience while in school … [Recently at the unschoolers camp] I got really interested in photography and I would have never known that I like this sort of thing if I was in school. I would have been learning stuff like weird maths terms and stuff that I actually don't really need in my daily life.

(personal interview, December 2017)

SDL is clearly based on the presupposition of equality by seeing the (un-)learner as capable and intelligent enough to identify their own learning project – i.e. finding something that matters to them – and then go about their learning without formal teacher or textbook. Unschooling therefore entails the Rancièrean assumption

> that there is only one kind of intelligence, namely the universal, and in fact anarchistic, intelligence of being able to learn anything autonomously; an intelligence, that is, which is shared by the scientist, the technician, the peasant, the craftsman, the musician, the painter etc. It is the intelligence of anybody.
>
> (Sonderegger 2014: 55)

In practically applying this assumption by verifying the learners' equality, unschooling

> allows children to follow their own interests and thereby assert their own individual will to learn. We don't teach an infant to walk, and nor do we teach children how to speak.[6] Instead, they simply will themselves into doing so. Why should any other learning be any different? One can offer support and encouragement, but learning itself is to be considered quite literally as the process of emancipation.
>
> (Springer 2016: 254)

This is also similarly stated by Pashwa Jhala, who unschools together with her two children:

> the foundation of this approach is based on trust and respect. It sees children as intelligent, social and curious beings by nature … and recognizes that when their freedom is respected, and their emotional needs met, they are able to navigate their own lives, learning and explorations in a peaceful and joyous way.
>
> (Jhala 2018)

There lies an inherent anarchistic, anti-authoritarian ethos in unschooling in that there is no authority in form of the 'expert' (be it a teacher, parent or any other figure of authority) to tell the unschooler what to learn, how to learn and what to do with what s/he has learned. What we can, however, identify in the unschooling approach is the figure of the ignorant schoolmaster who provides encouragement to the unschooler if and when needed, and/or helps to create spaces and opportunities to verify the unschoolers' equality. This becomes evident in the following account by unschooling parent Sharmila Govande during the 'reimagining education' unschoolers meeting and workshop held at Swaraj University outside Udaipur in May 2018:

> radical unschooling[7] is where you just let the child be. And let the child explore and learn whatever he or she wants to. It's a relationship between the parents and the child where you work on the child's interests, enhance the

curiosity of the child and just let it flower. So … you don't intrude too much in the child's life and believe that the child will decide and learn on his own.

Similarly, an unschooling parent taking part in the survey describes unschooling as follows: 'unschooling is when you trust the child's inherent ability and curiosity to find his journey forward and we as parents help and support'. Pashwa Jhala relatedly shares that 'our role as parents has simply been to provide a safe and loving context, and offer support or information when asked' (Jhala 2018).

Other unschooling parents who were part of the survey respectively described their parental roles as 'a friend', 'just one more member of the family rather than a parent', 'taking a back seat and letting the child explore whatever she wants and trusting her completely' or simply as 'being present'. Another parent further defines her role as 'finding a balance between being there for them [the children], yet not in an imposing way, guiding them when help is asked for and stopping the moment when they seem to no longer want it'.

This clearly shows the anti-hierarchical tendency and egalitarian ethos of unschooling in which

> parents completely surrender their role as authority figures and instead treat the child as an equal member of the household … 'The main principle of radical unschooling is to encourage children to be self-disciplined and self-motivated', says [unschooler child] Ishaan's mother Dola Dasgupta, who … is an active member of the country's alternative learning community … 'They figure out for themselves … they stretch their limits. The more self-aware a person is, the more empowered they become'.
>
> (Chhibber 2018)

This also becomes evident in the following description by Mohit Trivedi, founder of Mukt Dhara Multiversity,[8] a team member of Swaraj University (see Chapter 7), and an unschooling parent himself:

> unschooling is something where you are not in your child's way. It's more like, you are not the authority, the truth doesn't come from you. The truth is not coming from the supreme authorities. The kids are free to find their own versions of truths.

Here we can further see how unschooling challenges the prerogative of 'experts' and their privileged access to meaning and truth that is so characteristic of the OWW and which tells us 'that any meaning we may make for ourselves, out of our own experience, has no value' (Holt 2008: 18).

At the same time, in the numerous conversations I had with unschooler parents, I could identify a certain humility and sense of interconnectedness and interbeing, positioning the human being and human knowledge within a broader, more relational picture of the world and our role in it. For example,

Mohit Trivedi says about his own approach of unschooling together with his family:

> I also believe that we are not experts. We also have limited wisdom of this new paradigm [of unschooling], so we are also learning together with the kids and are evolving as parents ... What works in our own context might not work for any other unschooling family. So using our understanding of our context and needs makes unschooling more realistic and practical.

The result of this different sense of knowing-thinking-feeling-being in the world, which is a far cry from the OWW with its iron laws, hard facts and expert-certified truths, is to see, understand, practice and celebrate

> learning as a natural, joyful process ... Children are good judges of what they are ready to learn and when they are ready to learn it. Learning processes should therefore be 'child-led' rather than simply just 'child-centered' ... Children explore their own questions, at their own pace, and engage with a number of different spaces, people and relationships in their community.
>
> (Jain n.d.)[9]

Manish Jain's emphasis on interdependence (learning with and alongside people and communities) in the above statement shows further that unschooling is not a (neo-)liberal form of learning which only and exclusively focuses on the idea of the autonomous, rational, self-interested human being. In stark contrast to this, unlearning puts a lot of emphasis on learning with each other and alongside each other through getting as much exposure from the outside world as possible and pursuing peer-to-peer, collaborative- and community-based learning, as well as applying the learnings across concrete projects in the local community. These concepts and ideas have indeed been frequently invoked by unlearners during my conversations with them about what unlearning means and entails.

It is also in this emphasis on community-based learning in its widest sense – i.e. learning with, from and alongside as many different people as possible from all walks of life, backgrounds, etc. – that we can see much of the inherent political, anarchist nature of radical unschooling. As unschooler and blogger Idzie Desmarais shares, unschooling 'embraces horizontal ways of relating to other people, across age divides, and invites us all to question the oppressive structures we've been told are just and necessary' (Desmarais 2019). Here,

> the importance of family and community culture comes into play. Who is part of a child's life? What are their perspectives, experiences, and values? If children are surrounded by people who talk about and embody different ways of existing and living outside of the dominant culture, who discuss inequalities and structural violence, important history and current events, who work to unlearn their own prejudices and fight for justice, who care and learn and

struggle and include children in all of that – then that is what they will learn to do themselves.

(ibid.)

The concept of interdependence is further reflected in what Shikshantar refers to as 'families learning together':

the idea is that parents, children, neighbors, relatives, friends – and all those we consider as part of our 'joint/extended family – are each responsible for their own learning and are responsible for supporting and nurturing each other in our varied learning interests. We believe that children need to re-ignite passion and curiosity in adults and adults need to also do the same for children … Each of us can generate our own 'intergenerational learning webs' – an intricate set of multi-age relationships across different spaces where each of us (adults as well as children) can go to learn or unlearn what we want.

(Jain n.d.)

As Manish Jain further says,

we try to rebuild a larger connection with community, culture and ecology. A lot of it, at least in India, it's different to what I've seen in the West because there's a lot of individualised things there, but less sense of community building or commoning. We are trying to also focus on inter-generational learning spaces. I believe you need at least 3 generations exploring things together to generate the conditions for real wisdom and imagination to emerge. We need both together like roots and wings.

(quoted in Hopkins 2018)

The concept of intergenerational learning webs demonstrates how ANPED, as opposed to OWW Education, nurtures connections, friendships, sharing and learning between various age groups. This is opposed to the schooling system which puts only children of the same age together in one class. In turn, this strongly impacts how we socialise with others and leads us to make friends only with the ones who are roughly in the same age group – everything else is usually being seen as 'unnatural'. This often inhibits opportunities and chances for intergenerational solidarity.

Among the unschooling movement, the opposite is the case. As my friend Avinash Almeida, a 24-year-old unschooler, says: 'I have friends between four to 63 years. I think one advantage of our unschooling is that you just make friends of different age groups' (personal interview, May 2018).[10]

This also goes against the common stereotype that unschoolers would be isolated and have difficulties in making friends. Munish, an unschooler parent of two children, narrates how

we have a park in front of my house, and children get together every day and play there for two hours. On weekends, what I do is we organise trips for children. Everybody comes together to our house and we all together visit different places … Third, my children conduct workshops for other children. We go to schools and they conduct different kinds of workshops. So the whole day they are interacting with other people … There are lots of people to interact. They interact with adults, they interact with people older to them, younger to them, same age groups … School-going children mostly interact with their own age group. We get a chance to interact with all age groups.

Through the description of radical unschooling as 'families learning together', we can also clearly see the importance of exchanging the roles between 'ignorant schoolmasters' and (un-)learners. Therefore, parents and elders – who might be naturally thought of as taking on the role of ignorant schoolmasters – often find themselves on the other side, as unlearners themselves.

This has indeed been a common theme in many of the unschooler parents' reflections, as in the following account by Mohit Trivedi: 'children come up with lots of questions and we are not experts in all the fields. So we explore together. All we need to do is to be available. We can be self-designed learners together'.

As Sumi-Chandresh likewise says about unschooling with her son Qudrat, 'unschooling doesn't mean that we become Qudrat's teachers. Instead, we see ourselves as co-learners – sharing and growing together' (Sumi-Chandresh, n.d.).

Radical unschooling as way(s) of life

For most unschooling families, unschooling does not only designate a way of education and learning but indeed refers to a whole way of life that brings us closer to the pluriverse. One unschooling parent narrates accordingly how 'unschooling is a completely different approach to life, the way you understand childhood and children, learning and education, parenting and parenthood' (unschooler survey, February 2019).

As Mohit Trivedi further points out,

unschooling is not just limited to not sending your kids to school, it's a way of life. Once a parent asked me if both [parents] are working then how can they pull their kids out of the school and in reply I said that once we change our lenses through which we see the world, lots of unlearnings happen in us, and then our priorities change. We used to live in a city, and now we are living here [on Swaraj University's green campus outside Udaipur]. So during this transition our lenses changed through lots of inner churnings and then many things happened. We realigned our priorities. New possibilities started emerging. We were chasing all the goals in that [previous] life, and still we were not content. Now that we have stopped chasing anything, we feel liberated, we feel content. We have nothing to chase. My wife is not working, I'm working half of the week, and half of the week I'm with the kids. So it's like everything changes.

The unschooling way of life is also illustrated by unschooler parent Pashwa Jhala:

> we actually live on a very minimal budget. Jim [Pashwa's husband] works online for a small eco-goods company … It is very part time work but it funds our very simple life … renting modest places, cooking for ourselves, travelling by train. We feel that having lots of free time to be with our children, each other and friends, and have time to engage in whatever is compelling for us, is a luxury that hugely outweighs any pleasure we might get from more expensive choices. Eating out, going shopping or attending events is not of much interest to any of us anyway, and they rarely feature in our current lifestyle. Instead we opt for (and prefer) a swim in the sea, wading in rivers, or walks and picnics in the mountains … We also do not acquire much as it is not possible to travel with too many things.
>
> (Jhala 2018)

One survey participant similarly shares how

> unschooling in our case arose from dissatisfaction with the current function of society. Anyone on this journey needs to spare lot of time for their kids. We decided to let go of money to buy time. We both found a place far from the city where we work and live hence saving time of commuting and lifestyle changes to bring our cost of living down. In simple words, we bought time and let go of money. I must say it doesn't mean our quality of life has gone down. In fact, the quality of life improved and we got a chance to learn other skills.

Relatedly, as unschooling directly challenges the primacy of OWW Education and its anthropocentric knowledge base, it also and at the same time re-values and includes a broad variety of 'other' knowledges that exist across lifeworlds exceeding the OWW's ontological limits and often exemplify very different, closer and less hierarchical relations with nature.

Moreover, and on a less abstract level, we can argue that unschooling simply gives unschoolers more opportunities to spend time in, with and around nature. As my friend Qudrat Sumi-Chandresh, a 21-year-old lifelong unschooler from Ahmedabad, says:

> see, I was always connected to nature. And unschooling helped in a way to think about and question everything and by questioning everything I was somehow more connected to nature. And I think not going to school gave me freedom to travel, to explore different places and this made me more connected to nature. From the beginning I loved nature and I admire it and I try my best to not eat too much junk and not being a consumer. It's hard to not be a consumer but I try not to be one. So basically by not going to school it helped me connect more to nature because I could spend more time with trees and water and mud and other stuff.
>
> (personal interview, June 2018)

In a similar vein, a survey participant further shares how his unschooling family

> believes in getting connected to nature and hence we engage ourselves in various activities like gardening, maintaining small kitchen garden and some other experiments and our son has joined us and has picked up many things. He can identify many trees, plants, flowers and spices. He also seems to understand the importance of trees and bees and looks at them differently. I doubt that he could learn this from a textbook or in a classroom.

Another related perspective is shared by Mohit Trivedi, talking about how his daughter relates to nature:

> once someone asked her who are your friends, and she said that I have my friends here. This tree is my friend ... I was shocked by her answer. We are very anthropocentric, human-centric. So our friends can only be humans. For her, it's different. She said that this stone is my friend. This tree is my friend. So they socialise in their own way. We are anyways schooled and conditioned, so for us friends are limited, but for them it's very wide.

Through all these accounts, we can clearly grasp the connection between unschooling as ANPED and the pursuit of ways of life outside the dualist OWW. With the growing dissensus against the OWW as the only way of thinking-feeling-being, there also often emerges a different set of priorities that moves away from a mass-consumerist lifestyle. As such, unschooling provides the opportunity to develop a more grounded understanding of our situatedness in the world – not as superior, detached rulers of a passive world waiting to be measured, explained and conquered, but as active participants always engaged with others (humans and non-humans) in various ways of worlding.

Overall, the picture of unschooling that emerges is a way of seeing the world as radically open, brimming with potentialities and being constantly made anew. Reflecting the non-teleological nature of ANPED and unschoolers' inherent relational view of the self, Lyn-Piluso and Lyn-Piluso (2008: 89) highlight how unschooling

> allows us to recognize that society is a human creation – that it has no ultimate, articulate basis to which we can appeal, other than our own interdependency, and our powers of thought and imagination. This awareness frees us, and our children, to work toward transforming society as it stands.

At the same time, this awareness translates into a certain tendency towards and indeed confidence in dwelling in the here and now and being firmly in the present, rather than reminiscing about the past or worrying about the future. This became evident in a discussion among three unschooler parents regarding any worries about what the future would hold for their unschooler children without formal schooling, certificates and degrees. As Sharmila Govande says,

> I don't think ever since I have started unschooling I thought about this. Look at today, live today beautifully and don't really bother yourself with

tomorrow. Tomorrow will come and you will find your path. So actually, currently I am just enjoying my space with the kids and I am seeing them doing so many different things, so I've really not thought about that aspect. I have been a facilitator, I have come here [to the workshop] and I'm starting a learning space, I'm writing an article on Multiversity Alliance[11] and alternate examples to higher education, and I realised that I don't have to worry about anything. There is so much happening all across India for alternate schoolers, even alternate higher education, and it's growing, there are even more such examples. Much more is coming up by the time my kids want to think about higher education. And even if they want to go to the mainstream, you can give your boards to NIOS [Indian National Institute of Open Schooling] and so on. If you want to go to mainstream there are a lot of universities now who are accepting kids without these qualifications, without certifications. When you want something, you find a way.

Relatedly, Mohit Trivedi expresses that

we have no idea about the future … What will the real world be when my kid is grown up and we can't control that distant future? But we can take care of what's happening now. So if they are happy now, if they are content now, then it's the right path. If this current mindset of modern education cannot give any certificate of constant happiness even though they literally steal the best time of childhood to prepare these kids for something they have no foresight for and if there is no certainty, then better to take care of what we can do now in this moment.

Looking at these accounts, we can grasp how unschooling follows a prefigurative politics or what Simon Springer similarly refers to as a *politics of being*: 'unlike other forms of learning, unschooling isn't about transcendence; it is about immanence. We're here because we're here, so let's have fun and enjoy ourselves. There is significant radical and transformative potential in embracing such a politics of being' (2016: 261).

This politics once more demonstrates how unschooling does not follow any 'divine truth' or an already laid out, organic path on the way to become 'fully human'. As unschooler parent Dola Dasgupta puts it,

there are certain kinds of people who can unschool, who take to unschooling much easier than others. And I think, for me, it was easier to take this as an exploratory journey, like this is an adventure we are exploring. I don't know the answers. I don't know where we are going with it.

(Dasgupta 2020)

This is also why for unschoolers there are no expectations or need to justify whatever it is they learn to any outsider in terms of its future usefulness or its past importance. Instead, learning as a continuous and often spontaneous process assumes an intrinsic value, freed from the pressure to permanently compete with other students, to excel in exams and get a degree, or to impress relatives, friends and society with their achievements. As such, Pashwa Jhala describes how she observes in her two children

> an absence (at least until now) of a movement to strive for or 'become' something. In the conventional world perhaps this could be seen as a short-coming in some way, as a lack of achievement or attaining excellence. However, for me, this has been refreshing and moving to witness. I sense that there is something in the conventional praise, approval and expecta-tion model that often leaves us feeling that we are falling short, or that we only deserve love and acceptance by *proving* ourselves worthy of it in some way. Constantly looking outward for approval or recognition is not only unsatisfying and stressful, but it also prevents us from listening to, and living from, our inner radars ... from living by that which truly inspires or resonates for us.
>
> (Jhala 2018; emphasis original)

This free environment of learning comes close to Ivan Illich's vision of a *deschooled society*, in which

> only actual participation constitutes socially valuable learning, a participa-tion by the learner in every stage of the learning process, including not only a free choice of what is to be learned and how it is to be learned but also a free determination by each learner of his own reason for living and learning – the part that his knowledge is to play in his life.
>
> (Illich 1973: 16)

Radical unschooling and the repartitioning of the sensible

Bhupender, an unlearner at Swaraj University (see Chapter 7), illustrates how he started to unschool and practise SDL as follows:

> when I was in school, I was interested in a lot of topics and a lot of subjects and I had a lot of questions. I realised that they don't fit in one subject any-where. All these questions, all these topics, they are interconnected. And I realised that I cannot pursue this path in a schooling system. So I left school and started learning on my own. I started with arts, with drawing and then slowly moved into other topics that interested me ... I started learning about the universe, and then from there I started reading about quantum mechan-ics and then I started to use all of this and what I learned into design, and then from design I went into the philosophy of science and from there I got interested in mathematics. And I was able to see the interconnections in all of these things. Now if I go into a formal system, I cannot say where I can get all of this. So the only option I had was to pursue it all on my own ... I used my own critical thinking to understand how the world is working ... By

doing this, I was simultaneously understanding how I learn and what are my patterns and what best suits me.

From this description, we can gain several more insights. The emphasis on inter-connectedness shows how unschooling and its practice of SDL enable learners to gain a holistic perspective on any given topic and indeed on the world by actively finding and drawing connections, and hence thinking in more relational terms than the OWW Education system and its compartmentalisation of knowledge would ever allow.

As we have seen through Bhupender's account of his activities, moving forth and back between painting, learning physics, doing design, studying mathematics and critically making sense of the world,

> play, work, and learning are fused together as inseparable components of the continuous unfolding of life, where children [and adults alike] can start to develop a global sense of consciousness by immediately recognizing them-selves as part of a bigger web.
>
> (Springer 2016: 259–260)

The above account also shows how, by giving decision-making power and auton-omy to the learner, radical unschooling opens the field of learning to topics, ideas and issues far beyond the limited and subjective ambit of OWW knowledge. Herein lies the chance to finally come up with some of the excessive questions and identify some of the excessive answers which are thus far eclipsed by the onto-logical blindfolds of the dualist OWW and its various practices. As Akomolafe and Jain (2016; emphasis original) put it, unschooling creates

> the space for a whole new set of generative questions to be explored with learners … *What do you want to learn or unlearn? What problems would you like to solve in your neighbourhood? What dreams do you have for your community? What is your idea of happiness? Who are you and how is your life and your community related to other living communities? What are the products you use every day, how are they made, where do they come from, how can you make them?*

Another aspect of unschooling we can identify above lies in the in-built process of refining and changing learning methods and approaches based on what works on the individual level and depending on what the learner wants to get out of their experience, instead of prescribing and imposing inflexible, top-down learning approaches based on a standardised idea of 'effective learning' to meet predefined 'learning outcomes'.

Related to this, unschooling encourages children and adults alike to experi-ment; to take detours rather than to follow the most forward-looking path to 'success' and only pursue what has been proven 'to work'; to fail and to make mistakes. As Avinash Almeida says: 'we celebrate failure as equal to success.

This was a big shock in the beginning. It's where I learned that failure is not the end of the world, but an opportunity to learn from your mistakes' (Almeida 2018).

Lastly, Bhupender's account also shows how SDL actively nurtures and encourages the use of the capacity we all already have to make sense of our surroundings and the wider world without being dependent on teachers, experts, parents or other authorities. This once more re-affirms the presupposition of equal intelligence and shows how unschooling as part of ANPED and its ontological politics of equality indeed contains a strong element of subjectification by its inherent 'ethos' of questioning things, challenging common-sense assumptions, creating dissensus in the OWW order and developing ideas of what makes meaningful lives that far exceed the limits of the OWW.

At its most basic level, the practice of unschooling then breaks open the inherent contradictions of a 'democratic' OWW society and its schooling system, making visible the irony 'that in a society that sees itself as democratic, it would be taken for granted that children should be raised under conditions of virtual dictatorship' (Hughes and Carrico 2008: 167).

Geraldine and Gus Lyn-Piluso further draw on the 'radical potential' of unschooled children to contribute to a repartitioning of the sensible. They argue that without the art of 'unseeing' or 'normalising' they are taught in school, 'kids don't know what not to question; as a result, their artless queries can cut deep, exposing authority's most damning contradictions' (Lyn-Piluso and Lyn-Piluso 2008: 83). This radical potential, however, is not only confined to unschooled children but to unschoolers at large, as we can see in the following account of unschooler parent Sumi-Chandresh who is unschooling with and alongside her two children:

> we believe that to live a meaningful life, one must be self-confident, imaginative and be able to do things practically and sensitively … The dominant ratrace model of Development forces people to adopt the toxic worldview that they can survive only by exploiting themselves or others. We do not want to participate in or take any benefits from this kind of System. It is our conscious decision to seek out ways to disengage ourselves from it and to create our own ways of being.
>
> (Sumi-Chandresh n.d.)

This once more conveys the sense 'that an anti-capitalist world view threads through the [Indian unschooling] community' (Chhibber 2018), leading to 'a cooperative exploration of power, society, and the natural world' (Lyn-Piluso and Lyn-Piluso 2008: 83).

In the same vein, Manish Jain points out how

> unlearning starts with looking at the realities and possibilities of life from other points of view. It is about becoming more conscious of the different assumptions, abstractions, stereotypes, expectations etc. that influence how we understand the world, how we create knowledge, how we relate to each

other, how we act and how we grow. It is about resisting, and creating spaces to breathe.

(Jain 2003: 1)

At its best, unschooling then helps its learners to cultivate a habit and ethos, and develop and apply concrete strategies, that enable them to challenge and rearrange the OWW's various partitions and micro-partitions of the sensible in the same way they already challenge and move beyond OWW Education as one particular partition of the sensible.

It is in this context that unschooling

> can be viewed as direct action of the family against the institutional structure of school and ... in its most overtly political and activist-oriented manifestation, could even be viewed as a form of institutional sabotage, another anarchic technique to use against compulsory schooling. The process begins politically as parents and students choose to defy the expectations of compulsory schooling and instead invent their alternative.

(Todd 2012: 75)

Radical unschooling and the lessons of OWW Education

Many unschooling parents who took part in the survey I conducted based a part of the decision-making process to unschool their children on their own mainstream schooling experiences. Importantly, this was usually seen as the basis for offering and discussing unschooling with their children, and being open to and trying out the possibility of unschooling, rather than already making the decision for and on behalf of their children. As one unschooling parent states,

> it was my children who decided to unschool and I followed. They all did attend school (oldest till he turned 12 years, second for 10 years and my daughter was turning four when she decided that she didn't want to go to school). I would say, it was more of my children's experiences at school and my experiences as a teacher that took me towards unschooling.

Meghna, an unschooler parent from Hyderabad, further emphasises how unschooling lets the child make their own decisions, and as such the child needs to have a choice of going or not going to school – 'it's not like we're saying you're never going to school. That's not unschooling' (personal interview, January 2019).

Other parents who took part in the survey often describe how they decided together with their children to unschool after they saw how OWW Education made their erstwhile curious children into passive, often sad and frustrated students with low levels of self-esteem and self-confidence.

These cases also show how unschooler parents indeed act out of the presupposition of equality and take their children's opinions, feelings, thoughts, considerations and decisions seriously. More than this, they take their children as equals. As one survey participant puts it,

> unschooling is letting your child explore his interests in his own time and pace, with guidance from the parent when asked for it, also considering the child as a whole person and treating him with the love and respect which you would give to any adult.

This is in stark contrast to the OWW where children are part of the part that has no part. Indeed, to see children as irrational, unreasonable, immature, ignorant and less intelligent is one of the main legitimisations for schools to exist in the OWW – these 'deficiencies' are made into a 'natural condition' of the child that schools are supposed to address and improve by 'educating' and 'schooling' children to become equal consumer-citizens of OWW society.[12] Instead, unschooling creates the space and freedom for children to emancipate themselves and become subjects of their own lives.

As the survey with 16 unschooling parents from across India has further shown, all of them have gone through the entire mainstream education process, ranging from a college graduate to 8 out of 16 parents who stated that they completed their post-graduation. While four parents stated that their own schooling did not play any role in the decision-making process to unschool their children and two parents said it played only a minor role, nine parents stated that their own experience played a significant part in being open to and considering the unschooling path for their children in the first place.

Importantly, the negative experiences and critique of the modern education system were mostly related to the anarchistic postdevelopmental stance against OWW Education, rather than expressed through the idea that schooling does not adequately prepare children for the job market or their future role in a global economy. These themes did not feature in any of the parents' answers in the survey, which shows that unschooling is not seen and pursued as another means to provide children a 'competitive advantage' in the OWW by helping them to better acquire the kind of creative and innovative skills increasingly sought after by various OWW Development actors.

Instead, many parents emphasised how schooling erodes self-awareness and self-confidence. One parent describes how 'an average/low performance at school did lower my confidence levels', while another shares how

> I was always unhappy with the school atmosphere. It was very stressful, and I waited for it to get over every day. I thought things would change in college, but it didn't … just stress and bullying and depression … I hardly learnt anything other than crushing my self-worth.

Another unschooling parent also drew on the ingrained presupposition of inequality as a key characteristic of modern education:

> I don't like the concept of comparison and competition in schools. With my schooling experience, it has become so ingrained in me that to this day I

compare myself with others and feel I am not good enough. Another thing is with all the schooling, with others always telling me what to think, do, like etc., I am still struggling to get an idea of who I really am, what my likes and dislikes are.

One parent also relates the schooling experience to a 'lack of independence of decision-making and judgement', while another describes how OWW Education is based on stress and a grade-based, competitive education system rather than on real knowledge. Yet another parent states how 'the whole [education] system is just a business'.

Accordingly, the goals of and motivation behind unschooling were described by parents in coherent terms and ideas, including 'being a good human being'; 'being happy'; acquiring 'healthy self-confidence'; developing skills for 'self-reflection' and 'self-realisation', and abilities for 'caring for each other', 'self-directed learning' and being 'responsible'. As one survey participant further expounds,

> when we started we decided to pick our key values. We thought that if our kid hits the spot on those, then we are doing fine. Each family can have their own values that suit them. Ours were 'kind', 'happy', 'curious', 'loving' and 'loved'. We use these as our guiding thoughts and if our kid is fine on these core things, we are happy.

This demonstrates how unschooler parents emphasise more abstract values and ideas that give autonomy and freedom to the child instead of imposing concrete ideas, goals and related predefined learnings. In this line, one parent also answers that 'it is the child's journey and not mine to define goals. I am just the caretaker', while another survey participant finds that

> the main requirement [for unschooling parents] is a willingness to be open, acknowledging that each child is unique, and they are here not to fulfil parent's unfulfilled wishes, but to pursue their own growth. It requires some consciousness to understand this.

The most important benefits and positive characteristics of unschooling were described in a likewise manner and included spending more meaningful, quality time together and improving relationships between children and parents; seeing the child flourish in a context based on freedom and autonomy; reconnecting with nature; children becoming more and more independent and in charge of their own lives; abilities and skills for self-reflection, critical thinking and clearly communicating/articulating needs, issues, thoughts and ideas; discovering new skills, talents and passions; and more meaningful learning that is taking place (as opposed to OWW Education).

On the latter, one parent, for example, states that 'the most impactful experience so far is that he [the child] gets to understand the world and society through real intersections and experiences rather than through books. In simple words, learning by doing and through concrete experiences'. Similarly, another survey participant shares that one of the biggest advantages of unschooling is to 'learn without any pressure, whatever she [the child] learns she could understand the purpose of it and she could learn whenever it is required at the right time and learn at her own pace'.

Another parent emphasises how unschooling enables the family to 'work together as a unit. Spending so much time together – and more importantly mean-ingful time. Traveling together, experiencing new skills together, having a daily routine that doesn't involve dancing to the "wake up, rush, eat, sleep, homework, classes" routine'. Likewise, another survey participant highlights how

> we get a lot of time with each other, understanding how we function, we have time to explore so many areas of interest to both of us, we are mostly unhurried and under no external pressures to perform, submit, prove. It is an enriching way of life, we have even got connected with nature and animals and plants, growing our own food, making recipes from scratch, upcycling projects, DIYs ['do-it-yourselves'], we have gone a lot away from consumer-ism and status symbols for the sake of it.

Creating learning webs

The radical unschooling alternative to OWW Education challenges the exclusive monopoly of schools and colleges to define and distribute 'education' and 'knowl-edge'. Building on Ivan Illich and his conceptualisation of modern education as 'learning under the assumption of scarcity', Manish Jain draws attention to how OWW Education leads to the pedagogicisation of society as

> knowledge becomes a commodity that can only be obtained through schools (or some organized institutional program) rather than a natural aspect of Being in the world. People are trained/forced to believe that learning and the growth of cognitive capacities, require a process of consumption of services presented in an industrial, a planned, a professional form. This debilitating dependence created by modern education helps pave the way to a life-long dependence on other service monopolies, such as hospitals, courts and police, to organize our lives.
>
> (Jain n.d.)

In contrast to this, unschooling has a much broader view of what constitutes worthwhile education and knowledge and how to pursue learning. Consequently, once we start to think that children as well as teenagers and adults are intelli-gent enough to pursue any sort of education or knowledge they are interested in by themselves, alongside and with each other, then there is simply no need any longer for the existence of formal schools:

> if the means for learning (in general) are abundant, rather than scarce, then education never arises – one does not need to make special arrangements for

'learning'. If, on the other hand, the means for learning are in scarce supply, or are assumed to be scarce, then educational arrangements crop up to 'ensure' that certain, important knowledge, ideas, skills, attitudes, etc., are 'transmitted'.

(Illich 2008: V)

What is important here is to state again that the calls for unschooling do not mean that the learners should be left to their own devices pure and simply. At the opposite, a deschooled society would be embedded in what Illich refers to as 'learning webs':

the child grows up in a world of things, surrounded by people who serve as models for skills and values. He finds peers who challenge him to argue, to compete, to cooperate, and to understand; and if the child is lucky, he is exposed to confrontation and criticism by an experienced elder who really cares. Things, models, peers, and elders are four resources each of which requires a different type of arrangement to ensure that everybody has ample access to it.

(Illich 1974: 76)

Unschooling spaces which can help to 'bundle' these four – and potentially many more – elements of the learning web are needed to ensure that everyone has free and equal access to them. This is particularly the case for more marginalised communities living in urban and semi-urban areas.

As Matt Hern consequently puts it,

we also need networks of learning centres, community projects, libraries, youth centres, parks, pools, gyms, playgrounds, and museums of every possible variety. We need those networks to be alive in every neighbourhood, and they have to be commonly held and democratically controlled by everyday people.

(Hern 2008: 115–116)

The need for learning webs was also expressed by two unschooling parents participating in the survey I conducted. One of them states that 'the biggest challenge we face is a lack of resources like parks, open spaces, and other places which help the child to play freely and explore', and another parent reflects how there is a lack of a support system for unschooling

from the government, the education system, society. If there were more public spaces – libraries, museums, theatres, parks for kids to be in. Education institutions that are open to sharing their resources like courts, labs, grounds for unschoolers to experiment with truly inclusive practices. Society – neighbours, family, society at large needs to rewrite the idea that the role of a child is just to be in school. The number of strangers whose first question when they see a child is 'which school?' is astonishing. Isn't a child more than his school? Notice this and you will be shocked how much the school thought has become insidiously entrenched in us in relation to children. Why should a child have to explain himself again and again to everyone? And why does no one ask what he is reading or whom he visited last or what is absorbing him now?

One of the most important tasks for radical unschooling families then is to build a thriving '(un-)learning community' that provides various learning experiences and opportunities the children and adults alike can tap into as well as to establish a network of like-minded people.

One survey participant accordingly highlights how the biggest challenge in unschooling includes 'a lack of meeting with peer groups on a regular basis'. Seven survey participants further said that the biggest challenge they are facing is how their choice to unschool with their children is not accepted by society, community and often not even by parts of their own family and relatives. As one parent puts it, 'outsiders and some family elders are saying that I spoil my daughter's life'.

The annual 'Learning Societies UnConference' (LSUC), organised by Shikshantar and alternating local hosts together with many volunteers, provides one of the best opportunities to network with other unschooling families and co-create sustainable learning webs, as well as to practice and celebrate unschooling together. Every year held at a different place across India, around 1000 unschoolers come together for 5 days and co-create what postanarchist Hakim Bey calls a temporary autonomous zone (TAZ), 'a deliberately short-lived (or else precarious) spatial zone in which peak experiences and altered consciousness are realised, in a context of "autonomy" or the absence of hierarchy' (McLaverty-Robinson 2018).

The LSUC does not follow any pre-planned schedule but evolves with its participants. Every day, participants (children, teenagers and adults alike) can offer to host or simply join an extremely broad variety of skill sessions, discussions, workshops and fun activities based on their own interests and ideas. At the 2019 LSUC held in Paralakhemundi, Odisha, the list of sessions and workshops included, for example,

Permaculture; natural buildings and eco-architecture; tribal dancing; 'the story of cyclone Titli in Odisha'; 'emotional literacy through mindfulness'; 'experiential learning and inclusion'; 'how to compost'; 'exploring Macramé'; 'the power of the menstrual cycle'; 'medicine from kitchen spices'; 'exploring the dream consciousness'; Yoga; Tai Chi; 'You Lead' talks to share one's life journeys; non-violent communication; 'unschooling our parents' (hosted by unschooler children for other unlearner children); 'listening café'; storytelling; 'connecting through food'; dot painting; tennis; basketball; ultimate frisbee; 'learning cartooning'; making herbal kajal; palm leaf craft; heritage walks; 'adapting to the world of artificial intelligence'; 'what is happening to indigenous communities in India?'; 'tribal stories of Odisha'; 'learn the basics of Russian ballet'; contact improvisation; poetry; 'exploring death' sharing circle; 'theatre of the oppressed 101', and much more.

Apart from the manifold workshops and sessions, the LSUC is full of games, sports, poetry, songs, music and dance and an overall mood of enchantment with the world and celebration of life.

Another key element of every LSUC is the experience and exercise of self-organisation and mutual aid across many different areas such as cooking and distributing food; cleaning the dishes and managing the supply of clean water; maintaining one's own space as well as all public space; taking care of each other's needs; using resources in sustainable ways; creating a safe environment for women and children; settling differences and disputes in non-violent ways; following the motto of 'leaving a place more beautiful than it was before'; and – overall – experiencing what it means to live together in a large, joint community. As such, the LSUC indeed prefigures elements of a deschooled, (un-)learning society in the here and now.

Community-building and community-living then plays an important role for unschoolers. It is indeed one of the key ingredients to prevent unschooling from becoming a kind of self-interested, individualistic, secluded and elitist learning approach. As Manish Jain says,

> where we need to invest our energy and time, my argument is it's not in try-ing to fix schools but actually building communities where kids can wander around, they can find people to mentor them, they can find people who are passionate about life, they can have space to do experiments.
>
> (quoted in Hopkins 2018)

Most survey participants accordingly said that it is very important for unschoolers to be part of a larger community. As one parent for example suggests,

> if lots of families come together for unschooling then it can create a commu-nity kind of model where lots of work and time can be shared … I strongly believe unschooling takes lots of effort and needs lots of people from various backgrounds. If more people join then it becomes easier. I also understand it might create completely new issues and challenges, but the benefit should easily surpass in my opinion. An African proverb says 'it takes a whole vil-lage to raise a child'.

However, as long as these community structures only exist temporarily or to a very limited degree, radical unschooling among families is as of now – particu-larly in the urban and semi-urban areas – rather confined to the middle classes, as it is often easier for them to individually afford and get access to the learning web due to their social, cultural and financial capital.

Most of the unschooling families I met had one parent who could afford to stay at home with the children. Those families travel frequently, visit places of interest near and far from home, borrow or buy any required resources and tap into the networks of their relatives, friends, colleagues, acquaintances and other unschooling families (often with similar socio-economic backgrounds) to facilitate learning opportunities.

Importantly however, radical unschooling among families is only one possible way of doing unschooling and does not mean that it is reserved for the middle classes only. As Vidhi Jain, co-founder of Shikshantar, argues,

> the Homeschooling/Unschooling approach is not limited to a particular set of people. It can be flexibly adapted by anyone according to their specific context and needs. It is a highly customized approach. We actually believe that the village is a much better learning environment (with more nature and sense of community) and many children there are already doing a lot to design their own learning. It is more a matter of appreciating and re-valuing the real wealth and knowledge that resides in the village.
>
> (quoted in Purohit 2016)

While it is a challenge to extend the possibilities of radical unschooling particularly to less privileged families in urban and semi-urban areas, the fact that as of now it is mostly middle-class families who pursue it is not necessarily a drawback only. After all, both the people who form a part of the OWW in whatever subservient roles and identities (such as middle-class families), as well as the people with a history rooted in more egalitarian, post-dualist lifeworlds that are increasingly marginalised by the expansion of OWW Development need to (re-)gain and (re-)discover their own, equal capacities to create meaningful lives alongside others for significant change to take place. We can indeed say that both, although in different forms, roles and intensities, are marginalised by the OWW Development model which only benefits the infamous 1 per cent.

An essential first step in challenging the OWW then can be that the ones who have previously accepted their identities and roles in the OWW and formed an integral part of upholding its hierarchical order stop doing so. By renouncing their pre-assigned roles in the OWW, they delegitimise the presupposition of inequality which holds together the OWW and leads to its relentless recreation, intensification and expansion.

Historically, it is indeed the middle classes which have been mostly entrenched in the OWW ideology and urgently need, indeed, unschooling. It is not 'the poor' or the most marginalised who follow the most damaging consumerist lifestyle and waste most resources; it is not 'the poor' and the most marginalised who harm the environment the most (even if the SDGs try to make us believe otherwise); it is not 'the poor' and the most marginalised who usually have an interest in perpetuating the status quo; and it is not 'the poor' and the most marginalised who look down on almost anything except intellectual labour.

Hence, radical unschooling among families is an important step to challenge the OWW Development model and helps the ones who are a part of the OWW to act in solidarity with and alongside the ones who have no part and are already pursuing the ontological politics of equality in various forms and guises. Here,

I rather see this as a positive development in which unschooling will play an important role in the increased acceptance, recognition, visibility, support for and strengthening of other knowledges, practices, ways of life and lifeworlds closer to or already part of the pluriverse.

As we have seen then, unschooling is not only a different approach to education but entails the shift towards creating new paths towards the pluriverse. However, even getting on these paths often requires – at least initially – a huge investment in time, often as well as money, and a willingness to take considerable risks, given the experimental nature of unschooling.

One survey participant, for example, states that in order to be able to pursue radical unschooling, it 'requires a lot of inner work and complete financial independence'. Chhibber (2018) accordingly observes how unschooling 'does demand alertness to the child's interests, and the financial ability to supplement these interests. And since for millions, a formal degree is still a necessary entry point into stable careers, unschooling remains a safer bet for the elite'.

A considerable part of families with marginalised socio-economic backgrounds – the ones which are already completely dependent on the OWW-based economy – often struggle for survival on a day-to-day basis and simply cannot afford – without any support – for their children as well as for themselves to go on an unschooling journey full of risks and with an uncertain outcome. For a large, non-negligible part of OWW society, the existential, material grip that OWW Development holds on them is often so strong that it is difficult to start escaping from it, even when they are aware that it is mainly due to our voluntary servitude to the status quo.

Put differently, the more entrenched in and dependent on the OWW we already are, and the lower the position we have been assigned and resigned to within the OWW, the more difficult it is to start renouncing our pre-given OWW identities – not out of some false consciousness, but out of material realities. What is needed therefore is the widespread set-up of unlearning spaces which offer support, encouragement and access to the learning web across many more communities, particularly across marginalised, urban and semi-urban low-income communities that are completely enmeshed in and dependent on OWW Development and its exploitative economic model.

Summation

Radical unschooling among families is another example of ANPED in practice. In verifying the equal intelligence of their children, parents become ignorant schoolmasters as well as co-learners together with their children. Following the principle of self-designed learning as a key element of unschooling then leads to the transcendence of existing hierarchies of knowledge and the prioritisation of different knowledge(s) relevant to the learner's lives.

In turn, the pursuit of other knowledge(s), which does not merely reinforce ways of becoming good or virtuous consumer-citizens, nurtures and incites the radical imagination of families. This leads to ideas of what makes meaningful lives that far exceed the OWW's ontological limits. In this sense, 'if we strip everything away and boil unschooling down to its pedagogic core, it is really nothing more than another term for "life"' (Springer 2016: 260).

At the heart of unschooling then lies the idea that knowledge is not scarce and education not a commodity. Instead, there exists an abundance of knowledge, skills and learning resources that we can tap into:

> homes, offices, parks, farmers' markets, cafés, street corners and sidewalks, old age homes, dumpsites, urban farms, and festivals become enlivened, animated and charged dimensions of our learning landscapes – instead of blank frames that propagate a disenchanting anonymity. Learning is being recast as spontaneous, dispersed, wild, unstable, promiscuous, emergent, decentralized, distributed and most importantly, embedded as the concrete walls of schooling are dismantled brick by brick.
>
> (Akomolafe and Jain 2016)

Therefore, unschooling recognises the knowledge systems and relationships that formal education has made invisible. Many learning sources, indeed, are available locally and freely – and we can see and understand these more by using appreciative approaches such as unschooling rather than the deficit perspectives that permeate OWW Development and Education.

Moreover, as with ANPED in general, the importance of radical unschooling, in particular, lies not first and foremost in what is being learned and how it is being learned, but in the practice of the ontological politics of equality which rearranges social relations within the family, the community and – ultimately – society at large. Unschooling's 'politics of being' does not – as we have seen – move towards a preordained path but aims to create fulfilling relations and meaningful lives in the here and now.

In building their intergenerational, and often also transgenerational, learning webs which overcome various separations of age, gender or socio-economic backgrounds as well as many of the hierarchical separations between humans and nature, as well as in pursuing concrete practices such as learning with and taking care of their grandparents, farming and planting trees, singing and dancing, caring for animals, listening to others and so many more things, unschoolers are involved in *building and re-creating healthy local communities in the here and now*.

This is in line with anarchist philosophy on education, whose emphasis is not first and foremost on bringing about

> a pre-conceived alternative model of social organisation, but on laying the ground for the natural evolution of such a model by means of fostering the attitudes that underpin it, alongside the experiment of creating a microcosm of alternative modes of social interaction without the state.
>
> (Suissa 2004: 15)

However, for many who do not enjoy the typical privileges of the Indian middle class, it is important to have access to spaces and platforms – such as the

Creativity Adda we have explored in the previous chapter – which help to bundle the various elements that constitute the unschooling learning web. Therefore, radical unschooling among families is one particular form of ANPED that might not be suitable and indeed accessible yet for everyone.

The next chapter then lays out another model of ANPED in the form of self-designed learning spaces called 'Nooks', which provide marginalised communities across India with access to the learning web.

Notes

1 As Jain and Jain (n.d.) state, 'thinking as a jugaadi' 'implies resourcefulness, creativity, starting with what materials, contexts, etc. exist (especially with so-called waste) and finding solutions from there'.
2 This quote and all other quotes without further in-text reference, and which are not attributed to the survey among unschooling parents featured in this chapter, are taken from various discussions and conversations at the 'reimagination education' workshop held at Swaraj University in May 2018.
3 This, importantly, also distinguishes unschooling from homeschooling. The latter still follows a given curriculum and usually subjects children to external exams and certifications. In the end, homeschooling merely exchanges the authority figure of the school teacher with the authority figure of the parent teacher.
4 Both terms are common in the Indian unschooling movement and I will use them interchangeably.
5 For example through playing, observing, reading, watching online videos and accessing other online content, conversations with family members, community members or others, getting exposure through meeting people or visiting sites related to the matter of interest, doing an internship or apprenticeship, conducting experiments, etc. It is also important to stress that self-designed learning does not mean that unschoolers wholesale reject the idea of attending classes and courses and of 'being taught'. This can also, *by choice*, be part of the various learning approaches of unschoolers, however it is clearly not the primary or preferred means of learning.
6 Rancière also draws on this notion in order to substantiate his principle of equality, arguing that 'what all human children learn best is what no master can explain: the mother tongue. We speak to them and we speak around them. They hear and retain, imitate and repeat, make mistakes and correct themselves, succeed by chance and begin again methodically, and, at too young an age for explicators to begin instructing them, they are almost all – regardless of gender, social condition, and skin color – able to understand and speak the language of their parents' (Rancière 1991: 5).
7 The term 'radical unschooling' is used by Sharmila Govande to draw attention to the fact that there are different styles of and approaches towards unschooling with different, varying levels of 'intervention' by the parents or any other person in the role of the ignorant schoolmaster. Based on my conversations with and observations among the unschoolers' movement and my work with Shikshantar, I identified 'radical unschooling' as the most widely applied 'approach' towards unschooling.
8 Situated in the tribal area of Southern Rajasthan, Mukt Dhara Multiversity 'is a semi structured learning space in the midst of conventional colleges, it is curated to explore, understand and internalize the radical and holistic approach on education and health care' (Mukt Dhara Multiversity n.d.).
9 In this we can once more see the close affinity with Rancière's idea of emancipation: 'for Rancière significant studying and learning take place as self-learning and collaborative learning organically in the natural environments, without outside authorities' (Suoranta 2008: 9).

10 Based on my own participation in the Shikshantar Unschooler Winter Camp which I visited over two weeks in December 2017, I found it indeed remarkable how children of all ages would relate to me as an equal rather than as a 'senior' or 'person of authority' and would include me in their projects, games, conversations and the daily life at the camp without any reservations. Indeed, I felt that it was me, as a schooled person, who needed to stop seeing myself as unequal (i.e. superior and different) to them.
11 The Indian Multiversities Alliance is an initiative of around 50 organisations across India engaged in various alternatives to higher education.
12 As Gibson ([1951] 1966: 437–438; emphasis original) relatedly puts it, 'adults tend to think of children as beings of their own species with mental and physical powers in a merely *immature* state. The process of "bringing them up" is therefore interpreted as conditioning them to accept adult social values so that they will become adult beings well fitted to play their part in society'.

References

Akomolafe, B., and Jain, M. (2016). 'Name the colour, blind the eye: Reimagining education'. https://bayoakomolafe.net/project/name-the-colour-blind-the-eye-reimagining-education/.
Almeida, A. (2018). 'Swaraj made with clipchamp 1'. https://www.youtube.com/watch?v=jnccJu5EAdw&feature=share.
Bhave, V. (2008). 'The intimate and the ultimate'. In Hern, M. (ed.), *Everywhere All the Time: A New Deschooling Reader*. Oakland: AK Press, pp. 7–12.
Chhibber, V. (2018). 'Meet the unschoolers'. https://www.livemint.com/Leisure/UkN5wLDOLHMDqW0jCiQreP/Meet-the-unschoolers.html?fbclid=IwAR2ZiVV0ZiGIYRLsTIZrW9sQo06guRcGx1I8R80w1R1Ldnw4XFV5vYmgf8w.
Dasgupta, D. (n.d.). 'Facilitating reading, writing and math in unschooling'. http://shikshantar.org/innovations-shiksha/families-learning-together-unschooling/facilitating-reading-writing-and-math.
Dasgupta, D. (2020). 'EU215 Transcript: Unschooling stories with Dola Dasgupta'. https://livingjoyfully.ca/eu215-transcript/.
Desmarais, I. (2019). 'Yes, there ARE things every kid should know: Social justice and self-direction'. https://yes-i-can-write.blogspot.com/2019/08/yes-there-are-things-every-kid-should.html.
Gibson, T. [1951] (1966). 'Youth for freedom'. In Krimerman, L.I., and Perry, L. (eds.), *Patterns of Anarchy: A Collection of Writings on the Anarchist Tradition*. New York: Doubleday, pp. 436–444.
Hern, M. (2008). 'Getting busy'. In Hern, M. (ed.), *Everywhere All the Time: A New Deschooling Reader*. Oakland: AK Press, pp. 115–119.
Holt, J. (2008). 'Instead of education'. In Hern, M. (ed.), *Everywhere All the Time: A New Deschooling Reader*. Oakland: AK Press, pp. 17–20.
Hopkins, R. (2018). 'Manish Jain: "Our work is to recover wisdom and imagination"'. https://www.robhopkins.net/2018/01/31/manish-jain-our-work-is-to-recover-wisdom-and-imagination/.
Hughes, M., and Carrico, J. (2008). 'Windsor house'. In Hern, M. (ed.), *Everywhere All the Time: A New Deschooling Reader*. Oakland: AK Press, pp. 165–170.
Illich, I. (1973). 'After deschooling, what'? In Gartner, A., Greer, C., and F. Riessman (eds.), *After Deschooling, What?* London: Harper & Row, pp. 1–28.
Illich, I. (1974). *Deschooling Society*. London: Marion Boyars.

Illich, I. (2008). 'Foreword'. In Hern, M. (ed.), *Everywhere All the Time: A New Deschooling Reader*. Oakland: AK Press, pp. iii–v.

Jain, M. (n.d.). 'Reclaiming real Shiksha in our lives'. http://shikshantar.org/articles/rec laimming-real-shiksha-our-lives.

Jain, M. (2003). 'An invitation to the reader'. In Jain, M. (ed.), *Paths of Unlearning*. Udaipur: Shikshantar, pp. 1–3.

Jain, M., and Jain, S. (n.d.). 'Towards an organic learning community'. http://www.shik shantar.org/articles/towards-organic-learning-community.

Jain, V. (2016). 'Co-learning with Kanku'. https://medium.com/families-learning-together -magazine/co-learning-with-kanku-636e58966fda.

Jhala, P. (2018). 'Reflections on a nomadic unschooling life'. https://medium.com/famili es-learning-together-magazine/reflections-on-anomadic-unschooling-life-e32200208 d64.

Lyn-Piluso, G., and Lyn-Piluso, G. (2008). 'Challenging the popular wisdom: What can families do'? In Hern, M. (ed.), *Everywhere All the Time: A New Deschooling Reader*. Oakland: AK Press, pp. 82–90.

McLaverty-Robinson, A. (2018). 'Hakim Bey: The temporary autonomous zone'. https:// ceasefiremagazine.co.uk/hakim-bey-temporary-autonomous-zone/.

Mukt Dhara Multiversity. (n.d.). 'Home'. https://muktdharamultiversity.wordpress.com.

Purohit, T. (2016). 'Social innovators of Udaipur: Interview with Vidhi Jain'. http://vik alpsangam.org/article/social-innovators-of-udaipur-interview-with-vidhi-jain/.

Rancière, J. (1991). *The Ignorant Schoolmaster. Five Lessons in Intellectual Emancipation*. Stanford: Stanford University Press.

Sonderegger, R. (2014). 'Do we need to emancipate ourselves'? *Krisis*, 1, pp. 53–67.

Springer, S. (2016). 'Learning through the soles of our feet: Unschooling, anarchism, and the geography of childhood'. In Springer, S., Lopes de Souza, M., and R. J. White (eds.), *The Radicalization of Pedagogy: Anarchism, Geography, and the Spirit of Revolt*. London: Rowman & Littlefield, pp. 247–265.

Suissa, J. (2004). 'Vocational education: A social anarchist perspective'. *Policy Futures in Education*, 2 (1), pp. 14–30.

Sumi-Chandresh. (n.d.). 'Growing with Kudrat'. http://shikshantar.org/innovations-shiks ha/families-learning-together-unschooling/growing-kudrat.

Suoranta, J. (2008). 'Jacques Rancière on radical equality and adult education'. https://su oranta.files.wordpress.com/2008/05/suoranta_malta081.pdf.

Todd, J. (2012). 'From deschooling to unschooling: Rethinking anarchopedagogy after Ivan Illich'. In Haworth, R. H. (ed.), *Anarchist Pedagogies: Collective Actions, Theories, and Critical Reflections on Education*. Oakland, CA: PM Press, pp. 69–87.

6 ANPED in practice
Unschooling in marginalised communities

As we have seen in the previous two chapters, ANPED as unschooling comes in many different forms and guises. While the Creativity Adda is a semi-structured unschooling space which provides school-going children from marginalised communities with access to the learning web through the set-up of specific hubs and the involvement of dedicated facilitators, radical unschooling among families is an approach in which whole families learn together and create their own learning webs.

This chapter introduces yet another variant of unschooling in the form of self-designed learning spaces or 'Nooks' which cater to marginalised communities. Set up by Bangalore-based NGO Project DEFY ('Design Education For Yourself'), the Nook model of unschooling aims to follow a largely organic approach with as little facilitation and as much freedom and autonomy for the learners as possible. This, however, also brings with it its own challenges and makes the process of subjectification potentially more arduous and uncertain.[1]

The Nook model of unschooling

Project DEFY and its Nook model began as an experiment in 2014. When its founder Abhijit Sinha, an engineering college graduate disillusioned with the mainstream education system, moved to Banjarapalya – a small village on the outskirts of Bangalore – he started to interact with a handful of children who were keen to use his laptop. Finally giving in to their pleas, Sinha observed how the children would – without any instructions whatsoever and despite none of them speaking English, which was the default language set on the computer – learn to operate the laptop in no time, start playing and excelling in games and show each other how to use the laptop.

Encouraged by what he observed, Sinha decided to take his accidental experiment a step further by renting out a small room equipped with a few Wi-Fi-connected laptops, hand tools and recycled waste materials. More and more children, teenagers and adults from the community came to the space to see what it was all about. Instead of telling and teaching them what to do, or asking others to become teachers, Sinha simply let the community members decide for themselves what they would want to do with the space and resources he provided. As he narrates,

> In Banjarapalya, we saw what people do when you just leave them to their own devices. When resources are provided, and space is provided, they are able to build a routine around this space, which means there's time. And people were able to use the time, the space and the resources to create learning in the way they wanted. And once we saw that this can happen even without our presence, we felt okay, then communities can have their own learning spaces that we don't even have to run. That are probably not influenced by us, maybe in the beginning, but we are not managing them and telling people what to do. And that for me was a drastic philosophical difference from how systems are created usually. We created the first space in the village and we went to another village, created it there, we went to a refugee camp in Uganda and created it there. And everywhere the space looked very different.
>
> (personal interview, July 2018)[2]

Since then, Project DEFY – which formally started as an NGO in 2016 – has set up nine Nooks across India as well as one in Rwanda and is set to expand to Bangladesh, Zimbabwe and Uganda in the near future. The currently seven operational Nooks in India are situated in and around Bangalore (Whitefield, JP Nagar, Kaggalipura), Fort Kochi, Delhi, Proto Village (a self-sustaining, intentional community in Andhra Pradesh) and Kherat Jattan (Punjab). All of them cater mostly to marginalised communities, including those with religious minorities, socio-economically disadvantaged groups and people from lower caste backgrounds.

While Nooks are open to everyone from the local community they are situated in and strongly encourage intergenerational learning, there often is a focus on girls, women and youth aged 15–25. This is because girls and women in marginalised communities have even less access to any kind of education, and in conservative societies they are strongly expected to conform to stereotypical gender roles. Many women in the communities that Project DEFY works in are indeed often confined to the domestic household and their role of caretakers for the family, without any other possibility to explore and pursue their own aspirations.

Male and female youth coming to the Nooks are often either attending public schools that do not cater to their needs and interests or have dropped out of school either because they failed, chose to leave or were forced to leave due to the need to contribute to the family's income. Others might also have completed high school or college but did not find any employment opportunities or have not figured out yet what they want to do in life.

For all of them, the Nook – with its flexible structure and no specified timing of attendance beyond the induction programme (see below), its free-of-cost nature and its strategic location usually in the centre of the community – provides an opportunity to pursue learning projects relevant to their own lives.

Initially, Nooks have been conceptualised more as maker-spaces with an emphasis on building and creating things, which is also related to Abhijt Sinha's own engineering background and how he set up the first Nook in Banjarapalya. Every Nook still comes with this basic set up, which often serves as an entry point to help facilitate the shift from 'being taught' under the presupposition of inequality to self-designed learning under the presupposition of equality. As such, making and building things is seen by the Project DEFY team as a way both to attract people to come to the Nook in the first place, as well as an effective and powerful way to verify the Nook learners' equality. As Megha Bhagat, Project DEFY's Chief Growth Officer, describes it,

> in most of the Nooks you see the initial projects that are there, they are those ice-cream stick houses, or very simple boards. At the face of it, you see that there are so many ice-cream stick houses, and so it looks like they just pick up the simplest thing. But what we learned is that, just finishing a task, just being able to finish from start to end with your imagination, with your curiosity, is a sense of accomplishment that is unparalleled. You don't have a test, you don't have an exam to come and assess you, but just the fact that I started building a house today and I can create it by end of the week is such a huge sense of accomplishment, especially for these communities. It kind of changes the way they are thinking about themselves. So there is a sudden shift from 'because I'm poor I can't do certain things' to 'I'm capable of completing this as long as I can ask people and I have access to information'. This shift determines a lot about how they start processing education, how they start perceiving themselves, how they start perceiving their role in the families, because suddenly they accomplished something. And that accomplishment is enough.
>
> (personal interview, July 2018)[3]

As Abhijit Sinha further adds,

> creation is interesting because it gets you very quickly to dirty your hands. I feel it's a good progression to start with using your hands and then start to use your brain to think about things that you not usually do.

Building on the insights gained from the first unschooling experiments in Banjarapalya, all current Nooks are equipped with Wi-Fi-connected laptops, a broad variety of tools, recycled waste materials, various electronics and different arts and handicraft materials. Additionally, every Nook features its own specific equipment catered to the individual needs and interests of the local community by providing the Nook learners with a monthly resource budget they can use at their own discretion after coming to a consensual decision among each other. As Megha Bhagat says,

> one of the bigger things that happens is that every Nook monthly decides what it wants to bring in to the Nook as resources. All the members decide together. And here we've also seen shifts. We've seen if there are few

particular members who want to kind of bring in a certain resource because that's what they want to learn. And we've seen that the community has rallied and says 'hey you know what, lets save up the budget for two months and then we can buy this and bring it to the Nook'.

This further reflects the learner-led nature of unschooling in all of its forms. As with the Creativity Adda, the Nook model aims to encourage learners not only to be a part of the space but indeed to own the space. This becomes visible in many aspects, for example when learners decide how the monthly budget is spent, co-create their own rules and regulations for the Nook space, organise events and workshops and – ultimately – design their own learning.

At the heart of Project DEFY's philosophy then lies the notion of giving power back into the hands of learners by creating learning spaces that minimise hierarchies as far as possible and therefore also prefigure a much less hierarchical state of larger society. As Megha Bhagat accordingly says,

> Project DEFY is inspired by the idea of how the world would look different and how would systems change if you give power back to the people. So eventually for me, Project DEFY has come to represent what does it mean to take away hierarchies. How does access change, how does society look different if you take away control. And for me, when I look at control systems, I look at them from a very systemic perspective. Why is a person who is born into a certain family expected to continue in the same role? Why is it that a driver's son aspires only to be a driver? Or a girl whose mother is a cleaner, and a father is just doing some menial job, why is it that she aspires to just get into that. So for me it's a very capitalist way of controlling societies. Because there has to be a system that keeps them at that level, because only then can they feed into the upper class service model. And for me, DEFY just became a channel to change that.

Bhagat's description highlights how Project DEFY and its Nook model rejects OWW Education's socialisation function which keeps people in their pre-assigned roles and identities and therefore serves as a key practice to recreate and expand the OWW Development model. As Abhijit Sinha further points out,

> the Development ideology is, 'I am the intelligent person, I can help others. I don't even expect something in return. I do something from the goodness of my heart'. Actually, it is a lot of ego. You think you can change the lives of others without them affecting you. Without opening yourself to learning from them. So this 'I vs them' is the core difference here. We do not have that. We do not attempt to create micro-entrepreneurs, we do not attempt to empower people, we do not attempt to do shit. We want to see what they want to do … *That is why the Development sector and the Education system are very similar, right? One person has to teach and change the lives of others.* How egoistic is that? Are we thinking that they can't do it for themselves?

Do we believe that we are such messiahs that we can change it for them, and their lives will be better because of us? *The problem is not that they [ordinary people] can't think for themselves. The problem is that they don't have the possibility for it. All you have to do is help them have the possibility, and then you shut up and watch. That's the only role you can truly play.* All other empowerment stories are based on you imprinting what you want to do onto others. What you think is right. Eventually, all this fails. People have been trying this for decades.

(emphasis added)

Here we can clearly see how Sinha, in his own words, goes against the presupposition of inequality which lies at the heart of OWW Development and Education. Instead, Nooks are envisioned as ANPED spaces in which learners can apply their equal intelligence to something that matters to them.

(Un-)learning in the Nook

To co-create such spaces together with learners and verify their equality, Project DEFY has developed a common structure across all Nooks which consists of a 45-day-long, recurring *induction programme* for new learners and a recurring, three-month-long *goal cycle* system in which learners – individually or in groups – pursue their own projects based on their specific needs, interests and aspirations.

Instead of immediately asking learners to start working on their own projects when they come to the Nook, the induction programme – facilitated by Project DEFY staff – introduces learners to a variety of different, hands-on projects such as web development, 3D modelling, carpentry, metal works, music, painting, poetry, urban gardening, tailoring and robotics, as well as other fields based on the learners' interests. The specific areas explored vary from Nook to Nook and focus particularly on skills which the 25–35 new learners who are part of the respective induction programme batch – commencing every three months – have not experienced thus far and, looking at their background, often would not be expected to do.[4]

As Boicha Huidrom, a 'hopper' at Project DEFY who helps to set up new Nooks and facilitates the induction programme, says,

> when a learner comes to the Nook for the first time, they often already have some preconceived ideas of what kind of projects they want to do. But often they are not able to give a reason why they want to do this, how they are going to do it, and what they really want to do. In some way, we are all influenced by what we already know, what we have experienced in life, so this at times conditions us to stick only with what we know and what we think we can do, instead of exploring and trying out new things. At the Nook, we help the learners to unlearn the preconceived notions that society has taught them. We want learners to try out new things and explore what they don't know and

thereby find out what they really like and what they are actually capable of, which is far more than what they usually think.

(personal interview, August 2020)

Here we can see the importance of 'de-conditioning' the learners of societal norms and expectations, be it in relation to stereotypical gender roles or class- and caste-based assumptions which seek to pre-determine their roles and identities within the OWW. By providing learners from marginalised backgrounds – i.e. those who are thought of as less equal than others – with a strong experience of what they can possibly do and are capable of – and often across fields and areas they would usually not explore or would not be expected to engage in – the Nook model thus helps to verify their equality.

In this process, deep-seated gender stereotypes are also being challenged. As Abhijit Sinha shares his experience from one of the Nooks he helped to set up,

> the guys realised that the girls are building some skills that they don't have. So for some projects they were doing, they needed help from the girls. And they actually started collaborating with them. And they started realising that they are useful people. Women are useful too. That was a big realisation for them. Once that happened, we could actually see, maybe still not in the overall community, but among those kids, a new respect for the other gender. The girls also became confident to deal with guys and to not just give in to whatever these guys ask for.

As Sinha further says, one conscious strategy applied by Project DEFY is to target the most marginalised members of a community – such as, often, girls and women – first, before inviting others to join the Nook:

> we start with people who are most marginalised. Because that way we are able to break that sort of hierarchy that if you now come to the space, you are working in a space that is already being used by people who are most marginalised. That means you have to ask them, you have to take their help, it reduces that barrier.

Another important aspect of the induction programme is the facilitation of skill workshops, games, collaborative exercises and discussions to build the new learners' capacity for SDL and to help them make the shift from 'being taught' to 'learning alongside others'.

This includes the exploration of a variety of potential learning sources, from the skills and knowledge the Nook learners already have and are able to share with others and what is available in the broader, local community to the usage of various tools and technology; to familiarise learners – many of whom have access to a laptop for the first time in the Nook – with the basics of computers and the internet, and to let them explore how the internet can be utilised to find information and inspiration for their own learning goals; an introduction to useful online learning sources such as Udemy, Alison, Coursera, Skillshare, Khan Academy, Instructables and Arvind Gupta Toys; the set-up of individual email accounts (which learners often need to access free online courses and programmes); learning the basics of the English language (as online learning content and information is often in English); and an introduction to various software programmes and tools.

Here we can see that technology in general and the World Wide (learning) Web in particular play an important role in the Nooks. Abhijit Sinha accordingly emphasises how

> the internet gives you a line of sight beyond what you can see in your community. You can see far more. That is the reason to have internet. If you would have the same impact with a library that'd be great, but it doesn't seem to be … Technology has its place, it is part of society. The problem comes with technology when you start believing that it is god. It is what you work for, not the other way around. Technology must work for you, not that you create technologies just for the sake of it. So if these are resources that are available to people who have privilege, why should they not be available to people who don't. It may have good effects, it may have bad effects, but the fact that the very choice doesn't exist, isn't it very discriminating?

However, technology does not act as a silver bullet which simply replaces the 'all-knowing teacher' with the 'all-knowing internet'. As Megha Bhagat states,

> the concept has been that can we make technology not the ultimate tool, but can we get technology to facilitate life changes … We wanted to shift the model from should we give every person in the village or every person in the community a tablet or laptop or computer. What is the end narrative or the end game of that? What is going to be the impact out of me providing one tablet into every hand? Will that mean change in the person's outlook, will that ever mean change in how she or he is moving up the life cycle? These programmes have been implemented, the whole 'one child, one tablet'. So-called 'smart classes' have happened … One thing that they have not been able to prove is, what is the life cycle change?

The Nook model of unschooling therefore utilises technology in the context of what Murray Bookchin has termed a 'libertarian technics', and what Ivan Illich refers to as 'convivial tools'. As Illich (1973: 84–85) argues, 'there are two ranges in the growth of tools: the range within which machines are used to extend human capability and the range in which they are used to contract, eliminate, or replace human functions'. Convivial tools and innovation, therefore, 'will have to be efficacious in fostering people's creative autonomy, social equity, and well-being, including collective control over energy and work. This means that tools need to be subjected to a political process of a new kind' (Escobar 2018: 9).

In the case of Project DEFY, this political process is centred on the idea and importance of community-building and community-living that help to harness technology in particular ways based on values of cooperation, sharing, caring and mutual aid. Abhijit Sinha accordingly says that

> if computer and internet is enough, we would just install it in their homes. We need the people to come together in a place. That's what is more important. You can replace computers with other things … I feel the most important component of the [Nook] space are the people, not the computers, not even the tools. They are all replaceable. Look at how we function now in this country. We have lost most of our community spaces. The temples of today are shopping malls, they are not community spaces … We have no communities. We don't know our neighbours either. People who come here, they didn't know the person who's staying next door. Now they meet here in the space … The point is, learning from them and helping them learn … Everybody has something to teach, and everybody has something to learn. All we need to do is to get them in the same place. With a very clear idea that they are there to learn for themselves and to help others. That is how you build a community.

Consequently, rather than focusing on specific resources, materials, technology or learning content, it is, above all, the idea of creating a community of learners who can verify each other's equality which is at the heart of the Nook concept. One Nook learner accordingly highlights how for him one of the best aspects of the Nook is that he

> made so many friends here. We are helping each other, learning together, fighting together [laughs], anything. I enjoy it so much … Here are so many people, my friends are helping me and they encourage me and tell me how to improve.
>
> (personal interview, July 2018)

This also shows how unschooling platforms, due to the very nature of how learning happens, often develop into inclusive and safe spaces that bring people together. More than just being learning spaces, Nooks indeed aspire to become community meeting places that help people to better get to know each other, solve any problems together and improve life in the community without waiting for the intervention of outside 'experts'.

By encouraging learners to cooperate, better understand and support each other and work together in common projects instead of competing against each other, Nooks are able to bring people together who usually would not bother to or indeed avoid interacting with each other. One example of this is the Khera Jattan community in Punjab, where the Nook has become the only place for members of two warring factions that divide the entire village to come together and cooperate with each other. As Abhijit Sinha says, while violence has not vanished, it has reduced drastically since the start of the Nook.

Another example is Avalahalli village in Bangalore's JP Nagar, which is largely divided between a Muslim and Hindu area. While initially almost exclusively people from the Muslim part of Avalahalli, which is also where the Nook is located, came to the space and Hindus at times openly resented coming to the space because of its very location, this is also slowly changing. Especially young people from Hindu families increasingly started to come to the Nook and work together in projects with learners from Muslim families. In times of the rise of what we have termed virtuous neoliberalism, the creation of unschooling spaces as both learning and community-building platforms, therefore, is more important than ever.

The importance of community-building is also reflected in the induction programme, which aims to build a routine around social aspects such as group activities, entertainment and games and daily discussions and conversations among the learners.

While the daily discussions are initially facilitated by Project DEFY staff, learners are strongly encouraged to gradually take over from the team members, which will help them to develop a habit of questioning things and increase their self-confidence and capacities to articulate their own ideas and opinions. Discussions can include both specific topics suggested in advance and spontaneous, often random questions brought up by the learners which delve into philosophical, scientific, political, current affairs, local community-based, personal or any other issues that are of relevance to the learners. As Boicha Huidrom adds,

> one beautiful aspect of the Nook is that it brings learners of all age and various social backgrounds and life experiences together. They all bring with them different perspectives, ideas, and different solutions to problems. The daily discussions help to create a platform where everyone is able to freely share their opinion, feel comfortable, and discuss collective solutions to any problems and issues. That's why they play an important role to make the Nook into a free and inclusive learning space based on cooperation and mutual understanding and respect.
>
> (personal interview, August 2020)

The questions, topics and issues discussed by learners on a daily basis also pave the way for the final phase of the induction programme, which is to set specific learning goals (individually or – mostly and as strongly encouraged – in small groups) for the goal cycle which begins afterwards. To come up with a three-month learning goal that is relevant to the learners' lives and addresses their individual needs and interests requires a capacity for self-reflection, curiosity and questioning as well as a willingness to explore new things and be open to new experiences, the foundation of which is laid through the various elements of the induction programme.

The goal-setting process then helps the learners to find something that matters to them and to pursue this over the next three months in order to verify their equality. As Megha Bhagat points out,

> schools or any institution usually have to create goals through the exam system, or the academic curriculum, or through learning outcomes. But none

of them are decided by the students or the learners. None of them have absolutely anything to do with the person who is accessing it. They are pre-decided by somebody else and they are implemented and imposed on the audience. So at the Nook we completely change this by creating a goal-based system which is run through a project learning methodology … A lot of our work is concentrated on communities that are marginalised … so one of the big criteria for us is that we create project-based learning. The idea behind that is that it helps them to create relevant short-term, mid-term, long-term goals. And when you put goals for yourself, you are more driven towards them, instead of somebody else setting them for you. And you are more open to accessing help. Because you have set them, there is absolutely no scheme associated with 'what if I don't reach it'. And the goal you choose could be anything. We also don't go into curating their projects for them. You can pick up absolutely anything.

Over a period of seven days in the induction programme, learners are asked to decide their goals and form groups of three to five learners based on common interest. While learners can choose absolutely any goal they are interested in as long as it does not violate any of the core principles and values of the Nook – which are discussed and developed together with the learners during the induction programme – they can be generally divided into individual and community-oriented goals.

To provide some further guidance and orientation, the Project DEFY team members will introduce a slightly changed version of the Japanese concept of 'iki-gai' to the learners, which can be translated as 'a reason for being'. Individually, among each other and together with the DEFY team, learners will reflect on the three questions of 'what would I like to do', 'what am I good at' and 'what can help me sustain'.[5] The intersection of these three elements forms a person's ikigai.

Based on this, the learners will develop their initial goals which are further required to conform as much as possible to the 'SMAART' formula – Specific, Measurable, Achievable, Aspirational, Relevant and Timebound. All learner groups will then discuss their proposed goals with the local Project DEFY team and local partners or community members, which will ask, as Abhijit Sinha puts it, 'uncomfortable questions' about the learners, their ideas, dreams, challenges, needs and expectations:

when we ask people about their goals, initially everybody says basic things they believe they can achieve. And then we ask okay, especially with older people, we noticed that older people and especially women just stop having dreams after a certain point. In my experience, most of the time I have asked women over the age of 40 what they want to do, all their dreams are basically dreams of their children. I want my kid to become a doctor. But what do you want to do? We've done this several times, and it's going very deep, we have to ask them like what did you want to do when you were ten years old? Why did you give it up? What was the reason for not pursuing it? Like 'I got married, nobody would let me work, my parents told me to leave education', and so on.

> But that was something that was deep inside hidden, they would not talk about
> it because they don't believe they can achieve that. So then picking that up and
> saying 'okay, now do you want to make an attempt at this point'. Whether it is
> possible or not is a totally different question. Attempting is the first bit.

This reflects again how the verification of equality does not necessarily rest upon
the 'mastering of a discipline' but in the act of encouragement, trust and solidarity
of the 'ignorant schoolmaster' that makes the learner engage, discover, explore
and pursue any matter of interest.

In the Nook model of ANPED, the task of the ignorant schoolmaster is taken
up for the first three months by the 'hopper' who initially comes to set up a new
Nook and at the same time trains a Nook Fellow to take over from him once he
leaves and who is based at the local Nook for a period of 12–18 months. In this
period, the Nook Fellow – coming initially from outside the community and having already some experience in the area of alternative education – recruits and
trains a new Nook Fellow from the local community, who would usually be a
current or previous Nook learner him- or herself.

Interestingly, Project DEFY has changed to this model only very recently.
Previously, the hopper would select a Nook Fellow directly from the local community within the first three months of the Nook set-up.[6] However, looking at
how the different Nooks operated, it became clear that there is an extremely large
dependency on the individual Nook Fellow, which resulted in different development paths of the respective Nooks. While in some Nooks, learners would engage
in a wide variety of learning goals, advance from basic to more advanced goals
across the cycles and put more emphasis on projects which benefit the community
in one way or the other, in other Nooks the learners would often focus on a more
narrow range of individual goals where a majority of learners engaged in the same
kind of projects,[7] for example tailoring, electronics or carpentry, without much
notable progression towards more complex or new and different goals.

One of the main reasons for this is that some of the Nook Fellows – having no
structured training and practical experience in SDL before coming to the Nook –
struggled to support learners in the pursuit of learning goals they are not familiar
with themselves and therefore unconsciously promoted learning goals they either
knew themselves or that other learners were already pursuing. This at times discouraged learners from picking up and pursuing new and out of the box ideas and
projects or prevented them from taking their acquired skills and knowledge to the
next level.

In conversations with some Nook Fellows, I could indeed observe how a few of
them would struggle to describe the philosophy of unschooling and self-designed
learning, and how they would at times reduce learning in the Nook to using the
laptop and pursuing online learning courses. As some of the Nook Fellows also
had difficulties in facilitating engaging conversations and discussions among the
learners, this further hampered efforts in some of the Nooks to create a true 'community of learners' instead of individual learners who come to the Nook to pursue
their individual projects.

This shows that maybe it is not as easy as we thought to become an ignorant schoolmaster who emancipates others by verifying their equality. What became clear is that some of the initial Nook Fellows – selected mostly among Nook learners of the first goal cycle in a newly set-up Nook – were often not able to translate their own experience of potentiality through the particular projects they worked on in the Nook into the understanding and practice that learners can do anything and everything they want to do and that as Nook Fellows they can help others to learn what they themselves don't know.

In order to address these issues, Project DEFY has rolled out an extensive learning and exposure programme for all Nook Fellows which lets them discover different aspects and approaches towards SDL as well as to better understand the philosophy behind it. It consists of designated in-house training, training on the job, and increased collaboration with the Indian Multiversities Alliance network Project DEFY is part of. This is envisioned to help the Nook Fellows fulfil their role as ignorant schoolmasters who encourage and nurture the will of the learners to pursue whatever they want to do.

One of the current Nook Fellows is 30-year-old Deepika Ram, who started herself as a learner at the Kaggalipura Nook. She narrates how initially

> after a few days I realised that this place doesn't have teachers. I have to learn the things by myself. Actually, that part was a bit difficult for me, it felt difficult for me. Because I was not good in self-learning. So I felt that I need a teacher, I need someone's suggestions, guidance. Then slowly I adjusted to this place and started to learn by myself. Now what I am feeling is that actually, self-learning is good. Because in school and college they will say something, they won't give us the freedom to experience the things by ourselves. But here we get the experience. It's a good place … When I am trying to convince people to come here, I am telling my own story.
>
> (personal interview, July 2018)

One of the most important tasks for Deepika Ram and the other Nook Fellows is to help learners find their goals and support them throughout the goal cycles in their self-designed learning journeys without acting as teachers. Instead of imposing learning goals and projects on the learners and solving problems for them whenever they get stuck, they provide guidance, support and encouragement to the learners.

Once learners have finalised their goals, the Nook Fellow helps them to break down their three-month goal into concrete, hands-on projects. These milestones need to be achieved within a specified period of time and lead the learner or group of learners towards the completion of the overall goal.

For example, one learner group chose the overall, SMAART goal of 'designing & testing five prototypes of eco-friendly and affordable sanitary pads'. This goal was broken down into concrete milestones which included 'understanding Human Centred Design' (HCD), 'collect information and stories from local women', 'research different ways of making pads' and 'create five prototypes and test them'.

Together with the learners, the Nook Fellow then identifies learning sources which help them to accomplish their projects. In the above case, this included an online toolkit on HCD, a free UDEMY online course on 'Menstrual Hygiene Education', and a YouTube tutorial video on 'how to sew cloth pads'. At the request of learners, the Nook Fellow can also organise special skill sessions and workshops during the goal cycle which could be given by other learners, the Nook Fellow, Project DEFY team members or skilled people from the local community or from outside.

During the goal cycle, the Nook Fellow will follow up on the learners' progress through a weekly check-in, as well as through monthly presentations given by each learner group in which they are encouraged to share both their learnings as well as any challenges, difficulties and questions with other learners and seek help from each other.

Throughout the goal cycles, a lot of emphasis is indeed put on peer-to-peer and collaborative learning in order to foster the emergence of a community of learners. As Abhijit Sinha says,

> the people who are coming in, they are trying to do something that is hard for them … It's hard, so they have to take each other's help. A great community is one where you realise that you need other people's help and you realise that you have the capacity to help others as well. And we have lost all other places like that. I do not use the word social innovation or anything like that [to describe the Nook concept]. This is not new. It's just creating another excuse for people to meet, with a hope that they will benefit each other. It's not altruistic, it's actually very logical. It's not like someone from outside comes in and says 'okay I want to help this guy because "poor guy" needs help'. I need to help because he has to help me.

At the end of the three months, the learners will conduct an internal review and check if the goals have been achieved, often with the help of other community members and outsiders who have skills and knowledge in the respective learning goal areas. If learners were not able to complete their goals, learners can carry them forward to the next three-month goal cycle. Not completing the goal is not seen as something to be embarrassed about or indeed as 'failure', but as a great learning opportunity in and by itself. This is also why experimentation, taking detours and trying out new ways of doing things are encouraged by the Nook Fellows, even if this might not lead directly to the desired project outcome.

Learners who have completed their goals and want to continue to come to the Nook for the next three-month goal cycle can decide if they want to deepen their skills and pursue some more advanced goals in the same field, or they can decide to broaden their skills and knowledge by pursuing other goals which are or are not related to what they have done before. A community event for everyone then marks the end of each goal cycle, in which learners present their goals to the broader community and new potential learners are invited to join the next induction programme and goal cycle.

Although this varies from Nook to Nook, the learners, in general, pursue a wide variety of goals and projects. Areas of learning across the different Nooks include visual arts, tailoring, science, agriculture, technology, music, crafts, food and cooking, carpentry, metal works, construction, entrepreneurship, community problem solving, hairdressing, makeup and styling and much more.

As Abhijit Sinha shares some examples,

> one of the Nooks had a 17 year old who first designed a women's safety device by hacking an electric mosquito bat, and later created his own single-propeller glider that he controlled with his remote. The same Nook had an 11 year old who not only fixed his toy RC car, but also recreated it with a new body and hacking the inner parts together. An 8 year old at another nook refused to play any games but the ones he made on scratch. Tech has not been the only sort of project-area. Learners created kitchen gardens and grew plants. We have seen women create modern dresses, learning designs from youtube. We have also seen the creation of musical instruments using plastic bottles. Learners have created movies and released them on youtube. The list goes on and on.
>
> (Sinha 2018: 9)

Subjectification at the Nook

When I visited the Kaggalipura Nook, community members were engaged in a hydraulic project, making organic pesticides, designing and stitching clothes, glass paintings, jewellery design and henna drawing. In Bangalore's Shivaji Nagar, a predominantly Muslim community, I met mostly female Nook learners who were engaged in various beautician-related projects such as learning how to do makeup, hairstyles, etc.[8] As Sinha (2018: 9) puts it,

> in essence, we see Nooks create a strong sense of 'choice'. That what a learner does after the Nook is completely the learner's own decision based on his/her own interests. This may seem obvious, but it is important to remember that making choices is not everybody's privilege. The Nook has enabled learners to understand what they want, from moment to moment, and to pursue them. For some this has meant going for higher education in areas they were now interested in; seeking jobs that were in line with the future they want to create for themselves; creating businesses/enterprises to solve problems that matter to them. What is common and laudable is that they did not have to compete in doing so – instead they collaborated and helped each other.

However, when it comes to 'choice', the question always is from what one can choose. What I noticed in both the Kaggalipura and Shivaji Nagar Nooks was that a rather high number of female learners chose to pursue what we can call rather '(stereo-)typical projects' such as doing makeup, hairstyling or jewellery-making.

This seems to be a bit at odds with Project DEFY's aim to help learners pursue a process of subjectification that ultimately leads them to reject the roles on offer by the OWW and create their own (dis-)identities. However, as Abhijit Sinha illustrates, what the learners choose to do has to be seen in relation to their existing roles and identities when they start coming to the Nook:

> when people come here, they should be able to do or attempt things that they would not usually get to attempt, that they will be told not to do. And that works both in terms of skill and in terms of social behaviour. So this place [the Shivaji Nagar Nook], right, all the women, most of the women who come, have not been allowed to go and even learn stitching somewhere. Because they are not supposed to leave the house, they can't go alone. So that, coming here by themselves, doing things, starting a business, some of them want to start businesses and they are trying to do that, is challenging the social norm that has been expected of them. And the same is with skills. Trying to do things that are hard, and that you don't believe you can do or have not believed so far.

For 19-year-old Fareeha,[9] even coming to a learning space in the first place is a small revolution in and by itself. Coming almost every day to the Kaggalipura Nook for two years, she says that her family members, particularly her father, would not even have allowed her to go out earlier. Only by coming to the Nook and engaging with the community of learners, did Fareeha realise how the idea that girls should not leave the house was a deeply held and false belief she simply accepted and internalised for most of her life (personal interview, July 2018). Currently discovering and applying her passion for glass painting at the Nook, she says that since coming here, her self-confidence has increased drastically: 'now I feel like I can do anything'.

Fareeha further stresses that her communication skills have increased and shares how she is able to clearly articulate her thoughts, ideas and opinions. Being much more confident now about herself and what she wants in life, Fareeha adds that she also does not shy away anymore from direct confrontations with her father if he insists on her staying at home – 'I can easily fight with my father now … Only here [at the Nook] I learned how to overcome struggles in life'.

Overall, Fareeha says that becoming a Nook learner has helped her to acquire concrete skills relevant to her own life, to get out of her comfort zone and pursue her own dreams even against resistance from her family. Compared to this, she says that in school

> they just teach you what's in the books. We don't learn any real-life skills, and nothing is related to our lives. Here [in the Nook] I get encouragement and freedom, and I am motivated to explore new things. This is different from school. Here [in school], they punish you for your mistakes, there is no motivation to do anything.

Her next project, which is an example of how subjectification can gradually take hold, is to start playing the violin. Fareeha says that through violin as a medium, she wants to tell stories about people, for example, widows who struggle a lot and don't get enough support in society.

Another example comes from Niah,[10] a 33-year-old female learner who lives together with her husband, a truck driver, their two sons and her in-laws in Bangalore's JP Nagar area. She says that

> my husband and in-laws are very strict. They want me to stay at home and do only household work. At the same time, they call me 'useless', which makes me feel very bad about myself. It isn't fair, because they are the ones restricting me from doing anything productive in the first place.
>
> (quoted in Neusiedl 2020)

Niah is now learning English as well as the basics of accounting in order to earn her own money and become more independent. She adds that 'the Nook opens my mind and changes the way I think … I've experienced a world besides being a housewife' (ibid.).

While this can indeed be seen as an example of how some of the learners utilise the Nook as a space to create a better role for themselves within the OWW rather than outside of it, Project DEFY founder Abhijit Sinha emphasises how what happens in the Nook is a gradual and long-term process which differs from learner to learner and their specific positions within the OWW.

Depending on the frequency and intensity of their experiences of potentiality, the learners are increasingly questioning common-sense assumptions and developing their own ideas of what makes meaningful lives for them. This is not a one-off process – as we have also seen with the community-based Nook Fellows – but requires patience and the continuous verification of equality, which then gradually will result in the broadening of the learners' radical imagination and ultimately leads them to the anarchistic postdevelopmental notion that 'anyone can learn anything', which ultimately reveals the arbitrariness of the hierarchical order of society based on the presupposition of inequality.

A 17-year-old, female Nook learner for instance joined the Nook initially to learn English and then started to explore handicrafts and fashion design, which is something she would have no opportunity to do elsewhere. These experiences of potentiality made her realise her own equality:

> when I started to learn fashion design, I didn't have the confidence that I can stitch some clothes like this. But after coming here, after learning here how to stitch clothes I got the confidence that yeah *I can do anything*, and no one can talk [bad] about me, yeah I got confident from here.
>
> (personal interview, July 2018; emphasis added)

Similarly, a male learner describes how he

> didn't imagine that I can do so much. When I started to come here I realised that 'oh I have this talent, oh my god I made this, oh wow'. I didn't realise

that in my school. It was only about going school, coming home. That's it
… In school they explain or they teach. Here it is self-learning … so you can
learn without anyone's help. What we want to learn, we can do on our own.
It's easy … Here I realised that my talent was increasing and everybody is
supporting me, is encouraging me.

(personal interview, July 2018)

Overall, what becomes evident in how Project DEFY is approaching subjectification, transformation and change is that the team is very conscious about
hierarchies and how easy it is to impose ideas and knowledge on others rather
than having people creating ideas and experiences on their own, and often from
scratch. As such, the question becomes where 'creating space and possibilities' or
'providing exposure' ends and 'imposing views and ideas' starts.

Compared to other unschooling models such as the Creativity Adda or Swaraj
University, which we will explore in the next chapter, Project DEFY's approach
is more restrained, slow and cautious. As Sinha contends when asked about the
need particularly for marginalised women to gain more exposure and perspectives
in order to defy common gender stereotypes,

> while we want that to happen, we don't want to force it to happen. Because
> if I tell them, 'this is what girls are supposed to do, why are you doing it?', is
> that right? I don't think so. I think that is a discovery they have to make. Now
> think of this thing. How could you realise that people are equal, that you can try
> things that are not generally meant for guys. How did you build critical think-
> ing? These are privileges. These privileges you were able to build because the
> right people were around you, because you had access to information, you had
> access to the world, and you had time … Now these are barriers that they have
> to overcome themselves. Yes, beauty courses are probably very feminine in the
> social norm. But they will have to realise it themselves. And how will that hap-
> pen? It will take its time, it will take interesting people who come here. Like
> there are women coming here who are engineers. For the first time they are
> seeing women doing something like that. Now that is the very starting point of
> even believing that there are options. So while I would really love for them to
> take up hardcore science maybe, or philosophy or politics, it is something that
> I don't want to break it for them … I am not worried about the time. Let it take
> its time. If it's from the community it will have a far larger impact … I am yet
> to see a space which is curated and not coercive … Yes, I can accelerate it quite
> a lot. But accelerated processes, and I have seen this, continue only as long as
> the fuel is there. Only as long as I am there. What if I'm not there tomorrow?
> What if DEFY is not there? What if none of these things that we can currently
> do for them is even possible? Where does the community go then?

Therefore, Sinha further stresses that 'the only outcome I care about is that they
achieve the goals that they set for themselves … I don't expect, or I don't enforce

what I think would be good for them'. In this, he clearly follows the principle of Rancierèan democracy:

> once you commit to working democratically, you have to take the leap of faith that says that people will make informed choices. And you must trust that if they don't make the choices that you think in the short term are the best ones for them … in the long run, the experience of being in control will make them more responsible the next time they are able to exercise power.
>
> (Brookfield 1995, quoted in Suoranta 2008: 9)

As such, Sinha sees even perspective-building and self-discovery as organic processes that have to originate from within the community rather than being curated programme elements facilitated for the community. The following statement by Sinha then very closely reflects the anti-hierarchical, postanarchist ethos of Rancière's presupposition of equality:

> people have to discover themselves … That process of discovery … your own realisation that this thing, this so-called exposure, is important. Understanding for yourself that diversity is important. Now, one could argue that this kind of thinking can only be created, that somebody has to tell somebody else that these options are available and so you should go and explore. I feel that it can happen naturally if people just have the time to think. It is controversial to say that, and it is hard to give any research evidence for it. But I believe learning does not have to happen from top to bottom. From expert to novice or a group of novices. I feel a group of novices can learn on their own.

Seen from this perspective, the Nook model of unschooling offers everyone the potential to create space in their lives for self-discovery and perspective-building, rather than providing these as in-built programme elements:

> we have this 24 hours routine you follow, and suddenly this space has a place in that 24 hours, where your routine is distorted and you can do something that you would not be able to do in your routine. It creates space and time in your life … Do not expect or believe that this is a shortcut … It is not easy. You are still living in an environment which is extremely conservative. This is just that ten per cent or five per cent of your time that you have that opportunity to be different. But somewhere it has to start. Some space has to be created in life to explore. Otherwise, you are 24 hours in your very limited environment. So whether it will create a change of that massive scale, whether the entire community will be changed while creating this five per cent time in some people's lives, we are still to see.

Consequently, while this may not readily and at once lead to the erosion of the OWW and its dualist ontology across each and every sphere of life, Project DEFY's Nook model is a prime example of how ANPED can reconfigure various micro-partitions of the sensible that bit by bit, and seen together in the bigger picture, dismantle the hegemony of the OWW Development paradigm based on the presupposition of inequality. As Abhijit Sinha says,

> maybe we will see changes in the community, in the way they think, and the mental shifts, probably a decade from now. If they start, if you know, kids are born, and parents don't already decide what the kid is going to do 20 years later, that's great. That is something it has achieved. Or maybe something totally different happens, who knows. You plant a seed, you can't expect what height the tree will grow to. Unless it is GMO [genetically modified organism]. Here we don't even know the seeds. And it's cool.

Ultimately, then, 'Nooks are not the final place of your learning journey. Rather they are the starting point, where you learn to learn, from your community, from the Internet and from yourself, and then move on into your own learning paths' (Sinha 2018: 6).

Summation

Project DEFY and its Nook model provide a decentralised, customisable and easily adaptable platform to facilitate unschooling opportunities for marginalised communities. This is achieved by bundling together important elements of the learning web in a physical space freely accessible to all, initiating a process of deconditioning through the induction programme and making learners interested in something that matters to them through the goal-setting process and then enabling learners to pursue whatever they are interested in through the recurring goal cycle system. As a result, Nooks let learners emancipate themselves by verifying their equal intelligence.

As we have also seen in this chapter, the Nook Fellow as ignorant schoolmaster plays a crucial role in this process. Especially in marginalised communities located in urban and semi-urban areas, which is where the majority of Nooks are located, the learners are conditioned by societal expectations and judgements and therefore need recurring, strong experiences of potentiality for the presupposition of equality to take hold. This includes the Nook Fellows themselves, who often are early Nook learners from the local community the Nook is situated in. They have internalised the presupposition of equality to various degrees and at times struggle to live up to the anarchistic postdevelopmental philosophy which says that anyone can learn anything.

With its flexible structure and open access for everyone in the local community, the Nooks are also an example of how unschooling can be balanced and aligned with the concrete needs of marginalised communities in the here and now. Learners can decide to come to the Nook whenever they find time to do so and, indeed, however often they can afford to do so, given that many of them at the same time struggle to make a living. Unlike the case of radical unschooling among families, the Nook model does not require a complete shift in people's ways of life at once but creates a space in the lives of people to start their unschooling journeys.

Although this is an approach that takes more time, patience and possibly efforts, it largely avoids any imposition on learners of what they should do and how they should live their lives while helping them to gradually realise and apply their own equality on a daily basis. Especially in marginalised communities, this seems to be a more feasible approach, given how deeply many marginalised community members are entrenched in the material realities of the OWW.

Looking at the stories of some of the Nook learners we have met, we can further see how subjectification becomes a long-term process that does not readily and at once lead everyone to disavow their pre-assigned roles and identities within the OWW. However, the more the presupposition of equality takes hold among the learners, the more arbitrary and unjust the hierarchical order of the OWW will look to them. It is hoped that this will lead to long-term changes in what the learners aspire to do and how they live their lives. At the end, true to the spirit of ANPED, it is, however, up to the learners themselves what they do with the insight of their equal intelligence.

Ultimately, with the conscious and permanent effort to avoid any hierarchies and to not put any impositions on the learners, the Nook model of unschooling perhaps comes closest to the ideal of ANPED rooted in Jacques Rancière's principle of radical equality. On the one hand, this makes the process of unschooling and its inherent potential of subjectification and reconfiguration of the field of experience much longer, uncertain and, in a way, more difficult. On the other hand, it can potentially be one of the most impactful and indeed powerful ways for people to realise and act out of their own equality in the long run.

The final case study chapter will introduce and analyse yet another model of ANPED in India. Swaraj University is a semi-structured unschooling space for young adults which combines the principle of SDL with facilitated workshops, learning journeys and various other curated and non-curated experiences.

Notes

1 I am currently working with Project DEFY to establish a new impact framework for its Nook model of unschooling and further develop and expand its approach towards unschooling. A large part of this chapter was written before I started working with the organisation.

2 Unless otherwise stated, all quotes by Abhijit Sinha have been taken from this personal interview.

3 Unless otherwise stated, all quotes by Megha Bhagat have been taken from this personal interview.

4 A Nook, whose size usually is around 1,000 sq. ft., can accommodate around 100 learners per day in 2 to 3 batches. The induction programme can have 2 batches with around 25–35 learners each.

5 The original elements of ikigai are 'what you love', 'what you are good at', 'what you can be paid for' and 'what the world needs'. The latter aspect will be incorporated gradually for more experienced Nook learners who have gone through one or more goal cycles already.

6 Before this reorganisation, Nook Fellows were referred to as 'Nook Managers'. The shift towards a fellowship model then also aims to have the Fellows in the Nook who come from the local community for a more limited period of time (18–24 months) so

that the position does not first and foremost become a routine job to 'manage', but an opportunity for various Nook Fellows to gain new exposure, skills and knowledge during the fellowship as well as explore their own interests and ambitions which they can take up after the fellowship. As Abhijit Sinha stresses, the Nook Fellow therefore always and ideally is a proactive learner him- or herself.

7 Such a cluster where the majority of learners engage in a limited number of the same kinds of projects then also indicates usually that they are more influenced by what other learners already do, what the Nook Fellow consciously or unconsciously encourages them to do or what they think they should do based on societal expectations, instead of discovering their own interests on a deeper level.

8 The Shivaji Nagar Nook is currently not operating due to a lack of funding.

9 The name has been changed to protect privacy.

10 Ibid.

References

Escobar, A. (2018). *Designs for the Pluriverse: Radical Interdependence, Autonomy, and the Making of Worlds*. Durham: Duke University Press.

Illich, I. (1973). 'After deschooling, what'? In Gartner, A., Greer, C., and F. Riessman (eds.), *After Deschooling, What?* London: Harper & Row, pp. 1–28.

Neusiedl, C. (2020). 'Education in Times of COVID: The "Nook" model for designing your own learning'. https://thebastion.co.in/politics-and/education/education-in-times -of-covid-the-nook-model-for-designing-your-own-learning/.

Sinha, A. (2018). *Unmaking Education Through Nooks*. Unpublished article.

Suoranta, J. (2008). 'Jacques Rancière on radical equality and adult education'. https://su oranta.files.wordpress.com/2008/05/suoranta_malta081.pdf.

7 ANPED in practice
The Swaraj (Un-)University model

While this book has focused mostly on the ontological politics of inequality practised by mainstream schooling, it is important to not overlook the structural role of
academia within the OWW Education system. As Eli Meyerhoff shows by tracing
the origins and genealogy of higher education across the centuries, academia is
another key institution of the OWW which 'supplements modes of world-making
that are associated with modernist, colonial, capitalist, statist, white-supremacist,
hetero-patriarchal norms' (Meyerhoff 2019: 4).

As with schooling, academia likewise narrows down the concept of 'education'
to fit within the OWW paradigm of Western, rational, scientific knowledge. It follows a competitive and grade-based system based on the presupposition of inequality, and – even more than schools – limits access to the various means of education
to those deemed having sufficient formal entrance qualifications as well as the
social and financial capital to enrol in universities and pursue a certified degree.[1]

The Indian Multiversities Alliance (IMA) is a platform of around 50 organisations
and initiatives that seek to re-invent higher education along the lines of unschooling and self-designed learning, and thereby also to make it accessible for everyone.
One of the IMA's founding members is Swaraj University (SU),[2] established in
2010 by Shikshantar, which is also behind the Creativity Adda we have explored
earlier. Not recognised – and not aspiring to be recognised – by any official body,
Swaraj uses the term 'university' in its name in order 'to challenge the notion of
what a university has come to mean' (Hasija 2017: 21).[3]

This is graspable not only in the fact that SU neither asks for formal qualifications to join the programme nor awards any degrees or certificates upon completing it but in the entire programme structure and its various elements, which this
chapter will explore in more detail below.

As we have seen, ANPED as unschooling comes in various forms and approaches
which cater to various circumstances and livelihoods. Radical unschooling among
families, for example, is mostly practised by those unschoolers who never or only
for a comparably short time went through formal schooling and who make the
decision to unlearn together with the explicit support of their parents and therefore
unschool together as a family. The Nook model, as another example, caters to
those who are most often still deeply entrenched in the OWW and only gradually
start to question its iron laws by becoming learners in the Nook.

Swaraj University, situated on a wooded, 15-acre farm-campus nestled in the rugged hills outside Udaipur, represents yet another approach towards unschooling. It caters to young adults aged 16–31 years old who most often come from urban or semi-urban spaces, have been mostly through the mainstream education system up to high school, college or university, and have already decided for themselves that they want to seek alternatives for both their education and their ways of life, away from the OWW Development paradigm.

As a two-year programme and platform which combines self-designed learning with facilitated workshops, and curated and non-curated programme elements and experiences around self-discovery and exploration, community-building, perspective-building and sustainable livelihoods, it targets those learners who already have a strong dissensus against the OWW but seek orientation and guidance to take the next steps and co-create their own meaningful lives outside the OWW.

It is no coincidence, then, that whoever joins Swaraj University is not called a student, but a *khoji* (seeker).

Programme structure and overview

Since its beginning in 2010, each year has seen a cohort of 15–20 khojis joining the SU programme. As expected from a programme based on the ideas of unschooling and SDL, it is structured in a very flexible, open way.

Over the first year, there are three 'khoji meets' taking place at the Swaraj campus. Ranging from five to eight weeks each, they include a mix of pre-planned workshops and facilitated activities, spontaneous projects and experiments by the khojis, and experience and knowledge-sharing sessions about the individual or group-based SDL projects the khojis pursue outside the meets. This is further accompanied by lots of arts, music, games, conversations and discussions, and spending time in and with nature all around the campus.

Collaborative skill-building workshops constitute an important part of the khoji meets. These range from an introduction to and gradual adaptation of SDL methods in concrete projects to

> workshops featuring basic entrepreneurial skills as well as other skills such as: communication, facilitation and group dialogue, computers, financing, marketing, cooking, sewing, farming, yoga, film-making, web design and blogging, desktop publishing, writing of proposals and business plans, documentation, working English, etc.
>
> (Hasija 2017: 25)

In between the khoji meets, the programme gives ample time (1.5–3 months each) for self-designed learning projects. This usually takes the form of individual or small group projects with a particular emphasis on mentorships:

> Swaraj University aims to revive the traditional approach to education in India, through a *guru-shishya parampara*. That is, learners being placed

one-on-one with mentors (also called ustaads) who share both a range of practical skills as well as personal philosophies/wisdom.

(ibid.)

Swaraj University's ever-growing 'database', consisting of hundreds of 'non-certified' gurus and mentors, then also goes against the hierarchisation of knowledge which is a central part of academia. The sheer variety of mentors and what in a more formal setting we could call 'visiting faculty' – including 'traditional artisans and village healers and farmers, jail inmates, children, mentally challenged adults, and others' (Jain 2013, quoted in Kothiyal 2018: 215) – and the fields they work in then further help to make visible ideas, practices, ways of life and lifeworlds outside the OWW. As a result,

> the khojis are again able to see our 'illiterate' elders and many others with practical know-how (who had been rendered invisible) with new appreciation, respect and connection. Even the animals, trees, mountains, rivers, soil and children can be our gurus.
>
> (Jain and Akomolafe 2015)

Another important element of the programme are thematic learning journeys in which groups of khojis travel together in order to engage with inspiring people and projects, dive deep into the rural life of India and live together with groups or communities that resist the OWW Development model in various ways while building their own alternatives.

As Rahul Hasija, one of four residential facilitators at SU, shares,

> the aim of the first year is to encourage khojis to unlearn their dependence on external sources of knowledge and to engage in co-creating their self-directed learning path. Khojis also learn basic jugaad (playful improvisation), planning, facilitation, media and communication skills, as well as identify a practice area to pursue in more depth. It is also the time to go deeper into their own stories, histories and understand one's own self – beliefs, values, patterns, fears and emotions, and not just one's own self, but also understanding these stories of the whole group that empowers them to support their peers ... There are various explorations and experiments to understand the meaning of Swaraj, and the core principles related to it, which are sustainability, social justice and holistic living. Khojis are exposed to different kinds of community contexts – rural villages, social movements, entrepreneurs and non-profit organisations.
>
> (Hasija 2017: 26)

While the first year provides much exposure, discovery and exploration for the learners to find something that matters to them, the second year then serves to verify their equality by pursuing what matters to them in depth through shorter khoji meets of around 15 days each and longer, uninterrupted periods of SDL time.

> The focus of the second year is on Deep Diving. The aim is to facilitate deeper learning around each khoji's emerging vision. It is in a way consolidation of first year's exploration into a live project they take up … Khojis are encouraged to take risks, to try new things out and not to be afraid of making mistakes. These projects can be anything – right from their dream ideas to ideas they want to experiment with in their communities, from a foundation of an enterprise to ideas implementation in existing organizations. We call it Alivelihoods. Usually the focus of existing universities is just to have learners reach livelihoods. Our focus is to increase the spectrum and include questions, ideas and deeper calling from the world that makes the khojis alive or the communities they intend to work with, Alive.
>
> (ibid.: 27)

Ultimately, SU aims to help khojis create their own meaningful lives alongside others, based on the presupposition of equality. This also becomes visible in the following account by Chetan Kanoongo, talking about his role as facilitator at Swaraj University:

> I think we go with this presupposition that everyone who comes over here as khoji, and in fact other people who come here as well, is capable of designing their own learning. Otherwise, this place wouldn't exist. And capable of leading their lives as well in a way that they want to. As facilitators, we go with that presupposition and operate from there and also keep in mind the larger vision of Swaraj, which is mostly around enabling skills, SDL skills, which can help them move towards this understanding that yes, I can design my own learning and based on that I can design my own life and lead it in the way I want to.
>
> (focus group discussion, January 2019)[4]

Swaraj facilitator Rahul Hasjia further highlights how the programme helps khojis to create meaningful lives outside the ontological limits of OWW Development by reconfiguring the distribution of the sensible:

> the idea from which Swaraj started was how we can challenge this ready-made world where everything is given on a plate and there is no critical questioning behind that and so, how can one be in kind of control of life. How can people design their learning – not just their learning, but their life. What kind of life do they want to live, where do they want to live, and so on. Usually, the only definition of success is to acquire more money, more power, more property. So how can we also challenge that and instead you yourself define – how can individuals define what is their idea of reclaiming. We use this word, 'reclaiming the spaces of our own lives', by understanding them, diving into them deeply, so that is one idea. So that wherever we go, wherever we live,

we kind of live our lives and live our work with a lot of co-creation and care for the people. So I think that is something very important.

In what follows, we will assess in greater detail some of the most important programme elements of SU and show how they interrupt and fundamentally go against the principles, goals and objectives of OWW Education and thereby lead to the reconfiguration of various partitions and micro-partitions of the sensible.[5]

Self-discovery and community-building

Self-discovery, or the process of starting to get to know oneself better as well as identifying one's own ideas of a meaningful life, is one of the most important aspects of the SU programme. This is because most learners who decide to join the SU programme initially found themselves in a state of confusion. In most cases they developed a strong dissensus against some or many practices of OWW Development already before joining SU; however, they did not know what to do with this dissensus as it did not automatically translate into *creation*.

As Yash, one of the khojis, shares about his two years at SU:

> to reflect with this confusion and to reach that clarity, that what I'm really seeking, what do I really want, what are my real needs and where do I want to head towards. So that process, that beautiful process, I learned in these two years.

Like Yash, most khojis said that a primary reason for joining SU was to seek orientation and direction in life, looking for new perspectives for personal growth and exploring new ideas of how to lead meaningful lives.

This was often related to a high level of disappointment and disillusionment experienced with the mainstream education system and wider society. Only in a few cases, however, was this explicitly linked to *failing* in school or at college, whereas more often it was connected to the *meaninglessness, irrelevance and lack of perspective of mainstream education*, no matter if the khoji failed or 'succeeded' in the mainstream education path.[6]

This disillusionment was encapsulated in statements such as 'I felt school could not offer me anything new, there were no learning opportunities', or 'in my third year of college I was very disillusioned about my future and frustrated with the hypocrisy around me'. Arjun, another khoji, further argues that 'in India, schools don't even promote to learn. They promote you to fill exam sheets and get marks. That's the reason people quit and try to find places like Swaraj University and other alternative spaces in India'.

Madhur further describes how his

> recommended future was to go study economics, something like that. But I wasn't really sure if I wanted to do that, like why study economics, or English, or any of such particular things. I always dreamed of doing something creative and having a creative career, but I felt quite unequipped to do

anything like that. I wanted an experience which would be very different and tell me something about myself which I don't already know.

(personal interview, September 2017)

Thus, while all the khojis-to-be explicitly or implicitly rejected being part of the OWW Development machinery, they were rather in a state of confusion and often even vulnerability regarding how they wanted to live their lives instead. Rahul accordingly says that when joining Swaraj, 'I was also lost, I wanted to figure out what I wanted to do [in life]'.

Therefore, self-discovery, including the capacity for self-reflection, plays an important role in the first year of the programme. Mohit Trivedi, a *mitra*[7] at Swaraj University, describes the process of self-discovery as follows:

> in year one, the first and second meetings are around understanding the self, so there are different tools and processes like 'tree of life'[8] or 'river of life' through which khojis try to connect with themselves, and there is lots of time given for reflection. Because this space is very quiet, in the nature, and you get lots of time to connect with your Self, to meet your Self. Sometimes it can become very difficult when you meet your Self and you reflect and introspect, your Self asks you lots of questions, and that makes you uncomfortable. So there is a community which holds you.

(reimagining education workshop, May 2018)

The aspect of community which Trivedi highlights here is another essential part in the khoji's path of self-discovery. Several khojis shared how the interaction with a diversity of learners, bringing with them their different stories and backgrounds, helped them to gain new perspectives, to shake off and re-build some habitual ideas and concepts and to learn new things about themselves.

Yash, for example, pointed out how SU as a close-knit community space made it possible 'to go deeper in conversations, on one's learning path, to go deeper with each other'. For him, a community space like SU symbolises a strong and trustful bond between people who can self-realise and complete each other: 'whenever, whatever is needed, and whatever is missing, we pour into each other'.

Relatedly, for some khojis the strong bonds evolving within a close-knit community that allowed trust to grow and vulnerability to be shared played an important role. As Surendra puts it succinctly, 'I started trusting human beings after coming here. That was the biggest challenge that I have overcome now' (personal interview, December 2017).

The establishment of trustful relationships – including learning how to build them and how to sustain them – then indeed is another important element of ANPED:

> trust ... is an affective relationship of vulnerability toward the other ... It constitutes a rejection of exchange relationships. Trust can arise only in a context where one considers others as more than vehicles for personal gain and, in

addition, as similarly motivated. Trust, then, both relies on and contributes to the presupposition of equality within a process of subjectification.

(May 2007: 33)

Whereas students in the OWW Education system are usually forced to compete against each other and therefore often mistrust each other, the community life of Swaraj is characterised by cooperation, mutual trust, support and solidarity. Mohit Trivedi further says that another

> difference to mainstream education is that at Swaraj there is no judgement. The difference is nobody is going to look bad at you. And there is scope for growth. Because your peer group will give you the feedback. What you are good at, what you are not good at. Where you have to work on, what skills that you have to learn or build. The most important thing is, it's the community who really helps you to uplift your capacities. That way, I think it's very different. And it's not performance-oriented. It's more about who you are. You don't have to be perfect, but you have to be authentic. And it's really very organic.
>
> (personal interview, May 2018)

This was also expressed by Surendra, who started an LGBTQIA[9] advocacy project during his time at Swaraj:

> in India there are already so many fears that we have if we are talking about alternate sexualities. But in Swaraj I got the opportunity to talk about it fearlessly, freely. There is no compulsion, no judgement, and there is no hindrance to do this. Everyone supports you. Okay you want to talk about it, let's talk about it. We'll discuss together. That was the first thing I received from Swaraj. A space where I could come up with my idea.
>
> (personal interview, December 2017)

This also highlights how the community-building part of SU creates a safe space where emotions and vulnerabilities can be shared, where self-exploration, -reflection and -discovery can happen and indeed thrive without fear, anxiety or the pressure to have to conform to certain standards and expectations.

For Yash, SU then also functioned as a safe space in order to experiment with and try out new things and challenges, giving him the confidence to take whatever he did forward and outside the Swaraj community:

> Swaraj also offered me that safe space. So I was like that if I cannot break this wall in this safe space, then how I can do it in the outer world. So that's why I broke it, and now even in the outer world or wherever I have to do it, then I have that confidence.

Perspective-building

Instead of aiming to integrate khojis into the existing order, Swaraj University strongly encourages khojis to question, challenge and deconstruct the various partitions of the sensible that make up the OWW. This perspective-building element indeed constitutes the second pillar of the programme. As Swaraj facilitator Rahul Hasija expounds,

> the idea was also that when the youth come here, Swaraj is not only the space for helping them to work on their dreams or just their interests, but it is also a space in which people would have to engage with different kinds of lenses to see the world. Be it sustainable living or social justice and injustice, food and food politics, so not just what their interests are. If they come and say okay I want to do drawing, for example, and I want to start earning and just do drawing, there will be these aspects as well which would be part of the programme. Of course, you don't need to take that forward, but these are part of the programme which we feel are essential and are important to understand what is the kind of world which is there, and what is the world we are dreaming of. And it's very important for that bridge to happen and it will only happen if there are these aspects there.

Here we can see how SU takes a much more proactive stance in terms of perspective-building and creating exposure than would be the case in the Nook model of Project DEFY or also in the radical unschooling among families approach of ANPED.

However, especially in the latter part of Hasija's statement, we can also see how the facilitators are conscious of not *moulding* students according to specific beliefs and ideologies. As facilitators and khojis both emphasised, it is up to khojis which – if any – of the ideas on sustainability, social justice, healthy living, etc., they take up in their own work, learning projects and life. Of course, they are strongly encouraged to do so through the many experiences, workshops, etc., and for many, these focus areas, which challenge the key assumptions of the OWW, are one of the reasons why they are joining Swaraj University in the first place,[10] but there are no formal criteria or pressure to conform to any of the ideas and values they are confronted with outside Swaraj and life on campus.

The perspective-building component of the SU programme is distributed across three strongly interrelated themes. These are 'sustainability and rethinking development', 'social justice and injustice' and 'food and food politics'. In the following, we will explore the first two themes in more detail which seemed to have a comparably strong impact on the khojis' learning and life stories.

One of the most impactful experiences for the khojis across the programme is the annual cycle yatra (journey), a week-long bicycle expedition around rural Rajasthan. Yash describes his cycle yatra experience as follows:

> in this cycle yatra, we khojis go to rural areas of Udaipur without phone, without money, and without food. And we also don't know the direction before.

Our facilitators just say on the day that now you have to go this way. And no one is notified that 'our khojis will come, and you have to give them space or anything'. We just go randomly for seven days and wherever we reach, we talk with the rural people. We talk with them, we build relationships with them, and we tell them that this is the purpose of our journey, and we are just trusting you, we don't have food, money, not even mobile phones. So we tell them that we want to work, if you have any work we can do and in exchange you can give us food and accommodation. But that's just a point of starting. 'We will work for you' – it doesn't happen in India. Because we have this very rich culture, as much as I have explored this in the rural area, they say 'no, no, no, we will take care of everything, you just stay and observe and you just feel like this place is your home'.

(reimagining education workshop, May 2018)

Yash's account shows how practical experiences such as the cycle yatra help to shatter the 'fundamental truths' of the OWW. As such, a recurring theme mentioned by several khojis was how they managed to (re-)gain trust in people through the cycle yatra and how they were able to realise that human nature is not inherently individualistic, selfish, greedy and competitive (i.e. 'homo economicus'). This is also expressed in Stanzin's description of his cycle yatra experience:

we went out for seven days; we took two pair of clothes, one blanket and the cycle. So we went through villages, every day we stayed in another village and helped the villagers with their daily work. Actually, we were mostly worrying about food. Will we be getting food or not? But we found that it was not difficult at all. Then we were walking and talking with the villagers, it was a good time. Before that I couldn't ever think of just going without money or anything, because I don't have trust in strangers. I can't just think they will give food to me and let you stay in their house. Then when I went there, they were very welcoming and there's much more than what we expected.

(personal interview, September 2017)

For many learners, the cycle yatra experience also opened the door to actually starting to pursue a more sustainable, less consumerist way of life, based on deeper thinking and enquiry into what is really necessary to have in life and what is superfluous. While many khojis were theoretically aware of these issues before the cycle yatra, actually going on the yatra 'forced' them to practise a more sustainable way of life using only a minimum of resources. As Arjun puts it,

in life I've never ever seen myself without money or a mobile phone. And me being a tech buff it's very difficult for me to disconnect myself from a mobile phone or even any technology for that matter. But it happened so organically, and it happened that cycle yatra really built the stepping stones towards me trying to accept the fact that what are actually necessities and what are actually luxuries. And that had been a real change-maker in my life.

The ample time allocated in the SU programme for pursuing individual or group-based SDL projects (5.5–8.5 months in the first year and most of the second year) then offers plenty more opportunities for the learners to design their own activities around rethinking Development and sustainability if they are interested in this area.

Five khojis, for instance, used two months of their SDL time to start a community-living project. They lived and worked on a farm, prepared and cooked their own food and hosted nature-connect workshops for children. In Nikhil's case, the SDL time he spent on an organic farming project interestingly led him back to a completely different, yet related field:

> some unexpected stuff also happened when I got more and more into farming – somehow, I found myself getting more and more creative on the computer again, like reigniting my curiosity, doing other types of programming. And I got really good in all this, better than in farming in fact. So then towards the end of the two years I started focusing on what can I do with the stuff that I'm really good at already, that is computers and technology and web technology, and how I can help with that in sustainability.
>
> (personal interview, October 2017)

Another important element of the SU programme is to help khojis forge a closer connection to nature, challenging the artificial, dualist separation between humans and nature. Here, the very location and nature of the campus of course helps to facilitate some closer connection to nature as the khojis – literally – live *in* nature. As facilitator Rahul Hasija states,

> it is an essential part of the programme to have some interaction with nature. We are part of the nature here around us, and how do we connect to different elements of nature, be it water, air, ether, fire, land. There are many processes we have like a water walk, we have something called nature quest where people take a question with them which is really burning for them and maybe not letting them sleep, and they take that question to the wilderness and they are there for 18-24 hours with that question, solo, fasting, so that is another element … We also have certain processes like this water walk, fire walk, climbing up the hills, sitting there silently for two hours without doing anything, going for a blind trust walk with peers, going with shepherds when they go for herding the goats, accompanying them, seeing their lives, talking with them, or just silently observing.

Facilitator Sonika Gupta further relates the immersion in nature with the idea of recognising the existence of more-than-human beings, drawing on the potential of a 'profane re-enchantment'[11] with the more-than-human world:

> I guess it's also related to another way of being. We are so used to just being surrounded by human beings and by things that human beings have created

and language and words and noise. But I think there is another way of being which kind of surfaces when we are in nature and we get in touch with it … And the second thing is that a lot of what we are creating in the world today is from the disconnect that we have with nature. I don't know what happens if I just buy a phone and throw it away after two months. One of the things that happens or what we are trying to do is to bridge that – to actually reconnect the dots and to be able to see what happens. So mentally we can do that. But only when I fall in love with something, then I actually care about it. Then I care when a hill goes down. Because I'm so in love with it. Otherwise, it's just a random rock. So I feel that is another thing – it has happened for me I know, and it happens hopefully for other people as well. Let me fall in love again with nature and really reconnect, so that there is care. And then things which otherwise would feel very difficult to do in my life, choices which may feel very difficult to make in my life, suddenly become easier because I'm so in love with nature and I have the courage to go through with it.

Overall, the Swaraj programme has a clear, direct and long-lasting influence on changing many of the learners' attitudes and behaviours towards a more sustainable, less consumerist way of life. An example of this is Asawari's project called 'Life Beyond Development' which the khoji started during the Swaraj programme and which continues to run till today:

> me and my friend Isha do workshops with children. We try to explain them the concepts. Because we believe that children are change-makers and if they get to know the concepts in a young age and grow up, they will engage in projects that will not harm but benefit the planet. This critical perspective about Development I got only in Swaraj. There's a workshop called rethinking development, so only when I came here I understood all of this. I understood how the government is corrupting us, how the society is corrupting us, how corporations are corrupting us.
>
> (personal interview, September 2017)

Social justice, another important pillar of the SU experience, is very much interconnected and indeed difficult to separate from the 'rethinking development' part of the programme.

Many of the learning journeys which are part of the programme are focused on exploring real-life issues around social justice. As facilitator Rahul Hasija shares,

> there have been many learning journeys where people have gone and visited certain communities, people who are kind of resistant, resilient communities. Last year one of the groups went to Maharashtra where they visited a few places. One of them was a traditional fishermen community, and they are threatened by the nuclear power plant there. Because of that, a lot of fishes die. So their livelihoods are in danger. So we went and lived with that community and very near to that, there is also the Mumbai-Delhi industrial

corridor which is being built, and the communities which are being displaced because of that, we also went to live with these communities.[12]

Here we can see how Swaraj University helps the khojis to have first-hand encounters with the dire consequences of OWW Development. As Avinash, another khoji, puts it, 'you're meeting people whose lives were actually displaced … It basically makes you rethink Development and also raises your consciousness on how much you are consuming, and can you make it to a minimum level' (personal interview, January 2019).

Importantly, as Rahul Hasija further expounds, the khojis do not come into those communities as outsiders and experts to 'suggest solutions', or as spectators that can only make sense of OWW Development-affected people as passive victims:

> the idea was not to go and interview these communities or give a solution, but it was just to go and live their lives, what kind of life they are living. And … not going with a single story that 'oh they are kind of resilient or they are activists or they are struggling or oppressed', but there are also many gifts that they have in their lives. So going and engaging with that, observing, just being there with them. So from last eight to nine years, there have been many such learning journeys. I once went to Gujarat where there were lots of communities protesting against a cement factory which was getting built there … There was a … long yatra on the idea of water and land, to understand the various land struggles people are going through, it was a peace march that happened and a few khojis also participated there.

In encountering local communities not as oppressed, passive victims, but in engaging with them on a basis of mutual respect and a realisation and appreciation of people's manifold skills and gifts, these experiences then sow the seeds for khojis to act out of the presupposition of equality which is based not on struggling *for and on behalf* of others, but *with and alongside* others.

The various activities and explorations across the areas of rethinking development and social justice challenge the various hierarchies between humans as well as between humans and nature and provide an abundance of new experiences to khojis that exceed the ontological limits of the OWW and often fundamentally change the khojis' way of seeing things and understanding the world.

Asawari, for example, says that

> when I came to Swaraj, I learned about sustainability, about social justice, about healthy living, and today who I am is because of the two years in which I learned things here. Especially how you can live in harmony with nature.
> (personal interview, September 2017)

Stanzin, who currently constructs mud houses utilising traditional architectural methods from across India,[13] further relates what he learned at Swaraj to a change in his perspective about community life in his home state Ladakh, situated in the Himalayas:

> in Swaraj they talk more about what is going on in the world, globalisation and so on. And Ladakh is newly opened to all that, we are still practising traditional ways of living and all this, so when I was there I started thinking about my place. What's happening now in Ladakh is that communities are breaking up, kids don't want to do farming, even me, I'm outside now. So I realised this and when I went back to Ladakh I started looking into these things and I did farming and in the future I also want to go back there and continue the traditional practices.
>
> (personal interview, September 2017)

On another level, the confrontation and deep engagement with other worldviews and perspectives also helped many learners gain the capacity and willingness to better understand their own position in the world in relation to others and, in this process, listen to varying viewpoints without prejudice. In this line, Avinash emphasises that 'also what Swaraj does, it makes you conscious of the person you are' (personal interview, January 2019). This goes hand in hand with the ability to perceive and see issues from different, new angles and listen to contrary opinions and points of views. Accompanying this was the notion of listening first before coming to a judgement on any issues and making time for and slowing down the decision-making and opinion-forming processes.

In sum, what both the perspective-building and the self-discovery pillars of Swaraj University achieve is to interrupt and reverse the mono-ontological occupation of the OWW, what facilitator Chetan Kanoongo refers to as 'the danger of spreading a single story'. Taken together, both aspects help to (a) discover and realise one's own needs, interests, passions and desires; and (b) to apply, understand and possibly further develop, question and change these in relation to the wider community, society and world. The result is what we can call an increased ability for self-awareness, as described by Kanoongo:

> what happens in our normal lives is that we end up sleepwalking the whole life without knowing that we are just conforming, we are trying to comply, we are trying to match certain standards and expectations set by some people outside, some authority. We try just to conform to those standards. So self-awareness is a way of enquiring about everything – one is obviously exploring the deeper truths of who we are, what are we doing here, who am I and all those questions – but also to know how I and my choices are kind of impacting the whole thing, not only me but people outside, people around me, nature, and to understand yourself as well. By understanding yourself you also understand what's happening around you and how you impact that, how the choices you make, the things you do, are related, are connected to you and your actions and your way of being. So that's why self-awareness and enquiry come into the picture and why it's one of the focus areas.

The combination of various self-discovery and perspective-building elements, based in large part on the khojis' own experiences and experiments, also ensures that rather than one (OWW-)story being replaced with another hegemonic *story*, the khojis are able and indeed critically self-aware enough to create their own, unique and individual – yet connected and related – *stories*. In continuously crafting their stories and bringing them to life, the aspect of SDL then plays a central role.

Self-designed learning

SDL serves as the practical verification, application and continuous affirmation of what the khojis absorb and experience during their meets and learning journeys. It provides them with the time, space, freedom and opportunities to explore, learn and pursue what matters to them.

In aspects of self-discovery, SDL serves as a powerful practice to help khojis get rid of the ingrained presupposition of inequality. Accordingly, Asawari, a former khoji and facilitator at SU, points out how a good deal of the programme is necessarily spent on deconditioning the khojis – or, in other words, in strengthening the khojis' will:

> the new batch, when they come to Swaraj, it's very new for them. Because they have been in the conventional world, so they come for the first time. The first year is about helping them stop depending on others and becoming more independent. We are introducing the new batch to the concepts of Swaraj, getting them slowly used to be a self-directed learner, because it's not easy. When in your whole life you have been told what to do, suddenly you cannot do what you want on your own. You need to process it first.
>
> (personal interview, September 2017)

Madhur, for example, shared how challenging it was for him as a 'schooled person' to stop relying exclusively on academic knowledge that he would habitually judge as 'superior'. He says that

> one very important thing at Swaraj was to break out of just the intellectual or reading mode of learning things. I wasn't sure how am I applying all of my previous learning. I think a lot of my identity and a lot of my ego came from the fact than I'm intellectually superior from other people, that I score better than them, I read more difficult books than them. Take away my concepts and books and grades, I don't know. I think it was a great experience to break that superiority thing in the head.
>
> (personal interview, September 2017)

One activity focused on deconditioning khojis and leading them towards the presupposition of equality is called *Eklavya Ghumantu*,

> an exploration of finding learning opportunities on the run. In India, learners are made to believe that learning could only be possible if there's an expert to teach you. So, the whole power of learning is shifted to that expert. Eklavya

Ghumantu is a process where khojis are encouraged to go on the streets to search for and find their own Gurus. There is treasure of learning everywhere and potential teachers are everywhere. Artisans, cobblers, barbers, mechanics, and repair artists – the streets are full of people whom we can learn from. The khojis have to find these teachers and learn from them. It challenges their notion of learning and whom to learn from, encourages them to use their creativity to find and engage their own teachers and introduces them to many everyday contexts in which people use their creativity.

(Hasija 2017: 27)

To facilitate such experiments and encourage khojis to take on such challenges is a key part of the facilitators' work. Sonika Gupta describes this role as follows, reflecting the ignorant schoolmaster's task of encouraging her learners to use their equal intelligence they all already and always have:

one aspect is largely the role of a gardener when it comes to individuals and to the group – seeing what is needed and where, and being able to provide that. As gardeners, we presuppose that everybody knows how to grow and wants to grow and has a seed that will grow in them. But, we look at and help with what might be needed, what support, and so on.

This was further echoed by Chetan Kanoongo who says that

because we are growing in a system that creates authority and dependency, sometimes we just feel that 'oh, I can't do it', or 'I'm not capable to design my own learning'. So that's where the facilitators come in. We step in as people who probably have all done a bit of self-designed learning ourselves in our lives. So we are working with the whole group and see what is needed for the group and what is needed for people, wherever they are in their lives, and how can they slowly and gradually move towards developing that understanding and owning their own learning, designing their own learning.

Gupta further draws on the importance that trust plays in this process, further reflecting how the ignorant schoolmaster engages in what we have termed a politics of solidarity:

people are being ridiculed, discouraged or in self-doubt that whether this is possible. I think that one thing this space overall does is, the message that keeps going out is 'we believe in you'. And I think they need to hear that, because so much they hear 'you are an idiot' and all of that. So, that is another role. And we believe in you, we believe in what you wish to create for your life, and we are creating it together for our lives.

Gradually starting to apply SDL in their lives with the encouragement of their facilitators who verify their equal intelligence, the khojis then are more and more able to discover their own interests, skills and hidden talents; they feel encouraged to explore new things and engage in and co-create new experiences; and they see failures as a (positive, important) part of this recovery and discovery process. In turn, all this leads to a tremendous growth in self-confidence.

Indeed, one of the most recurring themes that khojis mentioned in relation to SDL in one way or the other was how it helped them to increase their self-confidence and build trust in their own abilities and skills. Notably, all such statements have not been associated with exploring and learning a particular skill or working in a particular area but are rather related to the idea of 'learning how to learn' and the accompanying realisation that everyone is equally intelligent.

In other words, the khojis' learning journey does not end once a particular skill has been identified, but it continues and is open in many new directions and towards exploring many new possibilities across different, not necessarily related or in any way connected areas and fields.

The increased confidence and trust in their own abilities were directly expressed by several khojis through the association of SDL with freedom and the idea of being in charge of their own learning and life, and the possibility to follow their own passions and interests rather than having an authority from above that imposes a certain kind of knowledge or learning on them.

Nikhil further relates SDL, in his own words, to the shift from the presupposition of inequality towards the presupposition of equality:

> direct democracy, that kind of orientation, for me Swaraj and self-designed learning was very important in that. Moving away from a technocratic mindset to a more localised mindset and all. Moving away from thinking that only the experts have all the answers and they should fix everything to thinking that okay, the people can figure out their own solutions, give them some chance even if they are faltering right now. And favouring a more decentralised approach in solving problems. For me that was a big learning ... And yeah, that whole thing of thinking that I need this or that qualification, that went away.
>
> (personal interview, October 2017)

Here we can see how SDL is also an important cornerstone of perspective-building for the khojis, helping them to realise and practically verify that we are all much more capable than the authorities and institutions make us believe and that we can indeed co-create our own meaningful lives alongside others.

Some khojis further associated SDL with the idea of recognising, valuing and appreciating anyone and anything as a potential learning opportunity. As such, Arti says that

> before Swaraj, I felt so much inhibition, like how can I ask people to teach me anything. But right now it's just so easy. It's a very small difference, but it changes a lot. Things become really accessible – you start to see how much you can learn from your immediate surroundings, and you are also seeing that people around you have gifts as well.

This reflects again how ANPED works remarkably different from OWW Education, which is based on the idea that only certain people with certain kind of knowledges are valuable and worthy. This leads to a hierarchical society where people look down upon each other and ignore or simply are not able to see any value in other people. SDL then functions as a reverse image to these assumptions by making people such as the Swaraj khojis see other people and, in turn, the world through a different lens, which we may call a lens of abundance (of wisdom, knowledge, skills, intelligences, equality, value, beauty, resources, learning opportunities, etc.) instead of a lens of scarcity.

In sum, SDL seems to be key for khojis in what we can identify as themes of self-growth, increasing self-confidence, being able to self-reflect, developing a more positive outlook towards life, finding hidden skills and talents, seeking out and being open to new perspectives and ideas, being able to form one's own point of view and clearly express one's thoughts to others, curiosity and willingness to enquire and go deep, and questioning and challenging common-sense assumptions. All these themes have been stated by various khojis as forming an important part of SDL and how they practise it till today even after leaving the programme.

Most khojis stated that the overall Swaraj experience helped them enormously to gain and grow self-confidence and trust in their own abilities and skills, opening the door to learn, experience, try out and pursue new things and do indeed whatever they want to do in life rather than being told what to do. One khoji for instance says that 'it's like this made-up cage in my head disappeared'. Anuj, another khoji, describes how after Swaraj he is now 'confident enough to go out on my own and do anything', and Arti shares that she was able to 'reclaim her life', realising that 'I can create whatever I want to create for my life'.

This demonstrates how SU serves as a space to verify the learner's equality and leads them to the conclusion that 'anyone can learn anything'. As Samyuktha, one of the khojis, describes it:

> I started knowing what are my learning patterns, how do I learn well, and I was becoming more comfortable with myself, recognising and accepting what my skills are. The whole two years helped me in this process. The best part is that it gives you a push. There are so many fears that you have in your mind. The two years and the process give you a push to see what happens when you face those fears. You start doing things and you find that the fears you had about them were actually not as real as you thought.
>
> (personal interview, September 2017)

Similarly, Nikhil expresses how 'Swaraj empowered me to try and do things that were beyond the scope of what I thought I could do. It really broadens your options of what you can do' (personal interview, October 2017). Surendra further shares he is grateful to SU 'for kicking my ass and helping me to know that I have wings and I really can fly. I always had these wings, but I didn't know about it' (personal interview, December 2017).

Related to the growing confidence and trust in their own abilities and the insight to not take things for granted and accept their (subordinate, passive, pre-given) role in life that the OWW accords to them, some khojis also connected this with an, overall, more positive outlook towards life and the idea that the world is radically open and full of possibilities waiting to be realised rather than a pre-given journey full of obstacles that prevent self-realisation. Rahul, for example, says how

> one of the biggest impacts in Swaraj helped me in generating my reflections in a way of self-growth rather than self-critique. Earlier I was more like criti-quing myself ... it was more destructive ... One of the most important things, it gives me faith in myself.

Alivelihoods: Creating meaningful lives alongside others

Bringing the interrelated elements of self-discovery, perspective-building and self-designed learning together, one of the main goals of SU is to provide a plat-form for khojis to gain the self-consciousness, skills, experiences and self-aware-ness they need in order to start creating their own meaningful lives alongside others – or Alivelihoods – by letting them find what SU calls the khojis' (indi-vidual and unique) 'sweet spot'.

As we can see from the below account of facilitator Sonika Gupta, this is simi-lar to what in Nooks is pursued as finding one's ikigai:

> what do I love doing and I am good at doing; what does the world need, what are my values, and what are my needs. So four of these can come together. Most of the world goes around saying that you can't bring these together, you have to compromise here or there, turn something rather into a hobby or do charity. But I think what we are saying is that no, it's possible to design a kind of life where this is feasible, and here are some of us living it, so come meet more people who are living it and let's try how you can also live it.

In this we can see again the complete opposite philosophy at work when com-pared to OWW Education, whose primary objective is to mould students into passive consumer-citizens that fit into the pre-given, hierarchical roles distributed by the OWW.

Although the fields and areas the khojis are working in after the programme (often but not always the same areas they pursued during the programme) are extremely wide, overlapping and often unique, we can very broadly categorise them as (a) creating/facilitating community-based experiences; (b) sustainable living; (c) green entrepreneurship; (d) alternative education; and e) arts.

While there are also a few examples of khojis who joined social justice and other activist movements, this shows again how across unschooling and ANPED – as we could also see for instance in the case of radical unschooling among families – there is more emphasis on direct action and a prefigurative politics which creates ways of harmonious, meaningful living outside the OWW in the here and now instead of directly confronting any existing, oppressive power relations found in the OWW.

This is based on what Newman (2019b: 301) calls 'a micro-political transformation of the self' in which the unschoolers mostly do not directly confront the various manifestations of state power but subvert or refuse to participate in them. This negation of power leads to various redistributions of the sensible and thereby sows the seeds for wider social transformation.

Anuj's work, for example, combines the fields of sustainability and entrepreneurship. During his time at SU, he started his own social enterprise *Takli*, working together with weavers and artisans to provide sustainable and sustainably made clothing. Takli's aim is to avoid the chemical and mechanical pollution and work involved in clothing by reviving old-style, traditional hand-made clothing techniques and skills.

As such, Takli is much more than just a 'business' in the conventional sense, but an initiative that goes against the 'progress myth' of OWW Development and the pressure to produce everything as efficiently (i.e. automated) and large-scale as possible. Further talking about his work and the impact it has, Anuj says that it benefits the local community in Indore he is working with as it helps to protect the traditional occupations of weavers and artisans from extinction and gives them flexible work they can combine with family and household work:

> now instead of becoming wage labourers, they can continue their crafts … Now we have around five to six weavers who approached us themselves because they wanted to go back doing what they were traditionally doing and apply the skills that they have. And now they are all very satisfied with the work they are doing and the ease with which they are able to do it, because we also work in a way that we don't have a set standard. We don't force them to produce a certain amount every day. They do it at their own pace and the way they can do it.
>
> (personal interview, February 2019)[14]

Drawing on SDL and what he (un-)learned at Swaraj, Anuj also encourages them to explore and experiment with new designs and fabrics rather than only following orders:

> when we are designing or building something new or developing a new piece, we leave it up to them to first see what new things they can do … We give them that space and we encourage them to try different things, explore it themselves and then see if it does or doesn't work out.

Overall, Anuj's '(non-)business model' defies common-sense expectations and ideas in the OWW where the focus is exclusively on selling as much as possible and making as much money as possible. For instance, Anuj further says that rather than having only buying customers coming to his shop,

> what I really like is that when there are some people who just have come to look around but end up becoming very good friends. And the kind of discussions which are followed with people about sustainability and various other things is the kind of impact that matters more than someone just taking a piece back home.

He adds that

> even more than experimenting with sustainable clothing, we are trying to promote how we can limit the amount of clothes that we are buying every year. So even when you are buying sustainable clothing, how can you minimise that as well to only the basic minimum that we need and not buy for pleasure or just for the sake of it.

This illustrates how a very different approach and mindset is at work which challenges some of the key pillars of OWW Development. As Anuj puts it, 'it's because of Swaraj that the thought is there to work with a cause and a purpose rather than just working'.

Arti's 'Alivelihood' is based on facilitating community-living experiments and experiences in her hometown of Nagpur which help to reverse the erosion of community ties which accompany the expansion of OWW Development. She says that during the Swaraj programme, her understanding of community evolved from including immediate family to neighbours and people in the local surroundings. This and what Arti calls 'the spirit of SDL' helped her to come up with a community-building project in Nagpur during her first year as a khoji, bringing some of the insights she gained at Swaraj to the outside world.

Since then, Arti has facilitated various experiences and experiments for her local community such as 'Dariya Dil Dukaan', a 'gift culture shop' in which people give away things which are of good quality and dear to their heart, but not necessarily needed, and in exchange they can choose something in the shop that other people gifted. Arti also co-organised various 'UNconferences' in Nagpur, which are smaller, regional versions of the annual Learning Societies UnConference (see Chapter 5) and provide a space and platform where people come together for a limited time to co-create their own agenda according to their interests and inclinations. As such, everyone participating in an UnConference can offer to host sessions and workshops on a topic or theme they are passionate about, without having to be an expert in the respective field.

Talking about the impact of her work in Nagpur, Arti reflects how

> we started a lot of circles, we started to do lots of experiments and that's how slowly and steadily our sense of community started to grow … A spirit of volunteering started to emerge, people started to come together … We did lots of experiments and now you can see a thriving community.
>
> (personal interview, February 2019)[15]

She says that the most powerful impact was to see how a community support system emerged in which people can now more easily tap into each other's skills and share their interests and talents with each other which otherwise are usually overlooked and ignored:

> now, we never feel that we are alone, and I think that's one of the powers of community which we started to see around us. And I also realised that there are communities already – it's just that we don't access them. We don't acknowledge them in our lives … There are people, it is just that I have to start interact with them and then the community emerges.

Overall, the manifold experiments and explorations of community life in Nagpur helped people to connect with and support each other, create a collective intelligence, develop a sense of solidarity and gain new exposure:

> there are people who felt they were alone, and now they found new friendships. They are finding that there are people like them who are doing different things and they can also do it. So that energy in a very intangible way moves around us and that is something that is extremely important. That is one of the major impacts I am sensing. And these people are also going out and explore new possibilities in their lives. So now people from Nagpur would go to unconferences and visit Swaraj University, and they are doing a lot of other things which they might not have done earlier. So they are being exposed to new perspectives of life as well. And I am also learning from them, they are learning from me, there is a lot of co-learning happening.

In this, we can see another example of how khojis themselves turn into ignorant schoolmasters, further creating the spaces and opportunities to verify other people's equality.

Some khojis like Rahul also create their own unschooling spaces. Building on the concept of learning journeys he encountered at SU, he recently started a project called 'Travellers' University', whose mission is 'to enable youth to uncover a range of learning/unlearning opportunities to understand themselves and their realities through encountering new worlds and challenge the institutionalization of knowledge, culture, and tradition' (Travellers' University 2019).

As with Swaraj University, there is an emphasis on perspective-building through gaining real-life exposure and experiences:

> we have always believed that 'travel is our best teacher'. When one steps outside their bubble, one gets to meet new people, see new places, learn new traditions and gain different experiences. When we travel, we experience or become part of a lot of things that we would have otherwise not been able to do. Travelling forces us to drop stereotypes, exit narrow-mindedness and leave superstitions behind to widen our perspective and horizon of the world and people around us.

> (ibid.)

Based on the SDL philosophy that everything and everyone offers a learning opportunity, Travellers' University believes that

> there is such extreme and varied diversity in India, that there is no end to learning. There is history, architecture, agriculture, environment, folk music & dance, traditional art and so much more to learn that we never get to read about in our textbooks.
>
> (ibid.)

The (un-)learning opportunities facilitated by Travellers' University then are intended to make visible approaches, practices and ways of life outside the OWW:

> through our learning journeys we are intending to give exposure of creative solutions and a new way to look at the world from the lenses of localization, renewable technology, sustainability, spirituality etc. holistically. Through these exposures we aim to enable the capacity to learn to unlearn and a life-long willingness to face new challenges in our learners.
>
> (ibid.)

Another way in which Traveller's University integrates key elements of unschool-ing and SDL in its programme is the focus on self-awareness and self-reflection we have also seen at SU. As Rahul says,

> one of the most important subjects is to learn about one's self. The art and sci-ence of introspection is an underlying theme in our programme. Through this we want to help grow our learners' confidence, creativity, resourcefulness, and passion for life. With direct support from the facilitators and mentors, learners gain lifelong skills in how to personalise, adapt, and follow one's own learning path which is self-paced. Learners decide the pace of their own learning – accelerating or slowing down in particular areas as desired. In this way, they gain more from each moment of learning by always working from a foundation of readiness and self-worth.
>
> (personal interview, January 2019)

These examples provide just a tiny glimpse into the various Alivelihoods that the SU khojis are creating during and after the two-year programme. Other fields and activities that khojis pursue include eco-architecture and natural building con-struction; organic farming and permaculture; running organic and healthy food outlets; running eco-resorts and agro-tourism projects; creating recycled and upcycled products and items; pranic healing, yoga and meditation; storytelling; film-making and photography; pottery and traditional crafts; nature conservation; taking care of animals; working with underprivileged communities in manifold ways; running their own unlearning spaces; engaging in open data initiatives; doing theatre, music and dance; and much more.

What all of these Alivelihoods have in common is that they challenge the deeply ingrained, various hierarchies among humans and between humans and nature that are key for the perpetuation of the OWW and its ontological politics of inequality. In other words, the newly created Alivelihoods contribute to various redistributions of the sensible and provide new ideas, perspectives and experiences that exceed the ontological limits of OWW Development.

However, it is anything but easy to pursue these meaningful lives when the OWW and its social and material realities still are dominant. Some khojis accordingly shared that the transition from the 'safe haven' of SU to the 'outside world' was very difficult for them. This was accompanied by a sense of disillusion and the charge that the Swaraj programme was somewhat romanticising or idealising the 'real life', as expressed by one khoji: 'there's a whole different world outside Swaraj. When we live in Swaraj it is a very cosy picture, we have enough time to sit with ourselves, we don't have to do anything if we don't [want to]'. Similarly, another khoji argues how 'the idea of following passions, SDL, of the [Swaraj] pillars are much harder to follow and obstacles much harder to face outside of the comfort zone of Swaraj'.

As McCowan (2019: 301) expresses this conundrum, 'how is it possible to create a democratic, inclusive and egalitarian space within an anti-democratic, exclusive and unequal society? And yet, how is the anti-democratic, exclusive and unequal society to change if we do not create alternatives?'

Given that we still live in a world dominated by the presupposition of inequality, in India and across the globe, the lifepaths that the khojis are choosing will never be 'easy' but often 'messy', sometimes precarious, and at times also contradictory – this is the price to pay for abandoning the hegemonic and hierarchical, unjust and exploitative OWW Development realm.

However, together with the many other anarchistic postdevelopmental initiatives unfolding in India and across the world, the khojis' stories, projects, learnings and Alivelihoods lay the foundation to rethink and practically overcome the hierarchies of the OWW in the long term on a broad basis, while often achieving this already on the micro-scale as a form of prefigurative politics in the here and now. As such, the khojis and their ontological politics of equality

> are challenging the language, lenses and labels of deficits, arrogance and inadequacy such as 'poor', 'primitive', 'illiterate', 'first-generation learners', 'backward', 'dropouts' which permeate the development discourse. They are unlearning the doctrines that forced them to see nature as monstrous and mute, needing the salvific intervention of technological convenience. They are holding a mirror to the face of their internalized 'white man's burden' which tricked them into continuing the game of 'othering' their own people. They are challenging sacred cow categories of nationalism, ownership/copyright, science, growth, technological utopianism, monoculture [,] beauty, etc. They are choosing not to cooperate with the established rules of the game and finding ways to hack the system … In short, they are discovering

many paths of walking out and walking on to possibilities for living beyond TINA-development.

(Jain and Akomolafe 2015)

Summation

Swaraj University provides another example which clearly demonstrates how ANPED and unschooling fundamentally challenge the core principles and 'truths' of OWW Education. The latter, as we have seen, aims to create subservient and authoritarian, competitive and individualistic, egoistic personalities. They often accept and fit themselves into hierarchies and unjust structures without questioning them ('there is no alternative'), lack self-confidence, feel that they are merely a small cog in the wheel without much power to create and shape their own meaningful lives and are very much dependent on others, especially on institutions and their expert advice.

In stark contrast to this, SU provides its learners with the platform to increase self-confidence and trust in their own capacities, leads them to an overall more positive outlook towards life, makes them more self-reliant, incites their curiosity to experiment and increases their understanding of different perspectives and worldviews.

The aspects of self-discovery, perspective-building and their practical application through the pursuit of SDL – held together through the Swaraj facilitators who act as ignorant schoolmasters – then all come together to help khojis realise and apply their equal intelligence in manifold ways.

In other words, Swaraj University acts as a catalyst that takes khojis from the stage of negation (of the status quo), in which they join Swaraj, to the state of creation, ultimately supporting khojis to create their own alternatives in the present. In the process, the khojis emerge as a new, collective subject that exceeds the ontological limits of the OWW and contributes to various redistributions of the sensible.

Notes

1 As Kumar (2012: 273) contends, 'if one looks at how much a student has to pay as Tuition Fee in some of the courses in universities managed by the state (which is, even so, much cheaper compared to the private universities), the impossibility of gaining access to higher education for most of Indians becomes obvious'.
2 In the words of Swaraj University co-founder Manish Jain, 'swaraj literally means rule over the self, but I prefer a more nuanced poetic framing as harmony of our many selves – with our inner world, with our diverse communities, with the natural worlds' (Jain 2015).
3 Swaraj University co-founder Manish Jain accordingly says that SU 'is proud to be 100 per cent undeemed and unrecognized by the government. This decision has been critical for us to retain our autonomy and freedom to innovate' (Jain 2015). This also reflects the overall anti-state stance of ANPED. As Jain says elsewhere, 'a politics and economics of monoculture underlie the modern Nation-State. The State functions by centralizing resources and power and spreading blind obedience. In the process, it

actually deprives people of local autonomy, kills local diversities and creates debilitating forms of dependence amongst the population' (Jain 2002: 3).

4 Unless otherwise stated, all quotes from the SU facilitators Chetan Kanoongo, Sonika Gupta and Rahul Hasija in this chapter are taken from a focus group discussion I conducted with them at Swaraj University in January 2019.

5 A significant part of the findings below derives from collaborative research I have conducted together with the Swaraj University facilitator team in order to provide an overall assessment of the programme. It is based on 36 extensive, semi-structured interviews conducted with past and current khojis held between January and February 2019. Out of those 36 interviews, I conducted 17, while the rest were conducted by and in collaboration with facilitators and other people affiliated with Swaraj University in various roles. Unless otherwise stated, all quotes by khojis in this chapter are taken from this research.

6 Indeed quite a few khojis shared that they were rather 'high achievers' in school or college.

7 The mitra's ('friend's') role at Swaraj University is to be a bridge between khojis and facilitators. In Mohit Trivedi's own words, 'the mitra offers "listenings" to the khojis. We kind of make that bond to the khojis. We are very much entangled with the programme, at the same time away from the programme. If the khoji has a complaint towards that structure or programme, they can share it with the mitra' (personal interview, May 2018).

8 'The Tree of Life' 'is a recovery approach, based on narrative therapy that focuses on culture, heritage, spirituality, strengths and hope. It originated in Zimbabwe to help traumatised communities find a safe place before talking about their problems – "the riverbank position". A tree is used as a metaphor for an individual's life and each part represents different positive elements' (Fraser n.d.).

9 LGBTQIA stands for 'lesbian, gay, bisexual, transgender, queer or questioning, intersex, and asexual or allied'.

10 In this line, we should also emphasise that as opposed to when they were *forced* to attend compulsory schooling, khojis have the *choice* of joining Swaraj University.

11 See Newman (2019a).

12 Other examples of recent learning journeys include 14-day trips to cities such as Indore and Nagpur to explore them as what SU calls learning cities. Khojis met with social entrepreneurs, activists and various individuals and organisations that work towards making their cities a better place and engaged in various collaborations. In one of the learning journeys in 2017, khojis went on a learning journey in Maharashtra to engage with the lives of sex workers.

13 See Das (2020).

14 All further quotes by Anuj in this chapter are taken from the personal interview I conducted with him.

15 All further quotes by Arti in this chapter are taken from the personal interview I conducted with her.

References

Das, B. (2020). 'Mad about Mud: These two travelling architects are building mud houses across India'. https://www.edexlive.com/happening/2020/jul/17/mad-about-mud-these-two-travelling-architects-are-building-mud-houses-across-india-13302.html.

Fraser, J. (n.d.). 'The tree of life'. https://www.slam.nhs.uk/media/386137/Summary%20poster%20of%20Tree%20of%20Life%20project.pdf.

Hasija, R. (2017). 'Imagine a university with no classrooms, no teachers, no degrees, curriculum or exams, founded on principles of self-designed and self-determined learning'. *Creative Academic Magazine*, 7, pp. 21–30.

Jain, M. (2002). 'Rediscovering the co-creators within'. In Jain, M., and Jain, S. (eds.), *Unfolding Learning Societies: Experiencing the Possibilities*. Udaipur: Shikshantar, pp. 1–15.

Jain, M. (2015). 'A philosophy of learning and living'. http://www.teacherplus.org/wp-content/uploads/2015/12/A-philosophy-of-learning-and-living.pdf.

Jain, M., and Akomolafe, B. (2015). 'This revolution will not be schooled: How we are collectively improvising a 'new story' about learning'. http://bayoakomolafe.net/proje ct/this-revolution-will-not-be-schooled-how-we-are-collectively-improvising-a-new -story-about-learning/.

Kothiyal, N. (2018). 'Swaraj: An alternative university'. In Vijay, D., and Varman, R. (eds.), *Alternative Organisations in India: Undoing Boundaries*. New Delhi: Cambridge University Press, pp. 205–224.

Kumar, R. (2012). 'The charge of neoliberal brigade and higher education in India'. *Journal for Critical Education Policy Studies*, 10 (2), pp. 258–281.

May, T. (2007). 'Jacques Rancière and the ethics of equality'. *SubStance*, 36 (2), pp. 20–36.

McCowan, T. (2019). *Higher Education for and beyond the Sustainable Development Goals*. Cham, Switzerland: Palgrave Macmillan.

Meyerhoff, E. (2019). *Beyond Education: Radical Studying for Another World*. Minneapolis: University of Minnesota Press.

Newman, S. (2019a). *Political Theology: A Critical Introduction*. Cambridge: Polity Press.

Newman, S. (2019b). 'Postanarchism'. In Levy, C., and Adams, M. (eds.), *The Palgrave Handbook of Anarchism*. Basingstoke: Palgrave, pp. 293–303.

Travellers' University. (2019). *Vision Document*. Unpublished document.

Conclusion
Crafting new pathways towards the pluriverse

I have argued in this book that in order to think the unthinkable and end the hegemony of capitalist Development which is at the heart of today's multiple and interconnected crises, we need to engage in a new kind of politics. This is all the more urgent as the neoliberal Development paradigm in India – with all its disempowering and oppressive consequences – is further intensified and accelerated by its fusing with a Hindu-nationalist framework aimed at creating virtuous market citizens.

As antidote to this toxic mix, we have established an emancipatory politics which sees the majority of the world's population not as unequal, incapable and inferior subjects – or rather objects – of the nation-state and its world-making practices such as Development, but as intelligent human beings capable of creating their own meaningful lives alongside others.

Drawing on anarchism and postdevelopment in general and the political philosophy of Jacques Rancière and Todd May in particular, the book has shown how such a framework of anarchistic postdevelopment shatters some of the most pervasive myths of what we have termed the OWW and its (neo-)liberal worldview.

In challenging and changing the OWW's hegemonic distribution of the sensible and creating new collective subjects who recognise and act according to their own and everyone else's equality, we have conceptualised anarchistic postdevelopment under the presupposition of equality as another, alternative world-making practice. Countering the disempowering stories and effects of OWW Development, this *ontological politics of equality* helps us to (re-)create new ways of life based on more egalitarian relations among human beings as well as between humans and nature.

Based on this, the second part of the book has shifted its focus to find ways in which the ontological politics of equality can be nurtured and strengthened in today's world. Here, I have highlighted the aspect of 'education' as one of the most powerful instruments to either recreate and reinforce, or challenge and change the deeply ingrained presupposition of inequality which holds together the OWW and lays the foundations for its practices such as OWW Development.

Accordingly, making sense of the modern education system as OWW Education, we have explored how the latter aims to 'produce' subservient, good consumer citizens who all too easily accept their subordinate, oppressive roles and identities within the OWW. As such, all current forms and guises of OWW Education are deeply entrenched in the presupposition of inequality by aiming to mould curious children into obedient, passive, authoritarian-subservient consumer-students that depend on the markets to earn a living and on institutions and their expert class to lead their lives.

To counter this, we have built a framework of anarchistic postdevelopmental education. ANPED stands in stark contrast to OWW Education by assuming and thereby verifying and enacting the student's equality at the outset, instead of aiming to bridge a gap between the unequal, less intelligent student and the all-knowing teacher. This, as we have seen, can only ever perpetuate and widen the gap of inequality.

Building on Rancière's figure of the ignorant schoolmaster and her practice of emancipation, I have argued that ANPED's main role lies not in teaching, distributing or imparting a specific kind of knowledge, but in co-creating with learners the spaces and platforms in which they can apply their equal intelligence to concrete learning projects that matter to them. This ultimately brings to life the anarchistic postdevelopmental understanding which says that anyone can learn anything, and therefore anyone is able to co-create their own meaningful lives alongside others.

We have then applied the framework of ANPED to the growing unschooling movement in India. As we have explored, this can take different forms, from radical and largely unstructured unschooling among families to formal unschooling spaces which provide learners with access to various elements of the learning web and cater to different segments of society along with their different needs.

The various examples of unschooling approaches have further shown how the learners undergo diverse processes of subjectification. As a result, unschoolers are increasingly taking control of their own lives and, as Saul Newman would put it, 'refuse powers' power over them'. Against all odds, they pursue their own ideas of what constitutes meaningful lives in the here and now, based largely on more egalitarian relations among human beings as well as between humans and nature.

This has become especially visible in the stories of the khojis at Swaraj University as well as in the vignettes from families practising radical unschooling together. The children at the Creativity Adda who explore and then pursue their own interests, aspirations and dreams and therefore defy societal expectations of what they should and can do are another example for this.

The case studies of the Creativity Adda and the Nook model of self-designed learning, in particular have also demonstrated how unschooling can potentially happen across all spheres and strata of society. However, to make unschooling a real alternative for everyone, what is needed is an abundance of various forms and guises of unschooling spaces that bundle together the elements of the learning web and make them freely accessible to everyone.

As I have argued, this is connected to the material realities of the OWW. As many people from marginalised backgrounds – particularly the ones living in urban and semi-urban areas without access to land and resources – remain so dependent on the dominant economic model, having at least momentarily no other way of making a living than selling their labour on the market, unschooling, with all its uncertainties, risks, experiments and overall paths that are not predictable nor plannable, still posits some big hurdles for them.

Therefore, unschooling does not function (nor does it portray itself) as a silver bullet to solve all problems – that is, as we have seen, the prerogative of OWW Education. However, what unschooling can do in non-middle-class contexts is to provide a platform to verify the equality of those thought less than equal to others, help grow their self-confidence and develop their skills and talents as well as their resilience that has been or is being eroded by the onslaught of OWW Development. Bit by bit, this tears apart the OWW's dualist ontology with its hegemonic distribution of the sensible and opens up new and at times unpredictable pathways, possibilities and potentialities.

Ultimately, the schooling and unschooling approaches towards education and learning embody two different stories. OWW Education is based, as we have seen, on the OWW's story of *separation*. Schools, after all, separate. They separate peers from other age groups and privileged students from less privileged ones; interconnected topics into clear-cut 'school subjects'; the acquisition of information from its real-life application; those 'who know' from those who allegedly don't; and 'superior' from 'inferior' knowledge. Schools also separate learning from life and learning for a (promised, yet to come) future from learning for the here and now. Finally, they separate children from nature, their local surroundings and their families, and take away the control of education from communities altogether.

ANPED as pluriversal practice, in turn, is based on the story – or rather on stories – of relationality, weaving together a rich learning web which is transgenerational (both across humans and across species), transcultural and transdisciplinary. This includes learning for and with life; identifying learning opportunities everywhere around us; recognising that everyone – and everything – possesses knowledge; facilitating learning beyond age and social boundaries; and breaking down the artificial separations that isolate schools from society and reduce learning to a sterile, classroom-based activity.

One of the central tenets of the relational pluriverse is the idea of *interexistence, interbeing and interdependence* – an understanding of the world(s) as perpetually and continuously in-the-making, in-becoming and in-flux, as opposed to the dualist OWW-understanding of a single, objective and natural World that pre-exists us. This goes beyond the truism that things interact with each other 'to considering things as *mutually constituted*, that is, viewing things as existing at all only due to their dependence on other things' (Sharma 2015: 2; emphasis original). As anthropologist Tim Ingold further argues based on this understanding,

> rather than thinking of ourselves only as observers, picking our way around the objects lying about on the ground of a ready-formed world, we must imagine ourselves in the first place as participants, each immersed with the whole of our being in the currents of a world-in-formation.
>
> (quoted in Escobar 2018: 87)

This understanding of 'being-in-the-world', which is clearly reflected in unschooling and its 'politics of being', therefore constitutes a powerful antidote against the OWW ideology that keeps on highlighting our own impotence to change anything substantial in the world as it is. In stark contrast to this, a perspective of interdependence lets us grasp how, as Kriti Sharma puts it, 'the world comes into being moment by moment, dependent upon our participation. This is why our being in the world – our participation in its making – is so central to its continued creation' (Sharma 2015: 4).

As such, all the various stories emerging through the different forms of ANPED – however small or large they might be – continuously come together and add to each other to challenge the OWW narrative of separation and TINA ('there is no alternative'). Instead of this, they make increasingly visible an abundance of alternative practices, actions, ideas, visions, ways of life and lifeworlds. These can catapult us into new, unpredictable, exciting, surprising, beautiful, scary, complex, contradictory, messy, intriguing paths not even considered possible earlier.

As Paul Kingsnorth puts it,

> I think that what I used to believe (arrogantly, probably) – that we could work together to create some grand new story for humanity – was just foolish. But that doesn't mean that lots and lots of small stories don't come together to form something bigger, which I think is probably how it always works. If enough people are questioning the way the world works and the values we have and the stories we tell ourselves, then what they will start to do instead will start to add up to something.
>
> (quoted in Emergence Magazine 2018)

Therefore, I believe, unschooling as a currently practised and increasingly popular form of ANPED in India and elsewhere constitutes the basis and the beginning – rather than the end – for us to start co-creating and crafting new stories that lead us on the many potential pathways towards the pluriverse.

References

Emergence Magazine. (2018). *The Myth of Progress: An Interview with Paul Kingsnorth.* https://emergencemagazine.org/story/the-myth-of-progress/.

Escobar, A. (2018). *Designs for the Pluriverse: Radical Interdependence, Autonomy, and the Making of Worlds.* Durham: Duke University Press.

Sharma, K. (2015). *Interdependence: Biology and Beyond.* New York: Fordham University Press.

Index

Absolute Return for Kids (Ark) 8, 69, 82–83, 85, 93; academies 87; Behaviour Management System 87; dealing with parents 87; pedagogy of 'choice' 88; pedagogy of 'competition' 89; schools in India 86, 89; use of Jolly Phonics 89–90
Acharya, M.P.T. 47
Akomolafe, Bayo 129
Alivelihoods 11, 180, 194–198, 199
alter-globalisation movement 47
alternative Development 19
Amsler, Sarah 68
anarchism 47; concept of freedom in 50; core principles of 47–50, 52; critique of domination in 48; role of education in 3, 49, 111, 152; view of human nature in 49
anarchistic postdevelopment 6–7, 43, 50; OWW Development versus 43, 62, 203; perspective on public schooling 90–91; presupposition of equality in 52
anarchistic postdevelopmental education (ANPED) 43, 100, 109, 121–122, 206; distinction from other educational approaches 104–106; as micro-political transformation of the self 195, 199; as ontological politics 107, 122, 138, 173–174, 205; OWW Education versus 120–121, 193–194, 200, 204; as prefigurative politics 110–111, 122; subjectification process in 142; *see also* unschooling
Arendt, Hannah 61–62, 123n8
Asian Development Bank 31
autonomía movement 47

Babones, Salvatore 30–31
Bakunin, Michael 49
Bey, Hakim 148

Bharatiya Janata Party (BJP) 17, 23–24, 26–27, 36–37, 70–71
Bhave, Vinoba 10, 38n6, 131
Biesta, Gert 7
Black Lives Matter movement 47
Bloch, Ernst 58
Bookchin, Murray 162
Bowles, Samuel 76

Call, Lewis 48
capitalist realism 3, 5
Chacko, Priya 22, 26
charter school 90
choice: in and of education 81, 84; in neoliberalism 88–89; in the Nook model 169–170; and school voucher systems 81–82
collective subject *see* subjectification
colonialism: and modern education 69, 99, 127, 177
consumer-citizens 5, 74, 77, 90–91, 93, 100–102, 144
consumerism 74, 81
convivial tools 162
Coronavirus pandemic 1–3; impact on school curriculum in India 70; lockdown in India 36
count of the uncounted 57
Covid–19 *see* Coronavirus pandemic
creative capitalism 85
Creativity Adda 9, 100, 111, 159; challenges of 120; children's council of 117–118; community engagement in 119–120; learning hubs and activities in 113–114; and the ontological politics of equality 115–116; philosophy of 112–113, 116–117; subjectification of learners in 120
critical pedagogy 104–106

Dariya Dil Dukaan 196
De Cleyre, Voltairine 49
de-conditioning: process of 161, 190–191
de La Boétie, Étienne 108
Dell Foundation 85
democratic politics 29, 54–55, 173
deschooled society 140, 147, 149
deschooling *see* unschooling
development: and education 8–9, 22;
    and equality 24, 27; Gujarat Model
    of 26; history of in India 20–21;
    as ontological politics 18, 32–33;
    participatory 19; and the presupposition
    of inequality 5, 29–32; and the rule
    of experts 29–31; *see also* OWW
    Development
Dinerstein, Ana Cecilia 58
direct action 49; unschooling as 143
disaster authoritarianism 2
disaster capitalism 2
Dongria Kond 46
dualist ontology 5, 34–35, 57

economic growth 1, 5, 8, 18, 20, 26, 31,
    72–73
education: government interventions
    in 22, 70–71; and learning 3;
    post-independence agenda of 22;
    presupposition of inequality in 104; role
    in OWW 8, 68–69, 70, 93, 102–104;
    role of 7
The Education Alliance (TEA) 85–86
Einstein, Albert 6
Eklavya Ghumantu 190–191
emancipation: and the presupposition of
    equal intelligence 60, 108–109, 132; and
    the state 20; and unschooling 144, 174
Enlightenment 34
equality: in liberal philosophy 5, 24–26,
    51, 60, 81; *see also* presupposition of
    equality
Erum, Nazia 92
Escobar, Arturo 8, 25, 32
Esteva, Gustavo 20
Eurocentrism 20, 71
explication 101

false consciousness 105
Ferguson, James 32
Fisher, Mark 3
Foucault, Michel 19, 33, 69
Franks, Benjamin 49
Freire, Paulo 100, 123n7
Fromm, Erich 92

Gandhi, Mohandas 10, 21–22, 26, 129
Gates, Bill 85
Ghosh, Jayati 2
Gibson-Graham, J.K. 56
Gilets Jaunes movement 47
Gintis, Herbert 76
Global Education Reform Movement
    (GERM) 69, 77–78, 93
Graeber, David 4

hidden curriculum 99–100
higher education 22, 75, 177; alternative
    139
Hindu nationalism *see* Hindutva
Hindutva 6, 17–18, 22, 35–36, 45–46
homeschooling 153n3
human capital 72–73, 80, 82, 86

ignorant schoolmaster 107–110;
    Creativity Adda facilitators as 114–115;
    in the Nook model 166; Swaraj
    University facilitators as 191, 200;
    unschooling parents as 136; *see also*
    Jacotot, Joseph
ikigai 165, 194
Illich, Ivan 102, 111, 140, 146–147, 162
Indian Multiversities Alliance (IMA) 139,
    167, 177
Indigenous communities 9, 50, 74, 127;
    knowledge of 9, 99; ontologies of 32–33
inequality: explanation for 103–104; *see
    also* presupposition of inequality
Ingold, Tim 205
institutionalisation of life *see*
    pedagogicisation of society
institutional sabotage 143

Jacotot, Joseph 52–53; *see also* ignorant
    schoolmaster
Jain, Manish 8, 55, 120, 127, 134, 146
Jain, Vidhi 130, 150
Jameson, Fredric 1
Jensen, Derek 7, 22–23

Kabir 10
Kalinga Institute of Social Sciences
    (KISS) 12n5
khojis 11, 178–179; fields of work
    of 194, 198; reasons for joining
    Swaraj University 181–182, 184; and
    sustainable living 185, 187, 189; *see
    also* Swaraj University
Kingsnorth, Paul 206
Klein, Naomi 2

knowledge: 'caste system of' 74;
as commodity 146; concept of in
unschooling 11, 56–57, 111, 128–131,
137, 146–147, 150, 152; distribution of
103; and Enlightenment thinking 34;
marginalisation of 9, 32, 55, 99; and
oppression 100; in the OWW 69, 73–76;
traditional 71
Krishnamurti, Jiddu 10
Kropotkin, Peter 49
Kumar, Rajiv 31
Kumar, Ravi 79

Law, John 5, 34
learning how to learn 110, 193
Learning Societies UnConference (LSUC)
114, 148–149, 196
learning webs 147–148, 151–153, 174,
204–205
liberal authoritarianism 30–31
liberal modernity 18, 20, 22, 25–27
lifelong learning 76, 83–84
lifeworlds: beyond Development 37, 50,
57, 59, 110, 116, 122, 137, 179, 206

Mahatma Gandhi Institute of Education
for Peace and Sustainable Development
(MGIEP) 72
Marcuse, Herbert 68
Marshall, Paul 87
Marx, Karl 70
Marxism: and concept of exploitation 48; and
Development 20; and education 104–106
May, Todd 5, 17, 24, 43, 55, 60
McGregor, Andrew 44
meaningful lives 11–12, 55–56; in the
OWW 73–74; and the presupposition of
inequality 28
Meyerhoff, Eli 177
microloans 27–28
Millennium Development Goals (MDGs) 8
Mills, James 70
minimum learning outcomes 86–87, 89–90
Mitchell, Katharyne 81, 84
modern education: application of business
language in 81, 93; authoritarian ethos
of 90–93; denigration of alternative
ways of life in 74, 77; depiction of
Adivasis in 69–70; de-skilling of
students in 8–9, 75–76, 83; as evidence-
based practice 7, 86; in Ladakh 70,
75; relation with equality and income
levels in India 76; standardisation of
77–78, 86; as Western hegemony 70,

72; *see also* education; public education;
schooling
modernity *see* liberal modernity
Modi, Narendra 23, 26–27, 29, 31, 33, 46, 71
mutual aid 2–3, 49–50, 110, 163

nai talim 21–22, 38n6
Nandi, Ashis 46
narrative therapy 56, 59; in anarchistic
postdevelopmental education (ANPED)
109–110; as anarchistic postdevelopment
tool 57; tree of life 182, 201n8
National Education Policy (NEP) 71,
86, 90; concept of early childhood
care and education in 83; concept of
multidisciplinarity in 75–76; concept of
school clusters in 82
nature deficit disorder 83
neoliberal Development 23–24, 26–28; and
nationalism 2, 17, 21, 23, 27, 33
Newman, Saul 51, 108, 195, 204
NITI Aayog 31, 79–80, 82
non-human nature: connecting with 113,
116, 137–138, 145–146, 182, 186–188;
marginalisation of 34–35, 74
non-power 51–52
Nook fellows 166–168, 174; *see also*
Nooks; Project DEFY
Nooks: as ANPED spaces 160; description
of 157–159; and gender equality in 161;
goal cycle system of 160, 164–168, 174;
induction programme of 160–162, 164,
174; learning goal examples 169; role of
technology in 162–163; subjectification
process in 170–172, 175; *see also* Nook
fellows; Project DEFY
Norberg-Hodge, Helena 70, 75
Nozick, Robert 25

occupy movement 47
Oksala, Johanna 33–34
Olmedo, Antonio 85
Omidyar Network 85
One-World world (OWW) 4–7, 34–37,
57–58; anthropocentrism of 44
ontological politics of equality 6–7, 43,
57–62
ontological politics of inequality 5–6, 17,
34–37
ontology 32–34
OWW Development 6, 34–37; and narrative
disvalues 55, 57, 59; *see also* Development
OWW Education 8–9, 69, 73, 76–77, 93,
101–104; *see also* modern education

Panagariya, Arvind 31
partition of the sensible 5–6, 54, 57, 59
patriarchy 35–36, 48, 177
pedagogicisation of society 9, 102, 108, 110, 146
pedagogy 77, 87–88, 90; of inequality 103; myth of 101; radical 108; *see also* critical pedagogy; Pedagogy of the Oppressed
Pedagogy of the Oppressed 100
Peepul *see* Absolute Return for Kids (Ark)
philanthrocapitalism 77, 84–85
Planning Commission of India 23, 31
Plumwood, Val 34–35, 60
pluriverse 4, 44–45, 50, 61, 122, 136, 151, 205
police order 29, 32, 39n19, 54
postanarchism 48
postdevelopment 4–5, 18–20, 32; affinity to anarchism 50; alternatives to Development *see* pluriverse; 'constructive' 44; cultural relativism in 45; and education 23; essentialism in 46–47, 49
power: anarchist understanding of 48; postdevelopmental understanding of 45
prefiguration 48–49
presupposition of equality 51–52; distinction from liberal notion of equality 60; as equality of all intelligence 53; as ontological politics 53, 57; *see also* ontological politics of equality
presupposition of inequality 5, 25–29; *see also* ontological politics of inequality
Project DEFY 156–157; philosophy of 159–160, 172–173; *see also* Nooks
public education: defunding and delegitimisation of 22, 78–79, 93; and inequality 103; perceived problems in 77, 103; privatisation of 69, 78, 82, 85; *see also* education; modern education; schooling
public-private partnerships (PPPs) 80
public-private partnerships in education (ePPPs) 22, 68–69, 79–81, 82, 93; role of philanthropic actors in 84–85

radical ecological democracy 47
radical unschooling 10, 127, 153n7; anti-authoritarian ethos of 132–133; examples of learning projects in 129; goals and perceived benefits of 145–146; as middle class phenomenon 149–151;

as ontological politics of equality 128, 136–138, 142–143, 152; as 'politics of being' 138–140, 152; reasons for practicing of 143–145; role of parents in 132–133, 136, 151; socialisation of children in 135–136, 138
Rancière, Jacques 5–6, 9, 24, 29, 43, 51–55, 57–59, 90, 101–102, 107–108, 132, 175, 203–204
Rawls, John 25
relationality 205
relational ontologies 44–45
Ricci, Carlo 111
Rojava movement 47
Rousseau, Jean-Jacques 49

Sachs, Wolfgang 18
Sadgopal, Anil 78–79
Sahlberg, Pasi 69, 77
Samaddar, Ranabir 23
schooling 69; and capitalist development 8; and conceptualisation of children 144; during Corona pandemic 3; culture of 112, 115; and discrimination of minorities in India 92; explicative order of 100–103; 'for the poor' 87; and private coaching business 84; reduction of learning to the classroom 83, 128; socialisation function of 22–23, 110, 128–129; *see also* modern education; public education
self-designed learning (SDL) 112, 127, 131–132, 151–152, 178; practical example of 140–142; *see also* unschooling
Sen, Amartya 25
separation 205
Sharma, Kriti 205–206
Shikshantar 8, 112, 121, 131, 135, 148, 177
Sinha, Abhijit 156–158
society 106, 108, 129, 131, 138, 142, 147, 159, 193, 199
Springer, Simon 139
Sri Aurobindo 10
standardisation: in and of education 77–78, 80, 82, 86
students: as consumer-citizens 69, 74, 77, 83, 100–102, 129, 203–204
stultification: teaching as 101, 107
subjectification 59, 110, 204
Suissa, Judith 3
Survival International 46
sustainability 19
Sustainable Development Goals (SDGs) 8, 20, 150

Swachh Bharat Abhiyan 26
Swaraj principle 47, 179, 200n2
Swaraj University (SU) 11, 177–179;
   challenges 199; and community-
   building 182–183; cycle yatra 184–185;
   and human-nature relations 186–188;
   learning journeys 179, 187–188,
   201n12; philosophy of 180–181, 184;
   role of facilitators in 180, 191; role of
   self-designed learning in 190, 192–193;
   see also khojis
system hacking 121

Tagore, Rabindranath 10
Takli 195–196
teachers: in ARK schools 87–88; in
   Creativity Adda 113, 117, 120–121
   and high-stakes testing 82; as master-
   explicators 100–102
Thapan, Meenakshi 91
TINA (there is no alternative) 200, 206
Travellers' University 197–198
trust 182–183, 191
Tyagi, Akshat 74

Udaipur as a Learning City (ULC) 56–57
unemployment 103–104
unlearning *see* unschooling
unschooling: acquisition of basic
   knowledge in 130–131; as community-
   based learning 134–135, 149, 163, 168;
description of 111–112; different forms
   of 156, 177–178, 184, 204; as holistic
   learning 129; in India 9–11; learner-
   led nature of 159; for marginalised
   communities 174–175; *see also* radical
   unschooling; self-designed learning

Vedanta 46
virtuous neoliberalism 22, 26–27, 30, 70,
   91, 164
voluntary servitude 108, 151

Ward, Colin 31, 64n16
Western modernity *see* liberal modernity
Wilson, Kalpana 46
World Bank: concept of education in 68,
   72; and the District Primary Education
   Project 79; Education Strategy 2020 72;
   and ePPPs 80; Human Capital Project
   (HCP) 72–73; and the 'Strengthening
   Teaching-Learning And Results for
   States' (STARS) programme 80–81, 90;
   structural adjustment programmes of
   21–22, 78; World Development Report
   2018 73
world-making *see* ontological politics
   of equality; ontological politics of
   inequality
worldview *see* ontology

Ziai, Aram 19–20, 32